THE SKEPTICAL FEMINIST

To Joan ~

Barbara Walker

THE SKEPTICAL
FEMINIST

Discovering the
Virgin, Mother,
and Crone

BARBARA G. WALKER

1817

Harper & Row, Publishers, San Francisco

Cambridge, Hagerstown, New York, Philadelphia, Washington
London, Mexico City, São Paulo, Singapore, Sydney

FIRST EDITION

Designed by Donald Hatch

Library of Congress Cataloging-in-Publication Data

Walker, Barbara G.
The skeptical feminist.

    1. Walker, Barbara.   2. Witchcraft—United States—
Biography.   3. Feminism—Religious aspects.
4. Patriarchy—Religious aspects—Controversial
literature.   5. Christianity—Controversial literature.
6. Paganism.   I. Title.
BF1598.W35A3 1987 291 86-43024
ISBN 0-06-250932-2

87 88 89 90 91 RRD 10 9 8 7 6 5 4 3 2 1

Contents

Introduction
The Skeptical Feminist

The word *feminist* means different things to different people. Therefore it seems necessary to define the word at once for the context of these writings. Here a feminist is one who believes the moral and ethical standards of matrifocal, women-oriented societies are intrinsically better for more people than the moral and ethical standards of patriarchal societies such as our own. Matrifocal societies provide more emotional satisfaction and stability for a greater number than patriarchal societies do, and fewer irrational, destructive, or violent behavior patterns exist.

A feminist believes a world where socioreligious and legal systems are governed by women would be a more humane world than the present one, which is governed by men. There would be less greed, injustice, exploitation, and warfare. There would be more concern for posterity and also for the quality of life in the here and now.

Sound biological evidence supports these views. Among most mammals only females bear responsibility for the survival of individuals other than themselves. Females, as mothers or potential mothers, have a natural, built-in altruism not shared by males, who are more hostile than otherwise toward the young. The survival of any species really depends on the caring behavior of its females, not the aggressive behavior of its males. The sole biological purpose of aggressive male behavior is to sort out the stronger, healthier males. In the wild these are the only males permitted to mate and thus pass on their genes. It is nature's way of improving the breed. In human societies, however, even weak and inferior males are allowed to mate, so male aggression is unfocused, serving no purposes except those of oppression and destruction. It can even be turned against women and children, a phenomenon of species insanity in the biological sense.

All social animals receive their first socialization from the complex interaction between mother and offspring. Successful bonding in the adult group is founded on maternal bonding patterns laid down in infancy and early youth. Therefore the mothers, not fathers, are the natural models of social relationships, transmitters of social standards, and instructors in social behavior. Of course no animal recognizes any physiological father relationship. If an adult male helps to care for the young, it is only because of his sexual attachment to their mother and his willingness to imitate her behavior.

Female animals are naturally endowed with superior alertness, mental retention, and reasoning ability, to enable them to teach and support their young. The same intrinsic advantages have been noticed in female humans, though a patriarchal society usually dismisses them with a belittling term such as *feminine intuition,* implying a sort of magical comprehension devoid of consciousness. This is one of innumerable ways men try to support the myth that theirs is the smarter sex. Men have gone to great lengths to keep women from being educated, meanwhile insisting that women are impossible to educate—never noticing the illogic of their fear that women might do what they say women can't do.

Male chauvinism aside, it has been shown that women possess not only the sensitive awareness and the ability to make intelligent mental connections that comprise "intuition," they also have a good deal of hard common sense. Most threatening to male fantasy structures is the feminine common sense that may prick the whole balloon by identifying its hot-air source. In medieval Europe men could dispose of skeptical women by torturing and burning them, which served to keep women in terror as well as divert attention from any secret skepticism they themselves may have entertained. Yet skeptical common sense usually survives, even under suppression of that magnitude. Like the child in Andersen's fairy tale, there is always someone willing to observe that the emperor is naked.

A skeptical feminist, then, is most threatening to male ideologies. Spreading doubt about any aspect of the conventional wisdom is what stimulates its perpetual changes, even under the noses of those who regard it as an unalterable constant. All ideology is continuously changeable, by its very nature, because it is amalgam of human opinions. Its most devoted adherents, however, typically desire the illusion of perpetuity. This is one of the reasons men like to envision their God in a condition of eternal stasis.

Feminist skepticism on the subject of God strikes at the root of male prerogatives. All patriarchal societies place a father-god at the top of their inevitable hierarchy and use him as the ultimate prop for gender inequities. Men claim ascendancy over women on the ground that God decreed it. Because he is man deified, God always conveniently wants whatever his priesthoods want, even when they contradict each other or themselves.

As patriarchal religions struggle to adapt to changing social and political conditions, their God changes his mind fairly often. Men get together in council to decide what God thinks, and present their conclusions as new orders from above, even when the old orders have been so frequently countermanded that the whole doctrine has become absurd. Sometimes God is even made his own enemy, as in a war where both sides are confident of his help in gaining victory.

Of course the question that leaves God most vulnerable to skepticism is the basic one: is he really there? Somewhere, that is, apart from the human minds that envision him in so many diverse ways? Can he be said to have an objective, superhuman or extrahuman existence? If so, has he really communicated the details of his history, character, likes and dislikes, special commands, and so on, to a select group of men with orders to spread the word and govern everyone's behavior by it? Or did some men simply invent him to govern the behavior of others according to their own desires?

There are only two choices. Either God is a nonhuman living creature with a humanlike personality, actually able to establish communication with human beings, or else he is the biggest lie ever told, and the most lucrative for those who told it. Either God exists as generally perceived for the past several thousand years now, as an almighty father without a mother, or else his priesthoods have hoodwinked the rest of credulous humanity all that time to attain unprecedented heights of wealth and power.

The second alternative is less simplistic than it might appear at first glance. Enlightened skepticism calls into question much more than the straightforwardly "there" or "not there" condition of deity. Certainly a concept present in so many human minds for so long can be said to exist in a way—as ghosts, dragons, and elves exist in recognizable art forms, if not in objective reality. An abstract idea may be said to exist in this sense whenever articulate humans describe it to each other and more or less agree on its characteristics. As a child may imbue a teddy bear with a personality and respond to it *as if* it were alive, so we may bestow on God a personality drawn from our own collective consciousness and allow ourselves to be influenced by it *as if* it had a separate being of its own. It is this human tendency that religious leaders find eminently exploitable.

Existence in the collective consciousness is not nonexistence, strictly speaking. Beyond any doubt, however, it is wholly human. Throughout history human society and activities have been profoundly influenced—indeed, radically altered—by gods, demons, ancestral spirits, oracles, myths, symbols, and other manifestations of supernaturalism created from the collective imagination. Cultural changes, rituals, wars, marriage customs, taboos, naming systems, and numerous other social phenomena have been brought about by such causes, often because the ignorant believe in the literal truth of something that their leaders have fabricated.

One should be able to choose one's mental constructs intelligently, rejecting those that do not serve one's needs or that lead to social injustice. In the feminist view, God has been of both these varieties. If God is simply a collective concept, it follows that he is—and always has been—entirely controllable by men.

One may strongly suspect that this is the case. Even today men go on constantly explaining and reexplaining God to each other. Like ants working and reworking their anthill, they change his shape little by little. Each may aim at a slightly dif-

ferent pattern, so the collective result takes on its own lineaments. Men are never finished working on God; they describe
him incessantly, together with his alleged relationships with humanity, which have run the gamut from pitiless vengeance to
all-forgiving love.

Men have always tacitly admitted that they create their own
deities. Eastern sages long declared that true deity inheres in
the Self, and the Self (atman) is identical with God. Gnostic
Christians also admitted as much, copying their doctrine from
the worshipers of Hermes, Osiris, Orpheus, and other popular
mystery cult saviors of the early Christian era. In all such religions salvation was thought to depend on achieving total identity with the god through sacraments of communion and in-
vocational prayer, so as to partake of the same immortality. God
and self are interchangeable in the promises of Jesus (John
15:4*), which the Gospel writers copied from Hermetic and
Mithraic traditions. "The kingdom of God is within you" (Luke
17:21) was also a Hermetic doctrine before it was Christian.

Despite these precedents, Western religious thought has remained doggedly simplistic in its reluctance to probe "supernatural" and "spiritual" archetypes at their source, the hidden
depths of the human mind. Our consciousness finds it difficult
to comprehend itself. Perhaps this is why there is so little understanding of our obvious tendency to attribute social systems
to the edicts of parent images in imitation of our childhood
experience. It was a mother during the early several million
years of human existence, a father during the later several
thousand. God is a great deal younger than Goddess, because
for most of humanity's time on earth the only recognizable parenthood was maternal.

We are barely beginning to understand the enormous tragedy of the historical clash between the archaic mother religion
and the new, aggressive father religion, which took place from
approximately 1000 B.C. to A.D. 1000, and which drastically
changed the world. The sexist attitudes, injustices, and outrages
that plague our society today have their foundation in religious
imagery. The reason a feminist needs a skeptical view of father

---

*All Bible passages are quoted from the King James Version of the Bible.

religion is that sexism is the product of that religion, and will remain so as long as God is assigned a masculine gender.

About three thousand years ago certain followers of the patriarchal gods began to derogate and humanize, even diabolize, the world's goddesses, in order to promote the idea of masculine supremacy. Inevitably, this led to devaluation of women in general. The process continued with ever-increasing rigor as male priesthoods used military might to seize secular power, culminating in totally male-oriented cults such as Judaism, Christianity, and Islam.

Social miseries proliferated whenever and wherever the grip of patriarchal theology squeezed. Even today a conventional Western religious upbringing can permanently injure a woman's sense of self-worth, because of its barely concealed hints of female sinfulness, inferiority, and uncleanness. The fiction that Eve was the first sinner was used for centuries to impose guilt by association on all women. Women can fit themselves into the interstices of patriarchal religions only at considerable cost to their sexual identity, not to mention their common sense. For such reasons many modern women are glad to deny the validity of the patriarchal tradition and may experience a newly skeptical attitude as liberating.

In addition, modern feminist scholars have rediscovered the Goddess, whose archetypal image remains as fresh as it was four thousand years ago in the hidden mind of every individual born of woman. It is becoming clear that the feminine image of the divine has as much, if not more, psychological validity as the masculine one. In denial of their conventional training, people are beginning to ask: how could our ancestors have spent almost two thousand years envisioning a Father without a corresponding Mother?

The answer is, of course, that they didn't. In practice the Mother of God or Queen of Heaven continued to occupy the same position in the Christian pantheon as in the earlier pagan one, even when churchmen officially declared her nondivine (though somewhat mysteriously miraculous). Medieval Mariolatry provided some degree of comfort for downtrodden women, although it could not assuage their pain more than just a little, since churchmen declared Mary exempt from the supposed crimes and disadvantages of mortal women. Mary was sexless, sinless, and absorbed in her relational role of mother to the exclusion of all other roles. The God who had impregnated her without pleasure had usurped all her earlier functions, such as creatress, lawgiver, judge, protectress, nurturer, spirit of nature, inventor of the civilized arts. The church insisted that the multitudes who worshipped her as divine were not really doing any such thing, simply because the church had forbidden them to view her as a true Goddess.

The patriarchs favored an image of motherhood like that of the official Mary—all give and no take, impossibly pure, and always obedient to the Father's slightest whim. They were fond of pointing out that Mary (in direct contradiction to all that is known of maternal nature) never even protested against the Father's demand for her (their) son's cruel death. Tamely accepting all fatherly decrees, she found glory in humility: the same inglorious sort of glory that earthly mothers were expected to attain by devoting all their lives to unceasing care of husbands and children—though for this, too, they might be insultingly labeled possessive or overprotective.

Male scholars now must reluctantly concede validity to the archaic Mother Goddess, but they try to belittle her as an agricultural version of Mary. She is seen as the fruitful earth, productive but passive. Her inert soil awaits the ever-so-important planting of the godlike seed. Some even suppose that the Mother Goddess assumed preeminence only in prehistoric agricultural communities, because people associated the planting of the seed with human reproduction. This view of active "male" planting in passive "female" soil was particularly favored by fathers of the Christian church, whose God distinctly informed them that the human soul resides only in a father's semen, and a mother's body is mere soulless dirt where the seed can grow. Their God somehow neglected to tell them about the human ovum.

Unfortunately for the agricultural theory of matriarchy, it appears that the Goddess was the supreme deity long before humans discovered either fatherhood or farming. Men of primitive farming cultures tell modern anthropologists that the planting must be done only by women, because only women know how to bring forth life. And in the most ancient cultures it was assumed that women knew the magical trick of impregnating themselves, a trick that men greatly envied for untold millennia and tried to imitate in a thousand naive experiments, ranging from transvestism and self-castration to Tantric sex, where men strove to absorb female fluids instead of the other way around.

When agriculture was established it was closely associated with female creativity. Birth giving, however, was no less visible in preagricultural societies. Myths around the world speak of the Great Mother giving birth to the first people in the beginning, without any reference to a fertilizing male principle. Often the Goddess produces a whole living cosmos just to amuse herself, because she had found the previous state of formlessness or nonbeing rather tiresome.

Only a pitiful remnant of ancient Goddess religion passed into patriarchal literature such as the works of classical writers or the Judeo-Christian Bible. Feminist scholars seeking their roots in such sources are in the same position as black scholars seeking the cultures of their African ancestors in the writings of missionaries, who condemned those cultures as the creations of devils. Some attenuated notion of the older society might seep through all the bias, but it might be virtually unrecognizable.

Patriarchal societies spent centuries revising their sacred histories and destroying the older scriptures of the Goddess, to the point of setting whole libraries afire and slaughtering record-keeping priestesses. The process was crowned by early Christian vandals, who burned all books written by women to support their own contention that the female sex was incapable of thought, scholarship, or theology. Only a very few writings of ancient priestesses were allowed to survive, such as the Sybilline Books, provided they were revised to seem to predict the coming of the Christian deity.

Philosophy was declared unsuitable for women and feminine theology heretical, punishable by death. In such ways the thinking of half the human race—the more moral half, at that—was violently eradicated from collective knowledge. Bits and pieces of the Goddess were sometimes adopted, where they were too firmly embedded in the hearts of the people to be eliminated, under the guise of Christian saints or pseudohistorical queens. Others became incarnations of Mary as "Our Lady of Such-and-Such." Still others were diabolized as the "Queen of Witches" (Hecate, Persephone, Diana, Herodias, Lilith, Ashtoreth, and so on) or as dangerous spirits of water or woodland, night-mares or succubae, lamias or banshees, the mermaid, the White Lady, the Morrigan, or one of a thousand other tempting she-demons whose attentions men both dreaded and desired, for they were the stuff of all forbidden sexual fantasy.

The classical writers had already trivialized many aspects of the Goddess by breaking them up into bureaucratic pantheons confined to one department apiece, such as the love goddess, sea goddess, moon goddess, earth goddess, and so on, as if they were not assorted manifestations of the same deity. Hellenic Greeks and Romans also laid the literary groundwork for humanizing the transcendent Goddess so her myths seemed to be only old stories about ordinary women. A well-known example is Medea, a supposedly historical witch tragically undone by her ungovernable passion for Greece's legendary hero Jason, which drove her to various crimes and an inevitable punishment. Even though Pliny expressly stated that Medea was the ruler of the heavens, and Herodotus said she was the Parthians' Great Goddess, immortal and all-wise, these remarks were ignored in favor of Euripides' version of her as a human, eminently fallible woman.

Actually, Medea was the eponymous Mother Goddess of the Medes, an all-healer from whose name came the word *medicine,* embodying the feminine Wisdom principle anciently known as *med.* Another incarnation of the same principle was Medusa (Greek Metis), converted into a poisonous she-demon by patriarchal reinterpretation and slain by the ancestral hero of Athenian patriarchy.

Of course it was just as easy to humanize a Goddess as to deify a woman or a man. This sort of thing went on all the time. There was constant exchange between mortal and immortal in every religious tradition. Roman emperors were made gods (by other human beings), sometimes after death, sometimes during their lives. Firstborn sons were routinely called sons of God, especially when they were supposed to be conceived by a "virgin bride of God" or priestess in the temple after a sacred marriage in which the god's part was played by either a priapic statue or the high priest. Initiates into any of the numerous mystery cults of the early Christian era—including Christianity itself—were taught that the god was actually embodied in them as a result of the holy communion in which he became flesh of their flesh. To share his body was the essential rite of sharing his immortality. The church considered itself empowered to transform human beings into demigods (saints) by a few ceremonial words and gestures. Gods and demons could also become incarnate as human beings, such as Jesus or Heracles-Apollo, and could enter into or "possess" human bodies. Considering all the permutations and combinations of supernatural and mortal in human beliefs, an anthropologist from a nonhuman species would be justified in declaring that we humans invented all our deities as mirror images of ourselves.

For the female half of our race, however, the process was interrupted. Men have worked unhindered on the creation of their god for many centuries now, devising thousands of variations on the basic image and devoting to its greater glory all the best artwork, music, architecture, and literary skill, with expense no object, so the less imaginative majority can experience a male divinity via innumerable representations and symbols. If the same had been done for the Goddess over all these centuries, she would now be just as real, or unquestioningly accepted, as the present Judeo-Christian God or Allah is to the mass of believers.

Theologians have toiled endlessly at explaining God's will (as well as stating that God's will is unknowable). With their usual predilection for doublethink, men cheerfully overlooked all their own contradictions in declaring that God was really there, yet not really there. He was all-powerful and anything he wanted to happen would happen. Yet mere mortals could flout his authority and deny him his will—even, or perhaps one should say particularly, women. Men took it upon themselves to punish those suspected of defying God, apparently believing God incapable of taking care of the matter by himself. Yet he was depicted as implacably vengeful, arranging eternities of hideous torture for evildoers, even while he was also all-forgiving and all-merciful. His decrees were said to be immutable; yet humans prayed to him in the fond belief that their human words could make him change his mind. He created the unbreakable laws of nature, yet idly broke them whenever he wanted to toss off a miracle, usually to impress a few ignorant peasants. (He never staged miracles in places or times where they could be verified by trained observers). He was supposed to be the spirit of rationality, yet he was accessible only through an irrational leap of faith. He claimed to love his only-begotten son, but insisted on having the latter most cruelly murdered. He claimed all humanity as his beloved children, yet (according to the Old Testament) set one tribe against another in vast slaughters, ordering tens or hundreds of thousands massacred time and again in almost the same breath that commanded, "Thou shalt not kill." A curious God, indeed.

Women especially were taught from infancy to worship this God, with peculiar effects on their psyches. It was tacitly thought once women became thoroughly accustomed to envisioning the characteristics of men in God, they would be more inclined to see the characteristics of God in men. That is, they would be adoringly deferential to the gender said to be made in God's image and would view themselves as sinful creatures needing constant monitoring by the more godlike sex. God could be invoked to hold each woman to the vows she made, often unthinkingly, in the rosy haze of youthful romance: to care for an adult man as assiduously as if he were a baby, cook his meals, clean his house, wash his clothes, nurse his illnesses, and look after his every comfort (including sexual servicing and general obedience to his slightest whim), all for no pay except the kind of subsistence granted a slave or indentured servant.

Men devoted themselves to a vast cultural effort to overlook the essential services provided by women in every aspect of their lives from birth to death. Yet the achievements of every achieving man depended on female work. Almost nothing of any value was ever done by a man who had to take care of his own household and cookery, not to mention child care and other mundane chores of daily life. Indeed, most men took pride in their ignorance of such matters.

Patriarchal convention even managed to overlook mother-hood, the most vital of all human functions, on which the sur-vival and continuance of the species depends. The entire hu-man race was referred to as "man." Ancestors were collectively "fathers." Mothers were said not to give life to new individuals, so much as to give children to their husbands, so that male surnames and inheritances might be perpetuated. A woman with no husband to give her children to was not supposed to have children (she could never give them to herself). She was disgraced if she became pregnant, yet—irrationality com-pounded!—she was not allowed to terminate the disgraceful pregnancy either. Only men reserved for themselves the right to terminate the lives of other human beings, which they did with huge enthusiasm in their endless wars, crusades, and per-secutions. It was often asked, but never answered, why a God who wanted every child born in wedlock arranged for so many of them to be born outside of it. Men apparently identified themselves with the baby that must be taken care of, rather than with the mother who must do the caretaking. It has been remarked that if men had to bear and nurture children, abor-tion would never have been declared illegal and God would have been goodnaturedly in favor of it, just as he was in favor of killing inconvenient Canaanites, Midianites, Amorites, Ari-ans, Cathari, pagans, infidels, and witches.

In recent years women have been questioning not only the patriarchy's ambivalent attitudes about male-initiated versus fe-male-initiated termination of life, but also nearly all other pa-triarchal premises.

It has been clear for more than a century that Western re-ligion has been the prime stronghold of male domination in society. God's men have always been eager to enlist women as serving attendants, helpful proselytizers, loyal disciples, fund-raisers, providers of refreshments, and lower pillars of the church, but never as its policymakers. Some churches now con-sider themselves generously liberal in speaking of a Father-Mother God or proclaiming God devoid of gender as a sop to contemporary feminist sentiment. Some women have been or-dained as Christian ministers or Jewish rabbis. Such women, however, still must prove themselves dedicated servants of a traditionally male god and must accept exclusion from the higher executive levels of "his" organizations. As with many other male-dominated fields, women are grudgingly allowed in, as long as they defer to the men, mind their manners, do the more menial jobs, and keep their hands off the real money.

For such reasons many women become impatient and disgusted with the struggle against traditional religious structures. They turn away, to devote themselves to reconstructing updated versions of the long-destroyed Goddess faith, which is obviously more compatible with the feminine temperament.

In doing so, women should take care to distinguish the Goddess faith from crude superstition. The early Christian fathers effectively insisted on this point on behalf of their own church even while they were shamelessly adopting as many superstitious notions as possible from the ancient world's social environment—including the fundamentally superstitious idea that one can become immortal by ingesting the blood of an immortal being, or that supernatural entities can inhabit human bodies, or that solemn verbal invocation of holy names alone can produce real happenings, and so on.

However silly their own notions, churchmen nevertheless contrived to discredit the Goddess by mocking her cults' elements of magic that usually failed to work, prophecies that didn't come true, healing amulets that didn't heal, love charms that attracted no lover, or resurrection spells that, understandably, failed to bring the dead back to life. Even though Christians themselves appropriated nearly every kind of magic for their own use (inventing new canonical names for it to make it seem a novelty), they condemned the magic of the old priestesses either on the ground that it didn't work, and therefore was folly, or did work, and therefore proved the involvement of devils. Churchmen never bothered to resolve this logical contradiction before persecuting magic-working women. It was enough that they were women laying claim to the sort of spiritual power that the churches reserved for men.

Christians also condemned every other group of people with a world-birthing Mother Goddess concept or female holy images in their temples. Not only the beliefs of primitive peoples but also those of highly sophisticated societies were scorned by Christian missionaries as benighted heathenism, savage ignorance, and devil worship. The missionaries needed only to see a holy statue with female breasts in order to begin raising their accusatory cries against heresy.

If numerous followers of the "false" Goddess faith got killed in the process of imposing the "true" God's word on the heathen, Christian men were unperturbed. The survivors would be that much more easily converted, and the followers of the true faith kept busy relieving them of their lands and other property along with their devilish superstitions. Much of Western civilization was developed in just this way, from the third century A.D. to the present. The Judeo-Christian God has always been the world's greatest imperialist, because greedy men shaped him from the beginning in order to confirm and bless their own greed.

Superstition has been a constant element in all faiths, including the Judeo-Christian one, ever since humans began associating one thought with another. During the age of scientific enlightenment Christianity began to destroy itself from within by clinging stubbornly to outdated superstitious beliefs long after educated people had realized their absurdity. Much theological casuistry was devoted to upholding these crude concepts against the rising tide of reason in the nineteenth and early twentieth centuries.

It came down to an intellectual war between reason and faith, wherein faith could preserve itself only by claiming a special privileged status, set apart and out of the reach of rationality. So the church's official position came full circle from early Christianity's pretended allegiance to reason. More modern clergymen insisted that they felt no compunction to justify their illogical beliefs with reason, although their writings incessantly tried to do just that. Churches readily took advantage of ignorant folks' love of myths, miracles, charms, amulets, processions, pilgrimages, prayers, rituals, exorcisms, recitations, holy water, feast days, sacrificial offerings, and elaborately decorated idols, the worship of which, however, was always carefully defined as *not* idol worship. The manifestations of the superstitious mindset were usually perceived as the surest guarantee of Christianity's survival in an increasingly skeptical world.

It would be all too easy to justify the faith of the Goddess in exactly the same way—particularly because the myths, miracles, charms, amulets, processions, and so on, were largely invented by Goddess worshipers in the first place. But women should learn from men's historical mistakes. Men's history shows that a religion dependent on the credulity of the simpleminded does not serve humanity's best interests. Such a religion is too readily exploitable, too useful to callous commercialism, and ultimately a cynical predator on the very people it claims to help.

Therefore Goddess adherents should try to purge their faith of truly superstitious or irrational beliefs, which can only work to its discredit. Instead of insisting on the external, objective existence of the unprovable as an article of faith, those attracted to the Goddess should perhaps address themselves to an entirely new task, that of comprehending the real wellsprings of religion within the human mind.

Such an unprecedented approach to the religious impulse opens up an enormous field of inquiry and seeks answers to many questions rooted in human psychology. What do religious images really mean to us? Why do we think we need them? What is the psychophysiological nature of the so-called religious experience? Why do our most irrational beliefs seem so precious to us? What is the relationship between sensual experience and religious thought? Why have religions so consistently concerned themselves with sexuality in one way or another, positive or negative? Why are father gods credited with one set of characteristics and mother goddesses with a different set? What went on in the minds of the humans who created these divine parent figures in the first place, and why do a majority of humans never seem to outgrow their needs for such figures?

Like any other psychosocial phenomenon, religion can be subjected to commonsense analysis. As one of the most elaborate constructions of human language and symbolism, it is rooted in the deepest recesses of the individual and collective mind. For countless centuries, visionaries made the journey inward to those deep roots (most fundamentally bound up with the Mother image) by subjective methods, all the while fancying their progress to be outward toward a cosmic truth. Yet all the while they also recognized and spoke of the journey as a progress toward the deity in their own hearts. The attendant implication of universality seems to have been nothing more than the common psychological mechanism known as projection.

Today we know that whatever cosmic truth may be, it lies forever beyond the mental grasp of our species. We are no more capable of comprehending the universe than a colony of ants, walking over a computer, would be capable of comprehending the mechanism's principles or purpose. To insist that the universe must have a meaning that humans can understand is a kind of ultimate hubris, perhaps directly attributable to typically patriarchal glorification of the self, disguised as an all-knowing God.

We can't teach ourselves to control "cosmic forces"—a favorite buzzword of the superstitious—by the power of our will, any more than a cow could teach herself to speak human words. A cow's brain, mouth, and larynx are not genetically formed to speak human words. Neither are we genetically formed to see all the reality we would like to see. Even our most sophisticated machines can show us no more of the real universe than the tip of the iceberg; nay, a single pebble on the peak of a veritable Everest of unknown and probably forever unknowable truths.

Some individuals, finding an impersonal unknown too uncomfortable, choose to call the whole mystery Goddess or God, which gives it an illusion of accessibility, as a parent is accessible to a child. This is like the kind of magic that consists of putting names to things and then confusing the name with the thing itself, and supposing that control of the name will control the thing also. Such magic is the basis of all religious invocation and evocation, prayer, chant, and ritual addresses. It is hardly surprising in a creature whose first lesson in survival is that Mother, the lifegiver, usually comes when she is called.

But women grow up and become mothers themselves, thus taking on the archetypal characteristics of the Goddess as caretaker and nurturer, the one who is responsible. Females seem to be genetically programmed to act not because they are ordered to do so, but because they see that an action is needed (for example, a child is hungry). Women are naturally inclined to assume responsibility for the welfare of others. Men require more training in adult responsibility, because they share with other male animals a natural self-centeredness and a certain indifference to future consequences.

Growing up in the feminist sense involves putting away childish things, including both self-centeredness and the childish belief in magic, such as word-magic and other sympathetic forms that have been consistently failing for thousands of years to produce the effects they claim to produce. Because the theory underlying such magic is false, its practice can hardly be useful except in those cases where success can be attributed to deliberate fraud or coincidence or emotional factors, as in the cure of psychosomatic illness by a profound emotional experience.

It has been noted that ancient Goddess worship was bound up with magic of the crudest sort. After all, this religion arose with the dawn of the human species, as soon as humans became truly human and were able to view motherhood as a power that created and supported them. Our primitive ancestors were not deep thinkers, nor even very keen observers of natural cause and effect, as shown by their many erroneous convictions. Primitive folk tend to be highly conservative, which helps them pass along time-tested survival skills from generation to generation for thousands of years, but also passes along by the same route innumerable ancestral mistakes, which are similarly learned and accepted without question.

After the invention of writing, errors enshrined in the sacred mysteries of alphabetical letters became even harder to dislodge. Many were the centuries in which the words *it is written* were virtually the same as *it is so*. The Judeo-Christian scriptures, for example, convinced more than a hundred generations that the earth was flat, the universe was created in seven days, angels carried messages routinely between earth and a populated sky, virgins could bear children, demons could be ordered away by a spoken formula, blindness could be cured with spit, dried-out skeletons could be reclothed with flesh and made living humans again, all by the power of words. And because it is written, it was all "gospel truth."

Belief in the efficacy of verbal formulas and other magic often served as a symbol substitute for the desired power to change real circumstances. In humanity's primitive ignorance of realities that science later would make accessible to human understanding, magic—both religious and secular—seemed to help. Historically, Judeo-Christianity firmly aligned itself with the magical way of thinking when it so bitterly opposed the scientific advances that conflicted with its "received" traditions. The whole premise of Christianity was a superstitious belief in a need for salvation from God's sadistic hell, a salvation made necessary by the mythical disobedience of humanity's first mother, and somehow brought about by revering the memory and drinking the blood of God's ritually murdered son/self. Without the myth—the Eden story, the imagined hell, the vengeful deity and his peculiarly cumbrous mechanism of forgiveness—there would be nothing to be saved from, hence no salvation required.

Superstition may be described as any tendency to confuse human mental constructs with external reality. This is also one definition of insanity. Every humanlike personification of a nonhuman, impersonal cosmos may be called superstitious, including the ancient images of the Goddess herself. Modern Goddess faith, however, may be called nonsuperstitious when it recognizes the basic humanity of the symbol, seeking not to project the symbol onto natural phenomena so much as to combine it with perceptions and memories of natural phenomena within the mind. We know it is important and enriching to think poetically, but we need not mistake a poem for a factual report.

Nevertheless, Goddess imagery is indubitably useful and empowering for women struggling in this day to cast off the monstrous inferiority complex forced upon them by centuries of ingrained, unrelenting patriarchy. It helps to know of whole civilizations that revered the feminine principle ahead of the male; that regarded women as the holier sex, invested with superior wisdom and moral sense; that viewed humanity not as man but as womb-man. It helps to assert the femininity within one's self as an awe-inspiring power independent of any masculine influence. It helps to sense one's fellow feeling for nature as a personal communion with a transcendent Mother. For most women it heals some of the hurts that patriarchy has inflicted to envision the ancient philosophies of the Goddess, where respectable place was made for tenderness, sensuality, mother love, family ties, sex, fun, playfulness, and esthetic sensibilities especially appealing to women. We have only begun to explore the inner, unconscious world where such imagery can lead us. It is a rich and colorful world indeed.

For these and similar reasons, women need Goddess imagery in their lives. Men also need it, as much or even more. The Mother figure traditionally embodies tolerance, sympathy, and love. No paternal god ever encouraged such clear articulation of a humane morality as the nurturant Mother. It is precisely for such feminine qualities that Christians revere their concept of Jesus, whose legend presents him as the very opposite of everything macho. Men can't attain a fully mature, responsible morality—that is, a benevolent sensitivity to human needs—unless they can make contact with such feminine qualities within themselves. The Mother symbol draws the world in this direction more strongly than the Father symbol ever did.

Therefore true feminism implies and embraces a return to the idea of the supreme Goddess, once nurturant Mother of everything including all gods, who owed her their allegiance and respect as the author of their being. Because religious imagery is sexism's major medium of transmission, religious imagery must be consciously corrected to convey nonsexist attitudes.

In the process the mistakes of the past can be avoided. We can eschew crude superstition, which can only eventually destroy itself by setting up false convictions in opposition to demonstrable facts. Those who cling to false convictions—no matter how long established or canonical—place themselves in a vulnerable position and possibly subject themselves to crises of faith. Surely a system of religious imagery can be established on a firmer foundation than that, in view of what we now know about the workings of the human mind.

The inner experiences and thoughts of many women point the way toward a new and better morality. At least women are beginning to come together to share their perceptions, in defiance of the patriarchal rules that have always operated to keep them in isolation, divided and therefore conquered. Women together can remake the Goddess that arose naturally in the long infancy of the human race, when she was the only author-of-being that anyone knew. Patriarchy has had a long run. In the true test of humane values, it has failed. Now the great circle begins to close again. We wonder if ideological wholeness can be achieved in time to save us from ourselves.

PART ONE

The Virgin
Intimations

Names and identifying details have been changed.

Prayers

"Now I lay me down to sleep, I pray the Lord my soul to keep. And if I die before I wake, I pray the Lord my soul to take."

After this nightly request came a variable list of people whom I directed God to bless, though I always wondered why God should bless them just on my say-so. It seemed to me that God would make up his own mind without any interference from me. I seriously doubted my power to change the mind of even one grownup, let alone God.

I began to wonder, what did it mean to bless? The people I recommended to God's attention seemed quite unchanged by any blessing or lack of blessing. How could one tell when the request for blessing was answered, if it ever was?

I asked, and was told that God's blessing made people good and happy. Then I began to drop assorted individuals out of my list, which was growing too long anyway. Grandparents, uncles, aunts, cousins, and miscellaneous acquaintances seemed good and happy enough for all practical purposes. A nightly blessing could hardly make much difference, even if God paid attention to me.

Many years into my own adulthood, I finally discovered the original meaning of *blessing* from the old Saxon *bleodswean*: to sanctify an altar by covering it with blood. Even the Bible told of altars consecrated in this way for the use of deities, whose principal food was the blood of sacrificed animals. To this day blood is poured out in kosher killing for Yahweh, who ordered his people not to eat blood, because that was to be set aside for offerings to himself.

As a child I certainly didn't want anyone covered with blood, but not having any clue as to the word's past or present meanings, I went on wondering what it meant to be blessed. Was I blessed? Sometimes I was good and happy, sometimes not. Most of the time I was not aware of any excess in either direction. Was it impossible for me to be consciously happy except when God specifically remembered to bless me? Was this only when other people asked him to? What would happen to me if he forgot?

Again I had an uneasy, insecure feeling about God. If my unhappiness indicated God's displeasure, then surely he was especially displeased with me when I was most visible to him, visiting his own house, the church. For each visit I was turned out of the play clothes that I felt comfortable in. I was made painfully clean. My hair was screwed into pigtails so tight that the skin of my face was drawn back. My dress was starched so stiffly that its folds rattled. My feet were encased in tight white socks and shiny, pinchy "good" shoes. My hands were hampered by white gloves, which I was ordered to keep clean, though somehow they always turned grubby around the fingertips within the hour. Thus arrayed, already sweating, itching, and suffering, I was conveyed to the house of God to endure another endless session of physical immobility and mental ennui.

If God knew everything and could read everyone's mind, then he knew perfectly well how I disliked visiting him. I suspected that I was not a good candidate for blessing, because my relationship with God was not the best. Nothing I could do would change the way I felt about Sunday mornings. And why should I ask God to bless me if he didn't want to? Was he not supposed to know best? Who was I to tell God what to do?

This thought led me to closer consideration of my bedtime prayer. I asked God to keep my soul as I slept. Did that mean it went out of my body during sleep? Was he supposed to return it to me so I could wake up? I wondered what would happen if I did die before I woke. If I had omitted the prayer the night before, would God refuse to take my soul? What would become of it then?

Sometimes I tried to articulate these questions to those who were teaching me about God's mysterious ways. Either they misunderstood me, or they answered me with platitudes that enlightened me not at all. When I asked what would happen to my soul if God failed to take it, I was hastily reassured that there was no possibility of that, none whatsoever; I was not to be afraid. This left me more perplexed than before. I hadn't been afraid, just curious. Not the question, but the answer planted a seed of fear. If God failed to pick up my soul, then was its fate so terrible that it couldn't even be mentioned?

I thought it a distinct possibility that God would ignore me when it came to the crunch, because he had so many other people to take care of who seemed to get along with him better than I did. I wanted to know what to expect but no one would tell me. I was reminded of the time I went to the hospital to have my tonsils out, and they told me I wasn't to worry about what to expect; everything would be perfectly all right. It wasn't perfectly all right at all. It was horrible. From this I learned that whenever adults told you not to worry, you were in for a really bad time.

I wondered about the efficacy of prayers in general. I was told that when you wanted something really badly, you should pray for it. Like Santa Claus in the department store who usually produced on Christmas morning the very things you had told him about, God would answer prayers. God, however, proved less dependable than Santa Claus.

Every time I prayed for something specific, my request was refused. If I prayed for sunshine on the day of a picnic, it rained. If I prayed for the return of a beloved toy that was lost, it stayed lost. Clearly God wasn't listening to me.

When I placed the problem before adult authority, I was told that God couldn't be expected to answer every prayer. Many prayers were about trivial things. Maybe God was too busy to bother with those. There were more important prayers to be attended to, serious, sincere prayers, matters of life and death.

But I knew God couldn't be relied on to answer those either. I remembered the severe illness of one of my aunts. Everyone in the family earnestly prayed that she would survive. She died anyway. Then there were resigned sighs: it was God's will, he had decided to take her to heaven. So what difference had the praying made? If God went ahead and did whatever he wanted, regardless of people's prayers, why did they bother?

I began to get the feeling that prayers were really nothing but expressions of a wish, as when I fantasized some feat I knew to be impossible: "I wish I could fly" or "I wish I could be a fairy princess." A prayer had the same aura of unreality. It was just a thing you said. I stopped expecting answers. Good things happened or bad things happened no matter how you talked about them to God. He wouldn't care whether you thanked him or reproached him. Why should he? How could it matter to him what mere people thought of him? Surely it wasn't God's place to try to earn the goodwill of people by catering to their wishes.

Or was it?

The Father

When I first walked into the Sunday school room in the church basement, I got a terrible shock. Facing me on the wall hung a life-size Crucifixion scene with a decidedly unattractive Jesus dripping blood and twisting his face in obvious agony.

Children of those long-ago days were not so blasé about gore and suffering as today's television-trained tots. I had never seen a graphic representation of torture. The picture shook me so much that I felt it physically. That first day I hardly listened to the teacher, so occupied was I with fighting my inner queasiness and trying not to look at that tormented, half-naked body—yet compulsively looking, again and again, until every strained tendon and muscle was printed on my young mind's eye.

Later, when I had become more accustomed to the suffering of Jesus, I heard the teacher say that we children were ourselves responsible for his suffering, because we were sinful creatures like all the rest of humanity. Each time we were bad and disobeyed the rules of God and parents, we caused Jesus to suffer more, because Jesus wanted children to be good and obedient. My throat closed up in revolt. I absolutely would not take responsibility for this poor man's pain. I, too tender-hearted to step on a passing caterpillar as the other kids gleefully did; I, who wanted to pet all creatures, even spiders, which I carefully invited to walk over my fingers while the other kids exclaimed "yecchh!"; I was to be held liable for this awful torture of a grown man? Certainly not. Were not the men really responsible shown right there in the picture, their scowling faces in the background betraying their guilt? Moreover, who had ordered this hideous execution in the first place? Who but God?

In my secret thoughts I pondered this. God was supposed to be an all-loving Father, kinder than any human father, even the kindest. Yet this loving Father ordained a horrible death for his only-begotten son, who had never done any bad thing in his whole life. He had been a perfect son, a son of whom any father should have been proud. What was wrong with this Father? The teacher never told us, but it confirmed my suspicion that God wasn't to be trusted. Even if you were as good as Jesus and behaved yourself perfectly and did everything right, look where it could get you.

We were taught that when we went upstairs to the grownups' church, we would participate in a gruesome rite. We would eat the flesh and blood of this poor, tormented son. Though it had the appearance of bread and wine, we must never forget that it was really human flesh and blood.

It seemed that not even death could end the degradation God had ordained for his son. The poor man was not only crucified but even cannibalized by the same people who professed to love him.

I didn't know whether I loved Jesus. I was told that he died because he loved me, but that seemed a peculiar way to show love. I certainly didn't want to be expected to return the favor. Of one thing, however, I was very sure: I didn't want to eat Jesus, lovingly or otherwise.

At my first communion I gagged when the wafer was placed in my mouth. I feared I would be unable to swallow it and would disgrace myself. Everyone else seemed to take Jesus-eating calmly. Somehow I got the bit of paste down my throat, but afterward I felt none of the uplift and purification I had been told to expect. I felt soiled and guilty, as I thought one ought to feel after consuming human flesh. I couldn't believe this was really God's idea of the right thing to do.

In time I encountered other unsettling indications of God's ill will toward human beings, who, it seemed, were all his children in some mysterious way, even though Jesus was his "only-begotten" child. There was also the matter of God's treatment of his first son and daughter in the Garden of Eden, which boded no good for those who would come afterward.

God put a magic tree of knowledge where Adam and Eve could get at it. In his omniscience he knew in advance that they would get at it. Then he forbade them to commit the crime he knew they would commit and sat back to await results. After they disobeyed, as expected, he cursed them and all their innocent descendants forever, condemning every one of them to a hell of eternal torture. After many centuries and many generations of pitiless damnation, he relented enough to send the aforementioned son to earth to lift the burden of sin from some, but by no means all.

This "all-forgiving" Father seemed anything but forgiving. On the contrary, he bore a grudge longer than anyone could reasonably expect, and inflicted worse punishments than anyone could bear. All this for a disobedience that he had himself set up and made inevitable.

If he was really all-forgiving, why didn't he forgive Adam and Eve and everybody else right away and welcome them all into heaven all through the centuries and treat them kindly? Instead he blamed them even for being born, which I learned was a sinful thing to do despite the fact that you couldn't help it. And this God refused to forgive anybody until he was appeased with the blood of his unhappy son, poor good-boy Jesus. I thought, if I had a father as mean as that, I would run away from home.

And what was the real nature of the crime for which God imposed such sweeping, mind-boggling punishment? We were told that the stolen apple was only a symbolic apple. It really meant the knowledge of good and evil. But surely that was precisely the same knowledge that we were sent to church to acquire. If Eve hadn't filched this knowledge against God's orders, how could we now tell right from wrong? Did God want us to know or did he want us to remain ignorant? It was puzzling. If God told the world it was evil to seek knowledge, then why were we children sent to school?

We were also taught to plead with God, via the Lord's Prayer, not to lead us into temptation. Each time I recited this I wondered, why should he? The Garden of Eden story disquietingly suggested that he was quite capable of it. He had led Adam and Eve into temptation, though he blamed it on them and on the snake. Was God in the habit of leading people into temptation so he could make them suffer for it afterward? I feared it might be so. Why else would we be begging him not to do it?

I remembered my mother talking with other mothers about putting "temptation" out of the reach of small children so they wouldn't get in trouble. It seemed only sensible. Children were not as wise as parents in foreseeing possible consequences. Was God less kind and less wise than an ordinary mother?

I also remembered my father taking care to find out precisely who was responsible for an offense before scolding the offender. He wasn't unduly harsh or unfair. He never blamed anyone for what someone else had done. Though he was certainly neither all-powerful nor all-knowing, was he perhaps morally superior to God?

Fallible earthly parents, for all their fallibility, seemed easier to live with than God. They were kinder and more trustworthy. They didn't tease children with temptation to make an excuse for cruel punishment. They didn't give kids the rope with which to hang themselves. They tried to prevent problems with care and foresight. If God was such a good parent, why couldn't he have done even better?

I thought that surely with the merest flick of his omnipotent finger, God could have made a world full of people who were naturally good and kind and happy. Why hadn't he? Why the messing about with forbidden apple trees, a nasty Crucifixion, and an even nastier hell? In time I was told that all this somehow indicated that God wanted people to come to him of their own free will, so he left them free to choose good or evil for themselves. But this statement, like many others I was given on the subject of God, didn't compute. It seemed the cards were stacked against poor, ignorant, struggling people from the beginning. And what about all those generations between Adam and Eve and Jesus, who had never even had a chance?

Considering the kind of character God seemed to have, I did not want to come to him of my own free will. What I really wanted to do was avoid him at all costs.

And what was the reward we could expect if we did come to him? Eternal bliss in heaven. Well, what was that like? Though it was impossible for us to imagine such beatitude, it seemed that the bliss would consist of living in God's presence and contemplating his glory forever. I was not convinced that this would be such a great pleasure. I would rather contemplate the things I liked on earth: trees, grass, sunshine, flowers, snow, clouds, stars, animals. Even if God was the maker of all these, he would not necessarily be any more interesting to look at.

I also learned that God didn't particularly want to contemplate me. I was female, and females were only marginal people as far as God was concerned. The hymns that we were taught spoke only of the "faith of the *fathers*." They said "Christ receiveth sinful *men*." Jesus died for *men*, and "peace is made 'twixt *man* and God"; also, "ye that are *men* now serve Him." There was a lot about Christian soldiers marching as to war, bravely fighting the good fight, winning the victory, calling each other *brothers*. Fairest Lord Jesus was called the son of God and *man*, not of God and woman. This surprised me. I had received an earlier impression that there was no man in Fairest Lord Jesus' parentage.

One hymn said, "As *brothers* of the *Son* of *Man*, rise up, O *men* of God!" Another hymn seemed to oppose racial discrimination, but confined its message to the male sex: "Join hands then, *brothers* of the faith, whate'er your race may be; who serves the *Father* as a *son* is surely kin to me." Where were the sisters, daughters, and mothers?

It seemed God didn't talk to or about women. God had talked to Adam, Abraham, Moses, and various other prophets, kings, and assorted dignitaries, but he never spoke directly to any woman except Eve—and then only to curse her along with her female descendants. Neither did he ever speak to the one woman who was supposed to have been good enough to bear his baby. According to the annually retold Christmas story, God sent an angel to carry his message (and seed) to Mary, without ever troubling himself to visit her in person or to give her the opportunity to decline the honor. God seemed especially overbearing toward those who were said to be his favorites: son, mother of his son, or chosen people. I began to think it might be healthier to be overlooked by God than to be singled out for his special attention.

Then there was the matter of the world's nonhuman creatures, in which I was keenly interested. I was the sort of child who always spoke to passing dogs or cats on the street; tried to pat all the animals in the zoo; spent cramped, immobile hours watching what insects did; stowed garter snakes in my pockets, turtles in the bathtub, and salamanders in special homes under the back porch. The high point of my visit to the circus menagerie was having a friendly elephant fondle my hair with its trunk tip. I entertained visions of adult life on a farm, where I could cherish all the animals I wanted.

I was to learn, however, that even though the animals were called God's creatures, he seemed not to like them very much. One day this was brought home to me with startling vividness, and the realization set my feet on the path of dissent.

Dogs in Heaven

My dog died.

A bald statement: sad, but not shattering. An everyday event. Most people outlive their dogs, even a series of dogs. But this was my first dog. I loved him beyond anything else I had. He was my constant companion, my confidante, my precious. The touch of his warm, silky fur comforted and delighted me. His soft brown eyes always seemed to understand and sympathize. He watched me and trusted me; he wanted to be with me at all times. We were inseparable. Then death came, and separated us forever. I was desolate.

Shortly after this sad event, our minister came to pay a visit to my mother. While he was sitting in our living room with a teacup in his hand, I ventured to ask him about my dog. What would it be like when I met my dog again in heaven? Would he be waiting for me right beside the gate? Would his joyous bark be the first sound to welcome me, as it had so many times in the past?

The minister gazed at me in quizzical silence, as if he didn't understand what I was asking. Then he broke the news to me. My dog would not be waiting for me in heaven, because dogs didn't go to heaven. You see, my dear, dogs don't have immortal souls, so they can't go to heaven. They're only animals. Heaven is for people. When I got to heaven, I would meet again all the people who loved me. But not a dog. No.

It was my turn to stare in silence. This had never occurred to me. I couldn't quite take it in; it was too shocking. No animals in heaven? Not even one's dearest pets? Then was heaven like one of those terrible, sterile apartment buildings that wouldn't allow people to keep their dogs and cats and canaries?

I insisted that it couldn't be so. Surely God wouldn't be so cruel as to deny people the company of their beloved animals. Secretly, I thought of a number of relatives—technically loved ones—whose company had never meant as much to me as that of my dog. I would be willing to forego reunion with them, if only God would restore my dog to me. Couldn't I strike some sort of bargain with God? Maybe trade an uncle or an aunt for my pet?

The minister smiled gently at my childish folly and repeated his statement. No exceptions were made. God simply didn't take animals into heaven. I would have to realize that God knew best.

Perceiving how upset I was, my mother suggested that perhaps there was dog heaven, where good dogs could live happily under God's care. But that was of no use to me. I didn't want my dog in a separate heaven, where we couldn't be together.

Besides, the minister not only failed to pick up on her lead, he even refused to let her get away with it. He wanted to set the record straight, not raise false hopes with kindergarten fantasies. He was sure the way he and other male adults fantasized their heaven was the only Truth. So he put down my mother's kind hypothesis and firmly denied the afterlife of animals. I would just have to face the fact, he said, that my dog was gone beyond recall. I was to pray to God for the strength to accept his will in this matter.

To the astonishment of everyone, including myself, I burst into a storm of tears, stamped my foot, and yelled. At the top of my voice I told the minister that in that case, I wanted nothing to do with this mean old God and he could just keep his rotten old heaven for himself, because if it had no animals in it, then it wasn't worth going to anyway. Certainly it would be no fun for me. I would rather go anywhere, yes, even to hell, than be stuck in a petless heaven. Furthermore, I didn't care what he thought about it, because that was how I felt, and I couldn't help it, so there!

Then, conscious of having misbehaved beyond any hope of redemption, I ran to my bedroom and flung myself down to cry.

My mother was mortified. She apologized for me over and over, but the minister smiled indulgently and reassured her, displaying his tolerance for the foolishness of children. He told my mother not to worry. After all, I had a lot of growing up to do. He was not offended. He understood how I missed my pet. He was sure that in time I would come to see the error of my ways and would learn to accept things with better grace. Meanwhile, if there was anything he could do to help make it easier, anything at all . . . don't hesitate . . . glad to . . . Yes. . . . But he took his leave soon, and his visits were less frequent after that.

My mutinous thoughts went on. It was clear that God didn't love animals. We were told that God loved us because he had created us. But hadn't he created the animals too? If not, then who had created the animals? And if so, why didn't he love them? Was God the Father of every living creature, or was he not?

I noticed after the dog incident that our minister avoided my eye. He never forgave me, nor I him. I sat in his audience and glared at him, a small, grim face that never smiled at his jokes or softened at his consolations. I knew what others of my age had not yet learned: that the ultimate consolation was nothing more than an empty, bleak command to take whatever God dished out to you, without fuss or complaint.

Somehow it just wasn't enough.

Death

The first funeral I attended was that of my Aunt Lily. She had died of the dread disease whose name was not spoken in polite company: cancer. I was thought too young to see her in her last illness, but somehow I was old enough to witness her last public appearance as a corpse.

My parents dressed in black. I was arrayed in a new white organdy dress with a black satin sash: proper funeral attire for children in those days. We drove to a house I had never seen before. We were admitted by an unfamiliar young man, very tall, in a black suit and black tie. Even the handkerchief shyly peeping from his breast pocket was edged with black. He wore an intensely solemn, lugubrious expression. He said softly and mournfully to my parents, "She's in the Slumber Room," indicating a door at the end of the entrance hall.

As I followed my parents in that direction, I lingered, looking back over my shoulder at the tall young man. He was now leaning against the wall, examining his fingernails. His expression had changed to one of enormous boredom. His lower jaw was rapidly pumping a wad of chewing gum. He began to yawn and stopped himself as he caught my eye. His expression changed again, to one of hostility. He glowered at me. Abashed, I turned away.

We entered the Slumber Room. It was banked with flowers,

which exhaled an overwhelmingly sweet smell. There were many people, all in black clothes. The only other child present was my cousin, Aunt Lily's daughter, who sat by herself on a straight chair, looking bewildered and somehow shrunken. Her nose was a rabbitlike pink from crying.

The center of this large room was occupied by Aunt Lily in her coffin, illuminated by brilliant stage lights. At first I couldn't make out what this strange effigy was supposed to be. It didn't look like Aunt Lily. It looked like a papier-mâché figure of surpassing ugliness, thickly powdered and rouged, with a corrugated skin and scaly, birdlike talons crossed on its meager chest. For some reason it wore Aunt Lily's violet silk Sunday dress.

A woman said, "Ah, she looks so natural. Just as if she were asleep." Another woman answered, "Yes, she's at peace now. It's a blessing." Both women were quietly weeping. Not having seen grownups cry before, I was frightened; the more so, because they were obviously talking nonsense. If the thing in the coffin was Aunt Lily, she certainly did not look natural. If they were glad to see her at peace in this manner, then why were they crying?

Someone else said, "She's in heaven, poor dear." This was perplexing. I had understood that heaven was a wonderful place to be. If Aunt Lily was there, why was she to be pitied? Moreover, if she was there, how could she be here?

Someone else said, "A shame about the child." The group of adults looked toward my cousin, sitting alone on her chair, staring at the rug, immobilized in embarrassment. "Well, he'll just have to Find Someone." Another voice: "You really wonder sometimes why God takes mothers." Another: "They say he takes the best ones first, because he wants them near him." The first voice continued: "Yes, but it's hard on the child. A mother should live for her little ones."

I gathered that God had taken Aunt Lily away from her little girl because God wanted mothers and didn't care if a child was left motherless. Would God take my mother away from me? In sudden panic I went to my mother and took her hand. I hoped she wasn't good enough for God to covet. I needed her more than God did.

I heard the same things said again and again with minor variations. Aunt Lily was at peace, she was in heaven, it was too bad, she looked natural, she seemed asleep, what was the poor man going to do about the child. The poor man was my uncle, the bereaved husband. He now stood beside the coffin with either a tear or a large drop of clear mucus trembling on the end of his nose. This fascinated me. The drop did not fall. When would it fall? It clung, defying gravity. My uncle kept nodding his head and shaking hands with people who spoke to him. He said over and over, "Thank you. Thank you." What was he thanking them for?

People were filing past the coffin, gazing upon the effigy's face with solemn expressions. Some bent over as if to whisper to it or kiss it. Nearly every one of the ladies burst into tears a moment afterward. The gentlemen usually looked more solemn, if possible. I wondered if I would be expected to burst into tears. I didn't think I could manage it.

When my parents' turn came, Mother faced me toward the coffin and instructed me to say goodbye to Aunt Lily. Dutifully I said, "Goodbye, Aunt Lily."

"You can kiss her if you like," Mother said. "Daddy will lift you up." On her signal, Daddy lifted me up, so I had a better view of the body. Not only did it look uglier from that angle, but it also seemed to exude a nasty smell that was only partly disguised by the scent of the flowers. Putting out a reluctant hand, I touched the painted cheek and found it cold as stone. I began to cry and struggle in my father's arms, exclaiming, "I don't want to!"

"Shh, shh, you must be quiet," my mother hissed in my ear. I was hastily carried away and set down in a corner. I thought I must have done the right thing by crying as I left the immediate vicinity of the corpse. It had been easy, because I was afraid I might be forced to kiss it. Some people glared at me severely, however, and I realized that my response had been incorrect. Like my young cousin, who was studiously avoiding my eye, I kept still and stared at the rug.

A little later, people clustered around the coffin and a strange man made a speech. I assumed he was a minister because he talked a lot about God. He also talked about Aunt

Lily, calling her God's humble maidservant, a woman without pride, a patient toiler in the Lord's vineyard, who always put others before herself. (I knew from experience that Aunt Lily wasn't all that humble, patient, or self-effacing. She showed a sharpish temper when crossed and often snapped out hard words about her husband's behavior at parties.) The speaker went on to say that God had tested her with martyrdom, to make her one of his chosen elect. Robed in glory, she would greet other family members as they arrived in the Divine Presence. (Here the bereaved husband sobbed aloud.)

Listening carefully, I tried to understand the relationship between the thing in the coffin and the transfigured Aunt Lily who was in heaven, yet who was to be pitied. I couldn't make it out at all. I wondered what would happen to the effigy, at whom everyone gazed as if they thought it was the real Aunt Lily.

Presently, people went out to their cars. The coffin was closed and carried into a fancy long car with black-curtained windows. The tall young doorman sat in the driver's seat. He was leaning his head on his hand and seemed to be taking a nap, though his jaw was still lazily working his chewing gum. I wished I had a piece of gum too.

The cars formed a line, turned on their headlights even though it was daytime, and drove together to a cemetery. I was impressed to see that none of the cars in the cortege stopped or even slowed down for a red light. Since it had been drilled into me from earliest toddlerhood that one must never, never proceed against a red light, I knew this occasion was wildly unusual.

In the cemetery the speechmaking man spoke at even greater length. All the black-clad people were gathered around a huge, interesting hole in the ground. I would have liked to jump down into the hole, though I knew it would dirty my white dress, and I couldn't climb back out without help from above. It seemed the hole was meant to receive Aunt Lily's coffin. For the first time I realized that all the ground in a cemetery must be full of similar coffins, each containing a person or some facsimile of a person.

The talk, the sniffling, and the muffled sobbing at the

graveside went on interminably. I gazed at the trees and bushes, jiggled from one foot to the other, and began to feel ominous pressure in my bladder. Mother prodded me and whispered that I must stand still. After a long while the coffin was lowered majestically into the grave. The mourners departed, leaving Aunt Lily—or her crude likeness—alone in the earth.

Later we went to a strange kind of party. There was plenty of food and drink, but no one joked, laughed, or had any fun. Some people were eating and wiping away tears at the same time. My cousin didn't want to play any games with me. Funerals, I decided, were far more boring than otherwise.

On the way home I tried to resolve some of the day's perplexities by asking my parents questions. "Where is Aunt Lily really? In heaven or in the ground?" It appeared that Aunt Lily was made of different parts. One part remained in the ground and another part, the soul, went to heaven. The part that remained in the ground was the only one we could kiss and say goodbye to; the other part, which was invisible, could watch us. I felt a sudden guilty little chill, wondering if Aunt Lily's invisible part had seen me meanly refusing to kiss her.

Of course it was taken for granted that no part of Aunt Lily had gone to hell. The possibility was not even to be considered. I wondered how this could be known.

"If nobody can see or hear souls," I asked, "how do you know people have them?"

My parents glanced at each other. Then my father said something I knew was true: "We don't know. Most people believe it, that's all."

"Why?"

Again he looked at my mother. "Because they want to. Because it makes them happier, especially when they have to lose people they love, like Aunt Lily today."

Because none of the people I had seen that day had looked at all happy, I found this confusing.

"Is it fun to go to heaven?"

"So we're told," my father said tonelessly.

"Will I go to heaven like Aunt Lily?"

"Not for a very long time," my mother said quickly. "Not

until you're all grown up and get very old. You don't have to worry about it."

"If it's fun, why should I worry about it?"

My father smiled for the first time that day and said, "They haven't figured out the answer to that one yet." I knew he was talking more to my mother than to me.

Gazing from the car window, I tried to picture Aunt Lily flying around the summit of a lofty thunderhead rising behind the treetops. I couldn't imagine her so. The image was obscured by that of a big box descending into a hole in the ground. Where was she, up or down? Flesh or spirit? Did anyone really know?

This was the first time my all-absorbing childish eye had ever really had to witness the exposure of the adults' collective fear, confusion, and ambivalence about death. As on the subject of sex, so also on the subject of death I had been given disturbingly contradictory messages that upset me more than the plain truth could have done. Had I been told that Aunt Lily was just terminated, never to exist again, I would not have worried. Aunt Lily was only peripheral to my life, as she was also (truth to tell) to the lives of most of the people who considered themselves duty bound to appear in the presence of her corpse. I was disturbed by the hypocrisy of the occasion, the ugliness masquerading behind flimsy masks, no more effectively concealed than the stench of death was concealed by the scent of flowers.

I was disturbed by the almost palpable sense of my elders' inner conficts. Their protests of faith in an afterlife seemed insincere. I didn't mind grownups admitting their ignorance of anything. I didn't expect them to be omniscient. But I did mind when my built-in lie detector told me they were pretending to know what they didn't know or that they were telling me nonsense because they were afraid of the truth.

Adult rationalization about protecting children from unpleasant truths is a pernicious habit associated with a generally self-deluding society. It is not our children but ourselves that we try to protect with our euphemisms about basic matters: birth, death, and sex. Such euphemisms are typical of patriarchy, not of the past matrifocal societies where there was less fear and more honest acceptance of nature. Violent fantasy death is presented to children *every day* in, for example, cartoons, yet they are not supposed to know about the real thing. Is it any wonder that in such a society to grow up means to learn dissimulation?

Christmas

I used to be mystified by the slogan, "Put Christ back in Christmas." As far as I was concerned, Christ had never been in Christmas very much, except as its mispronounced first syllable. At best he was only the infant portion of the formal mother-child symbol, representing the foundation of human— not divine—love.

Had I been aware of the old pagan name of the Yuletide festival, *matrum noctem* or Night of the Mother, and the meaning of its ancient pre-Christian madonna and child idols, I would have understood more about my own special feeling for Christmas.

My family treated Christmas as an intrinsically secular holiday celebrating the best in human feelings of kinship, love, joy, kindness, and appreciation of blood bonds without any reference to the Christian myth except for an appearance at church services. Our celebrations had their own rituals, meaningful for us, and a generally Dickensian-English, old-fashioned Christmas atmosphere of indiscriminate goodwill. My mother was the Fezziwig who made it work.

My mother was the youngest of three sisters, all of whom raised their families within reachable distance of each other in different suburbs of the same city. Consequently aunts, uncles, and cousins were inevitably involved on Christmas Day. Christmas Eve, however, belonged to our household alone.

Of course the festival began long before that: as soon as we began drawing up lists and keeping secrets, when mysterious packages were hidden away on high closet shelves, and when rolls of bright wrapping paper and ribbon appeared. About a week before Christmas my mother and I had a wrapping session. Sitting amid a litter of paper, string, tape, tags, cards, and assorted decorations, we happily toiled together for hours over the gifts, remaking prosaic boxes and other objects into things of satisfying, if ephemeral, beauty.

The end result was magic: perfectly ordinary things transmuted into shining, dreamlike talismans. Contemplating the heap, my mother always remarked how wonderful Christmas presents looked before they were opened and how dull they seemed afterward. Yet to my mind, Christmas presents never really lost their magic. There can be no doubt that the gift-giving custom was and is the major source of children's happy memories of Christmas, the custom that fixes it in their minds for life as a benevolent, enjoyable time. Nonetheless, our traditions included much more than gifts.

The real excitement began on Christmas Eve, the *matrum noctem* of our pagan ancestors, who revered the mystery of birth above the character of the one born. I would wake on the morning of December 24th with the pleasantly squiggly inner feeling that this would be one of the best days of the year: a day of fun, irradiated by anticipation of the morrow.

The first project was setting up the tree in the living room. It was brought in from the back porch and nailed into its triangular stand, which was always draped in the same green felt skirts, forming the ground of the toy villages and railroad tracks beneath. Boxes of little painted houses, stores, barns, and fences would be brought down from the attic together with metal or celluloid farm animals, people, and road vehicles. These I assembled into a play landscape under the trees. I laid pocket mirrors on the green felt to serve as ponds where tiny wooden ducks swam and tiny painted horses drank. I tucked cushions under the felt to simulate hills. I arranged platforms, switchbacks, and sidings for the Lionel trains.

Each step of the whole project was much discussed and tested. The tree's best side must be found and turned to face the room. The light strings must be placed just so. Every colored bulb must be checked. Invariably some were burnt out, which rendered the whole string inoperative. Offenders had to be located by trial and error and replaced before the strings could be clipped onto the tree. When all eight bulbs in each string lit up each was then supplied with a star-shaped metal reflector supposed to minimize fire hazard by intervening between a hot bulb and dry pine needles. Carefully chosen color combinations of reflector and bulb were intended to produce a pleasing balance of colors for the whole tree.

Boxes of Christmas balls, tinsel, and other tree ornaments also came down from the attic and stood about the room all day, their contents gradually being attached to the tree. It took many hours. For a few years when I was very small I believed that Santa Claus trimmed the tree in the night because it appeared like magic on Christmas morning: a whole fairy-tale world of light and color where an ordinary end table had stood the day before. My parents soon dispensed with Santa Claus, however, and enlisted my aid in building this particular fairy-tale world. We all worked on it at odd moments throughout the afternoon and evening.

The finished tree was indeed a fairy realm, rather like Tolkien's City of the Trees: "In their many-tiered branches and amid their ever-moving leaves countless lights were gleaming, green and gold and silver." Each bulb illuminated its own mystic chamber in the branches. Some of them were washed in golden light like a sunset; some in the rich glow of red; some in dim sapphire blue or emerald green; some in natural colors brightened by a white bulb with a silver reflector. I used to move my dollhouse dolls through these colored chambers in the tree or construct my own pipe cleaner creatures to climb through their various levels and atmospheres of light.

I was shocked one year to learn of careless people who simply stood back and *threw* clumped handfuls of tinsel onto their Christmas tree. With us, each strand of tinsel was laid down with due consideration for the total arrangement and aligned with precise verticality amid the branches. Some areas of the tree, like a landscape, had waterfalls of tinsel. Others had only a gentle rain. We also hung twisted metal icicles, gold or silver on one side and blue, red, or green on the other. They were placed to dangle free and straight so they would turn in the slightest draft to make glints of movement in the tree's world of light and color.

Other decorations—holly wreaths, window candles, outdoor lights—were placed on Christmas Eve. Mistletoe atop a huge green glass Christmas ball about six inches in diameter that my grandparents had brought from England, was hung with a red ribbon from the dining room lintel. Pine boughs with silver bows were laid behind the Seth Thomas clock on the mantelpiece. Whatever the weather, cold or mild, a fire was lit and a specially chosen Yule log burned.

After dinner we sat in the glow of firelight, candlelight, and rainbow tree light, admiring our work. Sometimes friends or neighbors would drop in for a glass of eggnog or a little token help with the tree-trimming. My mother played Christmas carols on the piano and we sang.

At some point during the evening my father would withdraw in deep secrecy behind closed doors to do his own gift wrapping. He used only one material—newspaper. It was a family joke. Everyone deliberately commented on the vulgar appearance of his newspaper-wrapped offerings, admitting, however, that they were usually the most expensive. He would give my mother a costly cashmere sweater or a platinum bracelet, inevitably wrapped in newspaper.

Gifts were piled around the tree wherever there was room. Newspaper-wrapped items were buried, with many jocular pseudoinsults, underneath prettier packages. The total effect was duly admired. Stockings were hung by the chimney with care, and stuffed with odd little shapes above a round ball in each toe: the obligatory tangerine.

The last Christmas Eve ceremony was lighting the bayberry candles in the bathtub, where they could safely burn unwatched all night. In accordance with English custom, my grandmother always sent a pair of bayberry candles accompanied by the couplet: "Bayberry candles burned to the socket/Bring health to the family and wealth to the pocket." Two candles were placed exactly one foot apart in the center of the bathtub and left to burn through the night. To the best of my remembrance, they never failed to burn to the socket before dawn. As a small child

I used to make innumerable unnecessary trips to the bathroom during the night just to check their progress and bask in their rich bayberry scent and warm orange glow.

Of course, I would hardly sleep at all that night. I would begin at about 4 A.M. to wake my parents enough to ask if it was time yet, and to be told to go back to bed for a while longer because it wasn't time yet, and for the next couple of hours to make periodic checks, until somehow it finally became time, and we went downstairs in our pajamas and robes. The tree was lit and admired all over again. The stockings were emptied, the tangerines eaten. Gifts were opened one at a time, each receiving its measure of praise.

Then there were a few hours of miscellaneous activities: playing with new toys, perusing new books, trying out new games, trying on new clothes, phone calls, visits, and sometimes a trip to church or a gift-delivering errand. My mother and aunts held the Christmas feast in one of their houses. If it was my mother's turn she had to begin preparations early in the day. The table was decorated, the turkey stuffed, the desserts made ready.

In the afternoon, either the other relatives arrived at our house, or we got dressed and traveled to theirs. Then came another present-opening session. Children and pets became more excited than ever, running about underfoot, hardly knowing what to play with next.

At this time somebody always received the family Snowman as an unexpected gift. The Snowman was an ugly, bedraggled little figure of cardboard covered with cracked glittery white plaster, a cheap Christmas ornament left over from an earlier era. For some unknown reason it had been preserved through a number of generations. It was passed back and forth among our family members. Each year the previous year's recipient would box it, wrap it, and formally present it to someone else. As children grew up and married, new spouses would be given the Snowman at their first family Christmas. They were invariably baffled at receiving such an old, broken, unlovely object, until, amid much laughter, the tradition was explained to them.

When one cousin served in the Navy during World War II, the Snowman was sent to him overseas in his Christmas package. He kept it safe through a year of active war, and returned it the next Christmas, looking not much more war-torn than it had looked originally.

Dinner was half pleasure, half ordeal. One was urged to eat to the point of discomfort and beyond. There was too much of everything, The turkey came with five vegetables, two salads, coleslaw, potatoes, biscuits with honey, jellies, pickles, olives, relishes, cranberry sauce, chestnut stuffing, two or three kinds of pie, ice cream, nuts, mints, fruit, and finally cookies and ginger ale to settle the stomach. After dinner, when we were sufficiently recovered from this Lucullan orgy, we played games: cards, charades, board games, parlor games. There was more carol singing. We had a very good time until the overfed and overstimulated children began to show signs of exhaustion that the adults also felt but didn't show; then the party broke up with hugs, kisses, and good wishes all around.

On the whole ours were typical middle-class American Christmases: not unique, not sacred, not particularly religious. They could easily be criticized as commercial, and overindulgent. My mother used to say, "Christmas is for the children." Children were hardly expected to comprehend the improbable doctrine of a woman impregnated by a god without sexual intercourse or to recognize in the resulting infant a future man whose death would be ordered by that same god to induce himself to accept human beings into his heaven. Perhaps such doctrines would have strained even the uncritically receptive childish imagination.

My cousins and I were not burdened by any such incredulities. At Christmas we simply and openly reveled in our childish acquisitiveness and sensual enjoyments, through which, somehow, the festival was transmuted into beautiful memories and tender sentiments, which we carried forward in time to our own children.

I suspect that even people who think they put Christ in Christmas treat it, in practice, as a celebration of family feeling, bodily indulgence, and a catering to children's shallow joy. At Christmas most people pity the poor and lonely because they lack material goods and human relationships, not because they lack the salvation supposedly engineered by the Christ child, which was said to belong to all. In this we demonstrate an awareness that Christ is not going to make anyone happy in honor of the season. This responsibility must fall on human shoulders.

At other seasons few efforts are made to alleviate poverty or loneliness. The Christmas season alone is seen as "a kind, forgiving, charitable, pleasant time," in the words of Scrooge's nephew. Even God seems temporarily better disposed toward sinful humanity and might even briefly repent having created hell.

In my composite view of Christmas throughout the years of my life a few early Christmases stand out, not because they were noticeably different but because they were quintessentially typical. I remember one meditative Christmas night during my adolescence, the year I received a recording of Dvorak's *New World Symphony*, which was my currently favorite piece of music.

It was late. The guests had departed. My parents had gone to bed. I sat alone by the declining fire, bathed in soft, multi-colored Christmas tree light, listening to my new record. Snow was falling. In the rainbow lights outside the window the snow-flakes became glittering jewels of pink, ruby, amber, azure, and sea green. Enraptured by the combination of color, light, music, and the peace of being still and introspective after a long day of noise and activity, I passed into a waking dream as rich and strange as any Nutcracker dream young Clara ever danced through.

It was such a magical interlude that I have remembered it clearly for many decades. I can still see my young self dreaming in the old burgundy wing chair by that fire of rosy coals, chin on hand, absorbed in the heart-swelling organ chords of the *New World's* final movement. A family party, beauty of the senses, serenity, contentment: these made the essence of Christmas for me. Thoughts of the suffering Christ could only have been an intrusion.

Many years later, after I had read much and thought much, one of the meditative moods induced by the Christmas season brought me to a sharp insight into the roots of my culture. I had learned that the winter solstice festival was celebrated in much the same way in nearly all ancient societies, from Scandinavia to Egypt, with such trappings as gifts, lights, feasts, tree worship, holly, ivy, carols of praise, and so on. Always people were told the divine Virgin had brought forth her holy child of light, the old god's son, who would grow and promise a new season of nourishment and blessings for all and whose blood, drunk by his worshipers, would even guarantee their postmortem survival in a similar godlike state. All at once I saw the original reason for the pattern: people everywhere believed the new season could not happen at all unless they performed the annual rituals as their priesthoods commanded.

Today we may celebrate the old seasonal festivals, from the spring drama of the god's death and resurrection (Easter) to the annual postharvest propitiation of the ghosts of the dead (Halloween). But our ancestors didn't "celebrate." They *caused.* They believed the seasonal cycles would grind to a halt and the world would end unless each person participated as fully as possible in the ceremonies and every act of the sacred drama was perfectly performed.

Therefore, Christmas, or Yule, or Dies Natalis, or the Koreion, or whatever other of its many names one likes, was hardly just a religious birthday party. It was immanent and real to those who invented it thousands of years ago, long before it was seized by Christianity. When the sun was seen to rise higher day by day, toward a new season of seedtime and harvest, all could rest content in the knowledge that the observances had been done correctly, had met with the deities' approval, and had recreated the world yet again—until the next time the sun's warmth waned and required further support from earthlings.

The priests and priestesses were necessary; they alone had the mysterious star calendars that told when the performances must take place. That was their hold over their congregations. That hold is no more. It passed away with the passing of naive beliefs about the cycles of nature. As far as modern religion goes, there is no reason for Christmas. Only the incredibly dogged human propensity to cling to tradition holds it in its place at the year's turning point to brighten the darkest days of winter with a little family fun.

But perhaps the very fact that Christmas has gone secular

and commercial is directly related to the practical reality of its more recent implications. These might be the only real meanings Christmas has left. Children really are delighted by their gifts. Grown-ups really do enjoy watching their pleasure. The decorations really are pleasant to contemplate. The family feasts really are fun. The warmth of friends and relatives reaching out to one another really exists. Though a Christ child may be taken as mere myth or symbol, children are certainly real and motherhood certainly is, psychologically and physiologically, the fountainhead of love: a fact that stands in need of much wider recognition in a patriarchal and alienated society.

Religious or not, none of us now believes the traditions we carry on can affect solar cycles. No sane person still thinks religious rituals keep the heavenly bodies in their courses or stave off the dissolution of the universe. Therefore we easily forget that this assumption was once taken for granted by all our ancestors in every part of the world. Churches miss the point when they cling to primitive ways of thinking. Perhaps, after all, Christmas is not about gods or miraculous births or world-saving infants threatening evil kings. Perhaps it is only about people.

Baptism

My friend Patsy attended a parochial school. That automatically made her the neighborhood expert on spiritual matters. She could lay down the final decision in any child-to-child argument with her oracular "Sister said." It was generally conceded not only that Sister was infallible, but also that Patsy, through Sister, had a special pipeline to God.

One day Patsy emerged from her house, a vision in ruffles and lace, fastidiously abstaining from play because she might get dirty. She said that in a little while she was to attend her baby brother's baptism.

I asked, "What's baptism?"

Patsy regarded me with ill-concealed contempt. "Baptism is when babies go to church to get their right names, dummy," she said. "Everybody gets baptized. You have to. The priest puts water on the babies and prays. The babies always cry."

"Why do priests want to make babies cry?" I asked.

Patsy sighed. "They have to do it," she explained patiently. "If babies don't go to church and get baptized, then if they die, they'll go straight to hell and burn forever and ever. They'll scream and scream, but nobody will ever come to help them." This thought seemed to afford Patsy considerable satisfaction. I got the impression that the baby brother had somehow failed to measure up to expectations.

"But babies can't have done anything bad enough to go to hell for," I objected. "They're too little. They can't even walk yet. How could they be that bad?"

"Don't you know *any*thing?" Patsy demanded in exasperation. "Babies are sinful just because they get born. It's a sin to be born. You have to get baptized to take away the sin. Otherwise, you burn in hell forever and ever."

I was assailed by the uneasy feeling that I might be still burdened with the sin of birth. "If I never did get baptized when I was a baby, then even if I never kill anybody or rob a bank or anything bad like that, would I have to go to hell when I die?"

"Sure," said Patsy. "God made that a rule. Sister said."

I began to feel really frightened. What if I hadn't been baptized? I couldn't remember anything that went on that early in my life. Then, mixed with fright, came anger. "That's not fair," I said. "People aren't supposed to be punished when they haven't done anything wrong."

"It doesn't matter," Patsy said serenely. "It's the rule. You think you know better than Sister?"

I couldn't presume to know better than Sister. But I definitely disliked the situation that I, as an unbaptized person, might have to face. What would be the use of trying to be good if one were assigned to hell from the beginning?

I watched Patsy step daintily into her parents' car with her parents and her baby brother, who was already beginning to wail in a hopeless, despairing sort of way, even though he was being jiggled to make him stop. They drove off and I sat down on their doorstep to think.

This new information didn't fit at all with previous assertions that God was kind and loved little children. How could he love them if all children were born wicked? How could he be kind if he sent to hell all who missed this little water ceremony?

I knew the world was full of children who were never baptized in a church. I saw their pictures in my Round-the-World books. They didn't look wicked. They looked happy and smiling. There were boys and girls whose families lived in tents in great deserts far away, where people prayed to Allah and had no churches. There were little girls in India who got to wear beautiful saris but went to odd-looking temples instead of churches. There were black African children, brown Polynesian children, yellow Asian children—millions of them—who never got baptized. Were all those children fated to burn in hell forever?

It seemed that I could almost hear the heartrending cacophony of their screams. God would hear too, but his heart would not be rent. These little ones deserved no comfort if they had not managed to get themselves baptized in time.

But I wondered: if babies should die unbaptized before they hardly had any time to live and then ended up spending eternity in torture, what was the use of letting them be born in the first place? Would God throw away babies just to build up the population of hell?

Presently I got up and went home to ask my mother if I had been baptized as a baby. She said yes. I was infinitely relieved to find that my parents' foresight had outmaneuvered God and prevented him from sending me to hell for the crime of being born. I thought my parents showed considerably more care for my welfare than God showed. Why did they try to tell me that God loved all little children? Patsy and Sister knew the truth: God loved only *baptized* little children.

You had to be one of the elite or you were doomed. God did not like just any sort of people and did not like babies much at all.

Three quarters of a lifetime would pass before I finally understood why men—and therefore men's God—seemed to dislike babies. At last I understood that primal jealousy, never quite admitted but never wholly hidden, that made adult men so resent a woman's total commitment to her infant. The Madonna-and-Child was man's favorite image of love, but the Father had no place in it, and his plans for the Child's future were not precisely benevolent.

I saw that Patsy's "Sister" was the patsy of a long line of jealous fathers, stretching all the way back to the blessed Augustine, who had indeed decided that it was a sin to be born of woman, as a result of ordinary human passion. And woman was somehow to blame for the sin.

And I saw that great father of symbols, Freud, doggedly insisting that a woman must love her baby only because it was a tepid substitute for the penis she really wanted. Father Freud even went so far as to blame the child for the father's resentment and jealousy, referring to the unequal contest between them as an Oedipal "conflict," as if the rivals were evenly matched and the infant capable of attacking the father with malice aforethought. I saw Father Freud being believed, even by women, even by mothers, who really knew with every fiber of their beings how wrong he was.

And I read the vile words of the blessed St. Jean Eudes, who wrote in the seventeenth century that all pregnant women are justly humiliated "to know that while they are with child, they carry within them . . . the enemy of God, the object of his hatred and malediction, and the shrine of the demon."[1] I read of the early church fathers' detestation of motherhood, their contempt for "yelling infants," and their insistence that every baby's soul is devilish. I read the blessed St. Augustine's statement that God shows the evil nature of birth by placing it "between feces and urine." I learned that baptism, even up to the present day, is one of the last routinely prescribed rituals for exorcising a demon from a human body.[2]

And I began to ask myself who harbored the real demons: the mothers, most of whom loved their babies and wanted them comfortable, or the fathers, especially the celibate pseudofathers, who seemed to hate babies and want them to suffer eternal torture? If women had been allowed to create their own theology, surely no such absurd cruelties could have survived in the official dogma for so many centuries. Mothers would have dismissed the baptism rationale a long time ago.

NOTES

1. Marina Warner, *Alone of All Her Sex: The Myth and the Cult of the Virgin Mary* (New York: Alfred A. Knopf, 1976), 57.
2. Barbara G. Walker, *The Woman's Encyclopedia of Myths and Secrets* (New York and San Francisco: Harper & Row, 1983), 90, 586.

Superstition

My friend Patsy was a perpetual gold mine of information on religion. One day she told me about the magical Lourdes water in her grandmother's possession. Patsy said it was a sure cure for every illness and physical handicap. It couldn't fail, because it had been given to the world by God's Mother.

At once a vista of great possibilities opened up before my mind's eye. "Then it could cure everybody in the neighborhood," I cried. "Mr. Wentworth has gout. Billy Foley has bad eyesight. That old lady down the street is crippled. . . ."

"There's not that much of it," Patsy objected. "It's only a little bottle and my Gran needs it. She takes a drop every day for her arthritis."

Soon after this I faced a health crisis. It was the day before the school play, in which I had a crucial role as the Autumn Leaf. I felt myself coming down with a cold. I knew it would be a severe one—a stay-in-bed cold. Before my mother could notice my feverish state and order me to bed, however, I went to Patsy and implored her to help. I really did fancy myself as the Autumn Leaf.

While Patsy's mother and grandmother were out shopping, we sneaked into her grandmother's room. Patsy showed me the Lourdes water in a cut glass vial with a silver cap marked by a cross. It was more than half full. "She'll never miss a couple of drops," I said.

Patsy looked dubious, but she let me have the vial. "Okay, go ahead, but hurry up." She looked nervously over her shoulder, although she knew we were alone in the house.

I unscrewed the cap and touched the magical water to my tongue a couple of times.

"That's enough," Patsy said hastily. "Gran never does it more than once. Put it away now."

I waited for my return to normalcy. It didn't come. An hour later I felt more feverish than ever. At the dinner table Mother saw that I was sick. She stuck the thermometer in my mouth and then put me to bed, where I remained for the next three days. The role of the Autumn Leaf was played by an understudy.

When I was up and around again, I accosted Patsy. "That Lourdes water of yours is no good," I complained. "It didn't work at all. They've been filling you full of humbug."

"Don't blame me," Patsy snapped. "Maybe it just doesn't work for Protestants, because they're all going to hell anyway. My own Gran takes it every day, and she knows more than you do."

"Your Gran's Catholic, right?"

"Of course."

"How long has she been taking it?"

"I dunno. Years and years."

I demanded triumphantly, "Then how come she still has arthritis?"

Patsy didn't answer.

Another time Patsy told me about the St. Christopher medal she wore. Each member of the family had one like it. Whenever they went on a trip together her father made sure they were all wearing their medals, because these kept everyone safe from accidents during travel.

Once more I wondered why the whole world did not make

use of this marvel. It seemed a very good thing. A bit suspicious after the Lourdes water letdown, however, I asked, "How do you know it works?"

"It has never failed," Patsy said loftily. "We've never had an accident."

"Well, neither have we, and nobody in my family has a St. Christopher medal."

"You're just lucky, that's all."

"How do you know you're not just lucky too?"

"Look, stupid, these medals are blessed by the pope himself. You can't get anything that works better than that."

A few weeks later Patsy's nearly grownup brother went to meet some friends in a bar, got drunk, and drove the family car into a tree. He broke two ribs, and his arm in three places. Because of the wrecked car Patsy's father passed into an interesting but frightening state that seemed to border on homicidal mania. He gave every indication of wanting to destroy his injured firstborn, who was fortunately protected from paternal wrath by lying in the hospital, out of reach.

After listening to a colorful description of her father's frenzy, I asked Patsy whether her brother had been wearing his St. Christopher medal at the time of the accident.

"Of course," she said. "He always wears it."

"They why did he get hurt?"

She paused only an instant before replying, "He probably would have been hurt lots worse without it. I heard my mother say it was a miracle that he was still alive. You can't do any better than a miracle." But I could see that her faith in medal magic was a bit shaken.

Later, while wearing her own protective medal, Patsy faced a personal crisis of her own. Two of her toes were mashed in a carelessly slammed car door. The doctor hoped the damaged toes might heal, but warned that the injury could necessitate an amputation if matters turned out badly. Patsy was terrified. Her mother counseled her to pray to God and the Blessed Virgin, who always listened to the prayers of little girls. Patsy prayed as hard as she could for an unmutilated foot, promising in return everything she could think of, even her whole future life's service in a convent.

But God and the Blessed Virgin weren't listening to Patsy. Infection set in. The antibiotics that could have conquered it were still some years in the future. Patsy's toes could not be saved. The dreaded operation was performed.

While she was hobbling about on crutches, convalescing, Patsy told me of her disappointment. She had never prayed so sincerely in all her life. Yet her plea had been ignored. She was more than a little annoyed with God and the Blessed Virgin, but she defended them nevertheless.

"Sister says God tests people's faith by letting bad things happen to them sometimes," Patsy explained. "He did it to Job in the Bible."

"I know about Job. God was awfully mean to him for no good reason."

"My mother says I have to remember about Job and trust God."

"She told you to trust God before, that he always listened to little girls' prayers. But he didn't."

"Well, maybe I prayed wrong or something. Maybe I'm too sinful."

Patsy looked so miserable that I hated to see her distressed by guilt on top of her other troubles. "Why should it be your fault?" I cried. "You didn't do anything wrong, any more than Job did. I don't see why you should make excuses for God if he's mean to people. He wouldn't make excuses for you."

Apparently Patsy remarked at home upon some of the doubts raised by conversation with me. Some time later she told me, "My mother says I mustn't talk to you about religion anymore, because you're ignorant and superstitious."

I couldn't deny my ignorance, which was the very reason for my insatiable curiosity. But I objected to being called superstitious. "That's not true," I said. "Superstitious means believing in things that aren't real, like bad luck from black cats and broken mirrors, and impossible things done by magic, and fairies and ghosts and Martians. I know better than that. You're the one who's superstitious."

"I am not!" Patsy flared.

"You are too. You believe in magic that doesn't work. Lourdes water. St. Christopher medals. You believe in ghosts.

You talk about the Holy Ghost and dead people coming out of their graves. That's superstitious."

Patsy said there was no use arguing with dumb Protestants, whom God planned to send to hell for their ignorance anyway. I often wondered what it was that Protestants were protesting. I thought perhaps it was that.

And yet my observations indicated that Patsy's rather accident-prone family enjoyed less protection against disaster than many others who boasted no claim to protection. If they really were God's favored ones, I wondered, why didn't God treat them better, to show the rest of us that they were right and we were wrong? I thought God couldn't be trusted even by people who thought him particularly attentive to their welfare. If God wanted Protestants to abandon what Patsy called their superstition and become Catholics so they could be saved, he wasn't going about it intelligently.

I overheard another definition of superstition from my parents. In an adjoining room, not knowing I was near enough to listen, they were discussing the recent tragic death of a neighbor's little boy from acute appendicitis. "Sheer superstition," my mother was saying angrily. "Barbaric. Criminal. It ought to be outlawed. They ought to go to jail."

Because my mother rarely used such a forceful tone, my attention was caught. I listened. She went on: "I happen to know the doctor explained to them carefully about peritonitis and told them the operation was absolutely necessary to save his life. Yet even after the school authorities had sent him to the hospital, they took him home again and wouldn't let the doctors touch him."

"That's Christian Science for you," my father said. "They thought praying was better. They had faith."

"What good is their faith now?" Mother demanded. "Will it take the place of the son they lost but could have saved?"

"Don't ask me," my father answered. "I know it's all superstition and nonsense. But what can you do? It was their legal right."

"Should people have a legal right to kill their children?"

"No, of course not. But they do have the right to practice

their religion, even if it's a silly one. This case just happened to present a serious conflict of ideas. They couldn't handle it."

My mother was still angry. "So now an innocent little boy is dead because of their disgusting conflict of ideas. I say again, such superstition ought to be outlawed."

"Perhaps so," my father said. "The problem is to define superstition. As somebody once said—was it Mark Twain?—superstition is whatever the other fellow calls religion."

I was to discover that this definition held up well against the variously designated superstitious sects in America, which continues to foster its own myth of ideological uniformity when in fact its diversity could be better described as polytheism. In subsequent years I asked many people to tell me the meaning of superstition and never got any two answers alike.

The Not-So-Good Book

When I grew old enough to read the Bible, I worked hard at it because I was told that a close reading of it would answer all my questions. I surely wanted those promised answers. Over the course of a few years, I went through the Bible word by word, with care, three times. I found few of my questions answered, many more raised, and a most unsettling mass of what seemed to be errors.

I ran into absurdities from chapter 1 of Genesis, which said God made plants before there was any sun. I knew plants couldn't live without sun. It also said God made birds, fish, and other animals before he made male and female human beings, both together, as his final act. Chapter 2 denied this, saying God made man first, then plants, then beasts and birds, and finally he took woman out of her male pseudomother. Which was the right story?

God told Adam not to eat the fruit of the tree of knowledge, because if he did he would die the same day (Gen. 2:17). This was a lie. Adam ate it and didn't die. In fact, he lived 930 years (Gen. 5:5). The serpent told Eve the truth, that the fruit wasn't deadly after all. Instead it contained information that God wanted to keep humans from knowing, so they wouldn't become as wise as the mysterious "us" of Gen. 3:22—that is, God and some others. Who were these others? I didn't know, because one is never told, that the original word for God in these writings was *elohim,* actually a plural, polytheistic Goddesses-and-gods-together.

Whence came the famous apple? The Bible never said the disputed fruit was an apple. I would have been pleased to have known then what I only later discovered, that apples traditionally symbolized wisdom or immortality bestowed by the Great Goddess on her chosen heroes, and that the whole Eden story seems to have been derived from ancient Akkadian icons showing a man receiving the apple of life from the Mother of All Living, while her serpent looked on from the branches of her sacred tree. Not until much later did I make the connection with the innumerable Greek, Celtic, Norse, Welsh, and German myths about life-giving apples.

I would have been glad to have known about the Gnostic creation stories that were accepted as part of the canon early in Christian history but later eliminated as being insufficiently patriarchal. The second book of Enoch said it was not God but the Wisdom-Goddess, Sophia (Heb. Hokmah), who created man on the sixth day of creation. Like the Egyptian Goddess who gave each human being seven souls, Sophia gave the first man seven natures, making his flesh from earth, his blood from dew, his eyes from the sun, his bones from stone, his veins and hair from grass, his soul from breath, and his mind from clouds.[1] This was more esthetically pleasing to me than a simple mud figure.

The Gnostic Gospel *On the Origin of the World* also made Eve the original human being, "not having a husband." It was Eve's mother, the Goddess Sophia Zoe ("Wisdom of Life") who later created Adam and gave him a soul made out of her own breath.[2] I would have liked to have known that the title Mother of All Living, purportedly bestowed on Eve by her husband/

mother, was really a common title of the Goddess worshiped throughout the Middle East centuries before the Bible was written.

Not knowing this, I was puzzled by the title applied to a woman who had no children at the time and who later produced only three—all males. One of her first two boys, Abel, was killed by his brother Cain, because of a quarrel actually stirred up by God, who rejected the vegetable offerings of Cain the farmer but accepted the blood offerings of Abel the shepherd. God unfairly called Cain a sinner for omitting the blood sacrifice, even though Cain didn't have any animals to slaughter (Gen. 4:7).

After Cain murdered his brother, God marked him so other people would know they mustn't kill him (Gen. 4:15). Having been taught that murderers should be executed, I puzzled over this. I also wondered: who were all those other people? The Bible gave no indication that there were any people in the world yet except Cain and his parents.

However, one verse later, Cain went away to live in a different country with his wife, who could only have been a sister, even though no daughters of Eve were ever mentioned. Cain built a city and named it after his son, Enoch. (A whole city for only one family!) Enoch begot a son, grandson, great-grandson, and so on, always without any reference to wives or daughters. Where did all those necessary women come from? If they too were descendants of Eve and Adam, then the human race was produced by incest and inbreeding. If they were not, then the Bible lied in saying all humanity came from just one couple.

As far as the Bible was concerned, however, Eve had only one more child, Seth, a replacement for Abel. Seth and his male descendants also seemed to find wives somehow, and beget more progeny. Finally, the "sons of God" mated with the "daughters of men" to produce giants and great heroes (Gen. 6:4). This was the first hint that Adam was not the only son of God's manufacture. Here God had been making more of them all along! But for some reason the others were never named or described.

My confusion could have been resolved by a mere footnote

explaining that the term *sons of God* really meant other deities, or spirits, left over from Israel's polytheistic past. It was a common habit of all gods in those times to impregnate mortal virgins and beget mythic heroes. Bible editors left many passages unexplained, however, so as to maintain the fiction that the biblical deity was somehow different from all his neighbors and companions in the mythic heavens.

After making all creatures and seeing that they were good, God withdrew his seal of approval, saying, "I will destroy man whom I have created from the face of the earth; both man, and beast, and the creeping thing, and the fowls of the air; for it repenteth me that I have made them" (Gen 6:7). Apparently his change of heart was brought on by his displeasure at the behavior of a few of the human beings. I often wondered why he couldn't just correct the erring ones with his omnipotent powers. Instead he declared, "Every thing that is in the earth shall die" (Gen. 6:17). Well, he didn't quite mean that either. He changed his mind again and decided to save Noah and his family and samples of every plant (Gen. 6:21) and two of every animal, insect, and bird (Gen. 6:19), or perhaps it was seven of some and two of others (Gen. 7:2).

My credulity was so strained by this tale of God's dithering about Noah's ark that I would have been glad to have known it was only a third- or fourth-hand myth copied from earlier Babylonian scriptures, in turn copied from a Sumerian story about the flood hero Ziusudra (or Xisuthros), probably based on the ancient pre-Vedic flood hero Ma-Nu, whose ark bore the seeds of life through the waters of destruction between one universe and the next. Details of the ark's manufacture had been plagiarized from Babylon's Twelve Tablets of Creation. Noah was made the tenth descendant of Adam only because the earlier flood hero was the tenth king.[3]

In my opinion, one of God's best commands was "Thou shalt not kill" (Exod. 20:13). Alas, God didn't really mean that either. The words were no sooner out of his mouth than he turned around and commanded his Levites to massacre their own brothers, companions, and neighbors, until there were 3000 dead (Exod. 32:27–28). He said the people of Bashan must be entirely slaughtered, not one left alive (Num. 21:35). He told his warriors to invade the lands of Jazer and Gilead. On their triumphant return, the warriors were to be held "guiltless before the Lord." But if they refused, they would be severely punished as sinners (Num. 32:23).

God's warriors boasted of their destruction of many cities, when they "utterly destroyed the men, and the women, and the little ones, of every city," leaving none alive (Deut. 2:34). Under God's direction Joshua's armies killed all the citizens of Jericho, Ai, Makkedah, Libnah, Lachish, Gezer, Eglon, Hebron, "and of the south, and of the vale, and of the springs, and all their kings: he left none remaining, but utterly destroyed all that breathed, as the Lord God of Israel commanded" (Josh. 10:40). If all these people were also children of the same God who took note of every sparrow that fell, I thought, he was certainly the most bloodthirsty father anyone could imagine.

The Book of Judges said God helped the Israelites kill 10,000 Canaanites and Perizzites, 10,000 Moabites, 600 Philistines, all the followers of Sisera, 120,000 Midianites, 18,000 Benjamites, and numberless others. There were at other times vast slaughters of Ammonites, Philistines, Geshurites, Gezrites, Amalekites, Jebusites, Moabites, Edomites, and Syrians. God sent an angel to butcher 185,000 Assyrians in a single night (2 Kings 19:35). God's typical command (after he had forbidden killing!) was, "Spare them not; but slay both man and woman, infant and suckling, ox and sheep, camel and ass" (1 Sam. 15:3). He forbade any show of mercy (Deut. 7:2).

Even God's own butchers found him untrustworthy. Breaking his promises and covenants, he turned against the Israelites and allowed Abijah to slaughter 500,000 of them. Then he arranged for King Pekah to massacre 120,000 Judeans in one day and to capture 200,000 of their women and children for slaves (2 Chron. 13:17, 28:6–8).

On one occasion God killed 50,070 of his own people in Bethshemesh because they looked into the Ark (1 Sam. 6:19). On another occasion God struck Uzzah dead for daring to touch the Ark, when he was only trying to keep it from falling to the ground (2 Sam. 6:6–7). Oddly, despite all his exaggerated protectiveness toward the Ark, by Jeremiah's time God had inexplicably lost interest in it and forbade his people to visit it or even remember it, any more (Jer. 3:16).

God's punishments were usually outsize, even for trivial offenses. He killed 14,700 Israelites by a plague, for "murmuring" against Moses (Num. 16:49), and 24,000 Israelites by another plague for living with Moabite women (Num. 25:9).

God seemed to have it in for children in particular. At Elisha's request he sent savage bears to tear apart 42 children whose only offense was making fun of Elisha's bald head (2 Kings 2:23–24). He personally killed all the firstborn children in Egypt and even the firstborn of cattle to convince Pharaoh that the Israelites must be sent out of the country (Exod. 12:29). Yet this massacre was planned ahead by God, who "hardened Pharaoh's heart" so he would be sure to keep the Israelites until the killing was done (Exod. 11:9–10). God also said children would be punished for sins they didn't commit left over from their fathers or grandfathers "unto the third and fourth generation" (Exod. 20:5). Later he contradicted this ruling: "The son shall not bear the iniquity of the father" (Ezek. 18:20). The whole Christian idea of salvation, however, depended on the earlier ruling with its implication that Adam's original sin would be punished through every subsequent generation of innocent descendants—a notion that I resented profoundly. I could understand and accept punishment for my own mischief, but to be punished for some trifling disobedience of a remote ancestor was insufferable.

I was especially upset by God's rules for the treatment of girls and women. A bride found not to be a virgin must be stoned to death at her father's door by the men of her city (Deut. 22:21). If a slave woman was raped her attacker would be forgiven after making God an offering, but she was to be whipped (Lev. 19:20–21). Thus God seemed to approve of blaming the victim. A woman who seized a man's genitals, even if the man were attacking her husband, must have her hand cut off, and "thine eye shall not pity her" (Deut. 25:11–12). I wondered if such things were still done. If not, why not? Weren't they God's biblical laws, along with all that other rubbish about sacrificing doves and not eating unclean animals and so forth?

I did see that God's laws concerning menstruation were not observed. God said a menstruating woman is unclean and so is everything she touches and the bed she sleeps on and any person who touches an article that has touched her. A man who sleeps with her must live apart and be unclean like her for seven days (Lev. 15:19–25). Growing up in a largely Christian community, I saw no couples living apart for a week out of every month, and so I thought perhaps God's laws could be ignored after all. Still, God threatened the disobedient with some pretty spectacular consequences, including pestilence, consumption, fever, inflammation, extreme burning, blasting, mildew, hemorrhoids, botch of Egypt, the scab, the itch, the madness, blindness, slavery, plague, and barren lands, (Deut. 28) not to mention his postmortem hell. Such claims gave me pause. God seemed quite vindictive.

Elizabeth Cady Stanton called the Pentateuch "a long painful record of war, corruption, rapine, and lust," and said it was impossible to understand why this material should be considered appropriate to convert the heathen to Christianity.[4] Thomas Paine said of the Bible, "It would be more consistent that we called it the word of a demon than the word of God. It is a history of wickedness, that has served to corrupt and brutalize mankind."[5] I couldn't help thinking that people who actually read the Bible (instead of listening to sermons about it) must be forced to the same conclusions.

For example, the morals of God's pet patriarchs left much to be desired. Abraham acted as a pimp for his wife, gaining his wealth through her sexual affair with the pharoah while Abraham pretended to be her brother (Gen. 12). Abraham pleased God by showing himself perfectly willing to slit the throat of his favorite son as a sacrificial offering (Gen. 22).

God so detested the sins of Sodom and Gomorrah that he threw down a rain of fire to kill all the people, including innocent children. The only person he saved was Lot, but why Lot deserved this preferential treatment remains wholly mysterious. Lot's notion of virtue was to offer his two virgin daughters to a mob of men to be gang raped, in order to protect two male guests, strangers, from being bothered. Later on these same virgin daughters got Lot drunk and committed incest with him (Gen. 19:8, 32). When I read this story I thought, if I had been one of Lot's daughters, I would have seized the opportunity to take a telling and permanent revenge.

God loved Jacob, who tricked his dimwitted brother Esau into selling his birthright, fooled his blind father into blessing the wrong son, and worked magic to give himself an unfair share of his uncle's flocks (Gen. 30:42–43). God loved David, who tortured his enemies to death, killed 200 Philistines just to buy his first wife with their foreskins, and stole his second wife from another man, whom he arranged to have murdered (1 Sam. 18:27; 2 Sam. 11). Despite his questionable morals, David was made the founder of the royal bloodline of the Messiah. When I came to the New Testament claims that Jesus was this same Messiah, however, I was once again bewildered.

Matthew gave a full genealogy of paternal ancestors to demonstrate Jesus' Davidic descent through Joseph. Then two verses later he stated that Jesus wasn't Joseph's son. Then why the genealogy? Luke also gave a patrilineal genealogy for Jesus, with a completely different list of names. I wondered which one was supposed to be right for Joseph; obviously neither was right for Jesus. Matthew also gave Jesus two different names. He was supposed to have been named Emmanuel, but somehow he wasn't (Matt. 1:23–25).

The virgin birth doctrine was always muddy and confused, even among Christians, because most legendary heroes and all the pagan savior-gods of the early Christian era were virgin-born as far back as anyone could remember. It was de rigueur for a demigod, but such a trite story that not even the pagans could take it seriously anymore. Ovid remarked that "Many a man has made his way into an honest girl's bedroom by calling himself a god."[6] As I discovered later, Christians didn't claim a virgin birth for Jesus until the A.D. second century, and St. Augustine was still denying the doctrine as late as the fifth century.[7] Nevertheless, church authorities decided to insist on it, because it was the only way to convince communicants that their eucharistic meal was really god flesh, imparting its magical quality of immortality.

In the New Testament I encountered the well-known difficulty found by any alert reader: the apostles were poor reporters, constantly contradicting one another. Even though they might be expected to remember Jesus's last words accurately, they didn't. Matthew and Mark agreed on "My God, my God, why hast thou forsaken me?" (Matt. 27:46; Mark 15:34) evidently because one book was copied largely from the other. Luke reported a more trustful "Father, into thy hands I commend my spirit," (Luke 23:46) and John insisted on a simple "It is finished." (John 19:30) If these presumed witnesses of such an important event couldn't agree on its details, I thought it possible that they were not to be trusted on other matters either.

And so it seemed. The ultimate miracle of the Ascension, supposed to prove Jesus' divinity and therefore his efficacy as a redeemer, was ignored by two of the four writers. The other two mentioned it as an afterthought, but disagreed on its location. Mark said Jerusalem. Luke said Bethany. Acts contradicted them both, claiming that Jesus lived among his disciples for 40 days postmortem, then entered a cloud over Mount Olivet (Acts 1:3–12). Unaccountably, he made no effort to establish credibility by showing his resurrected self to anyone else, not even his grieving mother.

Matthew 10:10 said Jesus told his followers to go forth and preach, without shoes or staves. Mark 6:8–9 said his followers must go forth and preach, with nothing but shoes and staves. Matthew 7:7–8 quoted Jesus: "Ask, and it shall be given you; seek, and ye shall find; knock, and it shall be opened unto you: For every one that asketh receiveth; and he that seeketh findeth; and to him that knocketh it shall be opened. But Luke 13:23–24 said Jesus taught that only a few can be saved, for many will seek to enter in and will not be admitted.

The famous Sermon on the Mount was delivered on the mount only according to Matt. 5:1. Luke 6:17 said it was delivered on a plain. Matthew 5:15–16 said good works should be done openly, to be seen by others as plainly as a shining light. Matthew 6:1 said good works should be done secretly, taking care that they should never be seen by others. Acts said in one place that Paul's companions on the road to Damascus heard the voice of Jesus speaking to Paul but saw nothing (Acts 9:7). The same book said in another place that they saw the light but heard no voice (Acts 22:9).

The writer of Acts also contradicted the only apostle who bothered to report the fate of Judas, saying he bought the potters' field with his 30 pieces of silver, then suffered a fall, and "burst asunder in the midst, and all his bowels gushed out" (Acts 1:18). Matthew 27:5–7 said on the contrary that Judas gave the money to the priests, who then bought the field, and Judas hanged himself. I thought it disappointing that the last moments of the supervillain must remain forever in doubt.

I was also disappointed by the many contradictions and falsehoods in Jesus' speeches. He said several times that the world would end in his own generation (Luke 21:32). Obviously he was wrong. Though he claimed the title of Prince of Peace, he said: "Think not that I am come to send peace on earth: I came not to send peace, but a sword" (Matt. 10:34). He said he would accept no one as a disciple if he "hate not his father, and mother, and wife, and children, and brethren, and sisters, yea, and his own life also" (Luke 14:26).

Though Jesus claimed his followers would live forever in heaven, he also claimed that "Heaven and earth shall pass away" (Matt. 24:35, Luke 21:33). I thought it might be difficult to live in a heaven that no longer existed. I was also perplexed by the Gospels' insistence that the earth and everything on it would be burned up (2 Peter 3:10), in view of God's assurances that the earth would abide forever (Eccl. 1:4).

Considering Jesus' views on the imminent end of the world, it hardly seemed reasonable that he would want to establish a church. According to the much-discussed Petrine passage, how-ever—actually a spurious insertion written in the A.D. fourth century for political purposes—Jesus founded his church on an apostle named Simon, renamed Peter or "the rock," who had denied Jesus three times during his night of crisis. I won-dered why Jesus chose such a disloyal follower to be his rock. Later apologists rationalized Jesus' choice as a demonstration of his power of forgiveness. Yet the same church supposedly founded by Peter the rock was to declare throughout history that denial of Christ was the worst sin of all and to execute millions very horribly indeed for this alleged crime.

Perhaps one outstanding quality fitted Peter for the job: he was an indefatigable fundraiser. He would kill to get money for his sect. He caused the deaths of Ananias and his wife, Sapphira, because they tried to keep back a little of their money from a land sale for themselves, instead of turning all of it over to Peter. Peter's "young men" carried off the bodies and buried them. The apostles were imprisoned for this crime, but an "angel of the Lord"—or another sympathizer—came secretly by night and let them out (Acts 5:1-19).

As I understood the overall message, God had forbidden people to have eternal life, having thrown Adam and Eve out of Eden before they could discover the fruit of immortality (Gen. 3:22-23). Much later he changed his mind and decided to offer eternal life to a select group who believed God had sent either himself or his only son to earth so people could torture him to death, which made it all right for some of them to enter heaven and live like gods, even though heaven wasn't going to last forever. This would happen only if they ate plenty of God's son's personal flesh and blood, although God had once forbidden the eating of blood as a "perpetual statute" (Lev. 3:17). The whole story was often called "beautiful" or "the greatest story ever told." I thought it quite ugly. I would have agreed with Pliny, who praised the Roman senate in 97 B.C. for outlawing the "monstrous rites" of human sacrifice, "in which it was counted the height of religion to kill a man, and a most healthful thing to eat him."[8]

Years later I was able to improve my perspective on the Bible by doing a little research.

It has been pointed out more than once that modern society suffers from spiritual starvation. Yet embarrassing biblical "untruths and incredible, irrational dogmas," give no spiritual nourishment that the educated people can stomach, when theologians still insist that this collection of second-hand myth and biased history is a copy of God's speech—an assertion that can be accepted by only an ignorant laity.[9] Therefore fundamen-

talist Bible schools have been established for the express purpose of keeping students ignorant of the truth about how and
when the Bible's various books were written, (what their original sources meant), how extensively they were plagiarized and
forged, and how arbitrary was their selection out of a variety
of so-called sacred texts.[10]

For example, the book of Revelation was regarded as a fake
in A.D. 340, and the now-rejected *Shepherd of Hermas* was accepted as part of the canon by Clement of Alexandria, Origen,
and Irenaeus. Lactantius and others in the fourth century said
Christians habitually lied about their books and copied other
authors' material. Hierocles said the stories about Jesus were
stolen from an earlier biography of Apollonius. The bishop of
Tunis wrote as late as A.D. 506 that the Gospels were being
extensively changed in his day because they were written by
"idiot evangelists" and needed correction.[11]

One of the most pernicious errors perpetrated by Christian
fundamentalism is the belief that biblical material was written
down at the time it describes and was preserved intact through
the centuries. Nothing could be more misleading. New Testament manuscripts that the theologians call original are anything
but that. They are copies of copies of copies, no two alike.
About 1500 such pseudo-originals date from the fourth
through tenth centuries—there are none earlier—with more
than 80,000 variations. When all 4000 New Testament fragments are compared, more than 150,000 contradictions and
discrepancies appear.[12]

Despite these and many similar facts, well known to biblical
scholars, the Catholic church's Dogmatic Constitution of 1965
once more proclaimed God the author of the Bible, and declared all biblical books "accurate, true, and without errors,"
thus capping a long history of misdirection and obfuscation in
regard to the sacred texts. Pope Pius X opposed scholarly study
of the Bible at the beginning of the twentieth century. In 1893
the encyclical *Providentissimus Deus* of Pope Leo XIII "infallibly"
declared that a scholar may not interpret the Bible in disagree-
ment with church policy, and that the church authorities on the
subject were never wrong.[13]

Even though the Bible presents a picture of God in many

ways offensive to the modern sensibility, the clergy count on the assumption that very few laypeople read the Bible with comprehension. Most listen to what they are told about it. Almost none of the ordinary believers seek out and read the works of Bible historians, especially because their ministers often forbid this kind of education. Even a Christian scholar now admits that "the Christian community continues to exist because the conclusions of critical examinations of the Bible are largely unknown to it."[14]

I was to discover that all this denying and lying is very much in the mainstream Christian tradition, which has contradicted demonstrable truths throughout history and bitterly opposed the rising tide of enlightenment through the past four centuries. Galileo was forbidden to demonstrate the earth's orbit around the sun by means of his telescopic observations because the Bible said the earth is the center of the universe. For two centuries after Magellan proved the roundness of the earth, educators in Catholic countries continued to insist that the earth is flat because the Bible said so.[15] It has always seemed to me, however, that no book is sacred enough to call black white, or round flat, or killing virtuous, and get away with it. Gods no less than humans deserve to be called to account for their mistakes.

The Bible told me that an allegedly unknowable God had once made himself known to certain ancient Middle-Eastern nomads, though not to any of their contemporaries in the greater cultures of Egypt, Babylon, Syria, Persia, Arabia, Greece, or Rome. All the latter were left to struggle along with their "false" gods. If the real God had wanted to say something comprehensible to the whole human race, surely his advertising campaign was badly planned. Why should he have talked intimately and at such length to such a small group of humans in such a remote place and in such a severely limited time span, and why should he have given them so much misinformation about the world they lived in?

Before I read the Bible I had sometimes resented God's injustices, but I had not doubted his sanity. Afterward I began to think the world was being governed by a celestial lunatic.

Eventually I came to realize that the primary stuff of which gods are made is human language—a new, literal interpretation of the Logos doctrine. Humans create their gods by describing them to one another; by composing hymns and prayers, reciting holy names, praising and listing the gods' attributes; writing and rewriting their myths; telling each other what God wants. The Judeo-Christian God was a product not only of the Bible's millions of words but also of a further two thousand years of words, the prolix pronunciamentos of church fathers. Men built their God as coral polyps build their reef, slowly, always changing his shape with new interpretations, while simultaneously emphasizing his changelessness, pretending that all traditions concerning him have been solidly consistent from the beginning. It is absurd, but any absurdity may be accepted by a majority of human beings if the affirmative words are said often enough—and if enough dissenters are persecuted or killed.

If, as actually happened to the Goddess and her sacred literature early in the Christian era, every book of the Bible were destroyed and the world forbidden to speak of the biblical deity—why then God would be forgotten, just as the Goddess was forgotten after centuries of suppression and neglect. Humans would have to reconstruct him all over again. Perhaps now that we are in a more enlightened age, that would not be such a bad idea.

NOTES

1. Willis Barnstone, ed., *The Other Bible* (San Francisco: Harper & Row, 1984), chapter 1.
2. James M. Robinson, ed., *The Nag Hammadi Library in English* (San Francisco: Harper & Row, 1977), 171–72.
3. Sir James G. Frazer, *Folk-Lore in the Old Testament* (New York: Macmillan, 1927), 62, 64.
4. Elizabeth Cady Stanton, *The Original Feminist Attack on the Bible* (New York: Arno Press, 1974), 66.
5. Ruth Hurmence Green, *The Born Again Skeptic's Guide to the Bible* (Madison, Wis.: Freedom From Religion Foundation, 1979), 83.
6. Marina Warner, *Alone of all Her Sex: The Myth and the Cult of the Virgin Mary* (New York: Alfred A. Knopf, 1976), 35.
7. G. Rattray Taylor, *Sex in History* (New York: Vanguard Press, 1970), 259.
8. T. R. Glover, *The Conflict of Religions in the Early Roman Empire* (New York: Cooper Square Publishers, Inc., 1975), 26.
9. Miles R. Abelard, *Physicians of No Value: The Repressed Story of Ecclesiastical Flummery* (Winter Park, Fla.: Reality Publications, 1979), 4.

10. Howard M. Teeple, *The Historical Approach to the Bible* (Evanston, Ill.: Religion and Ethics Institute, Inc., 1982), 110.
11. Abelard, *Physicians of No Value*, 42–43, 79.
12. Abelard, *Physicians of No Value*, 44.
13. Teeple, *Historical Approach to Bible*, 24; Abelard, *Physicians of No Value*, 9.
14. Abelard, *Physicians of No Value*, 45.
15. Taylor, *Sex in History*, 176.

The Confrontation

If my parents had known how upset I was by the cruelties and discrepancies of the biblical God, they might have eased my mind by telling me his book need not be taken literally or that I could see him as scary but unreal, like Ruggedo the Gnome King in my favorite Oz books. Unfortunately my parents were brainwashed by their generation's social conventions into thinking children must be exposed to religious training even if their elders were not true believers.

My parents were not true believers. Sometimes they went to church, largely for social reasons. My mother enjoyed attending Christmas and Easter services, "to see the flowers," as she put it. No one paid much attention to any theological rationale for ecclesiastical customs. Still, adults had been taught to consider both sex and religious skepticism taboo subjects in the presence of children. Consequently my parents never shared their agnostic views with me. I was perceptive enough to know they were dissembling, and this worried me even more. I knew the things people didn't talk about were the things that most frightened them. The whole subject worried me so much in those early years that I swore I would never stoop to dissembling for any child of my own, and I never did.

The cover-up was so thick that my first hint of the possibility of skepticism came not from any personal contact, but from a *Porgy and Bess* song I heard on the radio: "The things that you're liable to read in the Bible, it ain't necessarily so." This was good news, but I didn't quite dare believe it. I was terrified of the heartless biblical Father who thought nothing of arranging his son's Crucifixion or ordering his soldiers to smash babies' heads against stone walls. He particularly detested females, and I was female. I was small, weak, insignificant, powerless, hopelessly outclassed. I was just one more of his throwaway people. He could crush me like a mosquito.

Yet out of this inchoate fear that God had it in for me, down in my core I was beginning to develop a certain cornered-rat defiance. In those prepubescent years I began to build up that reckless disregard of consequences that can lead a perpetual victim to suddenly turn on her persecutor. Temperamentally prone to take the side of the underdog, I saw the underdog here as myself and God as a bully, threatening me and always getting away with it because he was unassailably omnipotent. I had not the ghost of a sporting chance. It wasn't fair. It was intolerable.

I ceased to send my Now-I-lay-me-down-to-sleep messages. I had run certain secret tests and discovered that no attention whatsoever was paid to what I said. I felt foolish for having bothered when God obviously never intended to listen to me at all. Indeed, why should he change his mind about anything just because some pipsqueak like me humbly begged him? I might as well expect the Mississippi River to change its course at the request of a tadpole.

My growing defiance came to a head one night in my eleventh or twelfth year, during a violent thunderstorm. Suddenly I was determined to force God to hear me. I would be humble no longer. I would call his bluff and die for it. In my last moments he would know I despised and defied him. Ah, drama!

I knew God's preferred method of destroying his enemies was to blast them with lightning. There was plenty of lightning around me. If he wanted to vaporize me in my bed, people would think it an accident of the storm. My parents would grieve but they would never know I had brought it on myself. At the moment I was sure my destruction was inevitable. I didn't care. I had had enough and had gone beyond fear.

Eyes narrowed, fists and jaw clenched, I arranged myself carefully under my bedclothes, my arms at my sides. Because I truly believed in God's power of instantaneous retribution, what I did next may have been the bravest act of my life. Concentrating hard, gathering my inner forces, I hurled my thought straight up like my own invisible thunderbolt. I pictured it passing through the ceiling, the attic, the roof, through the rain and the lowering storm clouds, into God's teeth. The thought said, "I hate you. You're awful. You hear me? I think you stink."

I gritted my teeth, squeezed my eyes shut, and held my breath, awaiting the blast. When it didn't come, I cautiously let my breath out. I opened my eyes and stared up into the darkness. Still no blast. Again I threw my heretical thought aloft, with even more energy than before. Again I waited, every muscle taut. Nothing. I began to feel the prickly irritation of one who has made a grand, attention-getting gesture, only to have it ignored. Had I still gone unheard, even now? I tried again and yet again, with ever more insulting terms, until I couldn't think of any more ways to say it.

Finally I rested, weak from extreme tension of body and mind. A new thought began to seep into my consciousness. It wasn't only that God wasn't listening. He wasn't there!

Speaking, as it were, into the same celestial telephone that no one had answered, I sent up this new thought. "You aren't there," I said. "I don't believe in you." I said it out loud in the darkness of my room. I said it over again. I began to see the first faint light of true inner liberation in my mind. Lo and behold, the paternalistic tyrant that had made me feel so unworthy was only a myth! A decade of my life had been spent in secret fear and growing resentment of a threat that was really no threat at all!

I had imagined myself in chains, and the chains had turned to paper. I had imagined an inescapable, all-powerful enemy, and there was nothing but an impersonal void. It was all lies: God's boring heaven and sadistic hell; the terrible judgment at the end of the world; the Bible's unaccountable nonsense; the silly apple-eating incident for which I was supposed to be responsible; the immoral people who were God's pets and the moral ones who weren't; the punitive male authority who thought my female self unworthy of his attention but deserving of his punishment. All lies. I was free to live my life, to take responsibility for myself, to make my own decisions, and form my own philosophy. It was one of those rare moments in life, a moment of seeing the great light.

An indescribable sense of lightness and release came over me. In one instant I had ceased believing in the God whom I had given his chance to destroy me. I had challenged him, like a little kid thumbing her nose at a bigger, stronger one, and I had made a great discovery. The lightning was not his weapon; it was just a natural phenomenon, scientifically explicable. Space was not his home; not even the immeasurable abysses between galaxies. He lived nowhere except within the narrow confines of the human mind. Each individual mind, I suddenly realized, has total control over the question of whether it will permit an image of God to exist within it. Each individual mind can shape a deity to its own liking or shape no deity at all. In the long run it doesn't matter. Life goes on just the same. People are still people. The rules for social behavior are made by people, not gods. Gods don't enlighten us about the world we live in; people do. And that chorus of abject praise and flattery continually rising into the empty air from the devout all over the globe is demanded not by any God (for why would such a creature need it?), but only by people, who want adulation themselves.

These discoveries made me quite amazingly happy. The next morning I arose feeling light as air. I ate breakfast and went off to school appreciating the glorious sunny day fresh-washed by the night's rain, wanting to skip and sing in my new sense of freedom. Without anything showing on the surface, all alone I had undergone a sort of conversion in reverse. Contrary to the conventional claim that everyone needs a religious faith, my experience showed that what I needed was an absence of religious faith, or at least an absence of the faith that offended my common sense and oppressed my female being. After that night, never once did I return even for a moment to my former belief, nor did I ever wish to. A great weight had been lifted from me forever.

I felt like the child in Andersen's fairy tale: the only one in the throng who had seen that the emperor was naked.

Without ever precisely articulating it to myself, I had discovered that my society's image of male authority was unworthy of my respect. After years of puzzling over his ambivalent character, I had arrived at my conclusion. He was unfit to guide me through life. He must be cut out of my psyche like a malignant growth and thrown away before I could become a whole person. I think nearly all women seeking relief from the internalized oppression of patriarchy must take this step at some point.

On a subverbal gut level I had decided not to be intimidated by patriarchal arrogance, not to tremble before divine injustice, not to kiss the foot that trampled on me. God had been weighed and found wanting. In fact, I had found him wanting on even the most basic level of objective existence. He was a phantom bogeyman, like the ones that ignorant parents sometimes used to frighten children into obedience. But I had discovered that nothing supernatural has any power over one who denies the supernatural. Rejection is the infallible psychic self-defense.

All alone, I had found my way to the haven of nonbelief, and I would remain there, at peace in my central core.

Visions

Several times in my life I have experienced the phenomenon known as a vision: the phenomenon that lies at the root of every religious and mystical system and that is probably much more common than most of us may think.

I have even seen that ubiquitous Queen of Heaven image, in the form of a luminous White Lady with a tender smile and stars in her hair, balancing herself in midair and gazing directly and meaningfully into my eyes. Many have seen her before and named her according to whatever faith they have been taught. Even if I had been declared a second Bernadette of Lourdes by reason of my encounter with her, however, it would have been difficult to build a church on the site of her appearance.

I was sitting on a beach at the time, and the Lady chose to appear about twenty feet above the surface of the sea, about fifty yards offshore.

There are many kinds of visions, which most of us have experienced routinely. There are vivid memories, daydreams, fantasies, fever hallucinations, imaginative scenes of possible future events, impressions left over from sleeping dreams, and mysterious feelings about things, people, or places. We constantly see pictures in clouds, trees, water, rocks, and so on. Even the inner tableaux that pass before the mind's eye when we read, listen to music, or drift into a doze might be called visionary, in that we can see what is not really before us. All human beings create imaginative pictures of the mind: This human "hallucinatory" capacity is the basis of language, because there is no connection in reality between the words we hear or read and the objects we associate with those words. Yet none of these day-to-day manifestations of inward vision are quite like what might be called a true vision.

A true vision appears when one least expects it, without any artificial aids to the visionary state, such as drugs, fasting, prolonged meditation, or the like. A true vision appears in three dimensions and in full color, appropriate shadows and all, according to the direction of the light, seeming as solid and real as anything else in the environment. It is seen as clearly and as objectively as you see the page you are now reading. The only difference between one's experience of reality and the vision is that the latter is there to be seen for only a short while, and then it disappears and is never seen again anywhere.

A unique emotional response accompanies the true vision. One believes at the time that it is realer than real, a revelation of some deep inner meaning applicable to all of life, or the future, or the cosmos, or all of them together. It seems a sort of key, a pipeline to eternity, an overwhelming truth—even though one can never plainly state of what this truth consists. One only feels sure of its transcendent significance. A true vision is never forgotten. It is more firmly impressed on the mind than the most thrilling, traumatic, or otherwise emotionally loaded experiences of real life. Its details may be recalled with the minutest clarity, long after any other kind of memory has faded into the mists of time. Like the earliest infantile memories, which become the last ones left to the mind that is declining toward death, the true vision seems to tap a very deep part of the mind.

Being wholly subjective, such pseudoperceptions lie beyond the reach of scientific understanding at present. Therefore no rational explanation is offered for them. They remain in the catchall category of the irrational, which also includes the hallucinatory phenomena of insanity.

For this reason many normal people who experience such a vision are scared by it and led to doubt their own sanity, unless they can hang the experience on the familiar religious hook by calling it God, or Jesus, or the Virgin, or some other acceptable symbol of the traditional revelation. Even though we know the insane claim incessantly to communicate with God, Jesus, or the Virgin, this poor interpretation is all that our naive and emotionally impoverished patriarchy makes available.

People who don't have visions tend to be awed by people who do. The visionary may be immediately rejected as a crazy person, or, if known to be otherwise perfectly stable, credited with an inexplicable but temporary mental aberration. Alternatively the visionary may be embraced by the credulous as a special person in touch with unseen worlds and ethereal beings. It is often assumed that the visionary must thereby be empowered to foresee the future, describe life after death, perform works of magic, cure illness, or dispense good advice because some incomprehensible spiritual mana has rendered him or her somehow godlike.

In the past, religious authorities automatically presumed to classify and judge everyone's visionary experiences according to the party line. If an acceptably pious person saw God or the Virgin or an angel, and dutifully subjected its interpretation to the church, then the church might adopt the vision to its greater glory and inevitable profit—as in the classic case of Lourdes. If a secular or impious person saw visions, however, he or she was declared either crazy or devilish, sometimes both.

Now we know almost anybody can have visions without intervention from either the supernatural or the pathological. It is only one of the creative functions of the human mind.

Yet this is the last explanation the majority want to accept, because creativity may be puzzling and unnerving to those who don't share in it. The sane visionary may be seen as a kind of eccentric genius mysteriously set apart from common folk, *sacer,* taboo, even dangerous. One might suspect that the attempt to attribute visions to a divine source is an effort to defuse their dangerous mana and to reaffirm what the majority want to believe, namely, that deities are in constant communication with mortals. According to conventional religion, which pretends to speak for the majority, God used to chat with ordinary people all the time, but he has since given that up and now speaks only to duly elected officials, who subsequently relay his remarks to the hoi polloi.

The first true vision in my life, however, had nothing of the conventional divine about it. No standard religious authority would have wanted to adopt it, for it had nothing of Judeo-Christian imagery. On the contrary, it was entirely pagan and archetypal, though I was at the time ignorant of the feminine archetype in any form.

I was 13 years old, taking my dog for a walk in the woods after school. It was a mild spring afternoon. I liked the woods in all seasons, but I preferred spring and fall, free of the winter's biting winds and the summer's biting gnats.

I walked farther than usual and found myself in a large grove of pine trees that I had never seen before. I walked into the cool dark-green shadow of the pines and stopped.

On the brown carpet of needles at my feet lay something interesting: the shed skin of a snake. I had never seen one before. I squatted down and picked it up carefully. I thought it beautiful in its delicate transparency. As I studied the snakeskin, a gleam of sunlight came through the dense green roof of the grove and spotlighted a fleck of white near my foot. It was one of the forest wildflowers known as Spring Beauty, or Star of Bethlehem: a tiny white five-pointed star with hair-thin lines of rosy red in its heart.

Focusing on the snakeskin and the flower, I forgot my surroundings for a while. When I looked up again, there was a different slant of sunlight down the majestic aisles of pine trees. I faced a long, open nave between two lines of trees, a narrow space slashed by golden shafts of late sunlight reaching toward one enormous tree that towered over the others. As I refocused my eyes for distance and looked toward this tree through the corridor of lights and shadows, the tree suddenly became a woman.

It wasn't just a tree that resembled a woman; it was the woman herself. She was a hefty, hippy, bosomy, naked green woman with three heads and huge, powerful legs planted in the earth like a strange new version of the Jolly Green Giant. Her three faces were made of different configurations of the tree's branches, but they were true faces, not just the looks-like sort of faces that one always sees in tree branches. The face to my left was that of a young girl. The face in the center was that of a mature woman. The face to my right was that of an old woman.

As I watched, and as the tree moved slightly in the breeze, the young-girl face turned toward me and opened its mouth to speak. I held my breath, certain that her speech would be supremely significant. The word *key* popped into my mind. She would give me a word that would be a key. It was important for me to hear it.

But I don't know what the word was. The green lips opened and closed. There was only the sighing rustle of wind in the boughs, like distant surf. Then there was another shift, another slight motion, and I saw another wonder.

Out of the dark triangle of the giant woman's crotch, between her massive thighs, poured an endless stream of living things. All species of plants and animals were mingled in a mass flowing like the waters of a river. Within the mass I distinguished sheep, goats, horses, deer, rhododendron bushes, cacti, bears, birds, cattle, fish, vines, seaweeds, foodstuffs, and people. The three faces high above took no notice of this perpetual birthing. The enormous body seemed to do it automatically while the three minds were occupied with other matters.

The heads smiled, nodded, inclined toward one another, or tilted toward me. The eyes moved, sometimes looking at me directly with a sharp, intense stare. I longed to know more about this apparition. I wanted to listen for any words it might speak. But my position was becoming uncomfortable. I had crouched for so long on the ground that my feet were going to sleep.

Laying the snakeskin carefully on the carpet of pine needles, I stood up. When I looked toward the giant woman again, she was gone. The tree was just a tree.

I sat down on the ground again, trying to restore the changed angle of light by moving my head. Then I got up and walked a few steps this way and that, squinting at the tree. It refused to turn back into a woman. I could see which branches had been heads, or arms, or great pendulous breasts; I could see the belly bulge and the dark hollow where the crotch had been. But my eye refused to put it all together into a coherent picture. I visited the pine grove many times afterward and looked at that big tree in many kinds of daylight, but I never again saw the woman clear, living, and whole, her treeness totally metamorphosed into the Triple Goddess of my vision. True visions don't repeat.

I collected the snakeskin and the little white starflower. I put them in my pocket and turned homeward. It was getting late. The sun was almost down. As I left the pine grove, I looked back once. I saw the evening star, flickering through the small opening that had made an eye in the tree-woman's right-hand head, the aged one. If I had known anything about mythic symbols, I might have said the Crone was winking at me. But I had never heard of the Crone.

I went home in the soft violet evening light, wrapped the snakeskin and flower together in a piece of tissue paper, and stowed them away in the back of a bureau drawer. Years later I found them again, the tissue paper yellow and brittle, the contents powdery dry. I threw the package away, but the five-pointed star and serpent figures were indissolubly embedded in my memory. I have never forgotten a single detail of that afternoon's experience. No matter how many years have passed, I can always replay it in my mind like an old movie, unchanged, unembellished, still unexplained. Whenever I want to recall it—which isn't really very often—it is all there.

It was only after many years that I began to realize this had been a true vision, that is, an extrusion of genuine archetypal material from the deep places in either my individual unconscious or the collective unconscious of my race. At the time I had no idea that human beings had envisioned the Mother Goddess in much the same way for countless millennia. I had never heard of the Triple Goddess with her Virgin, Mother, and Crone forms. More than two decades would pass before I saw a picture of the Willendorf Venus, whose body resembled that of my tree woman. I knew nothing about Earth Mothers, sacred groves, fertility symbols, pagan religions, or tree worship.

It never occurred to me to describe my tree woman as the Goddess. I never thought of myself as a Goddess-seer. I accepted both her appearance and her disappearance without giving them any particular meaning. Like nature, she was just there, then she was not. Perhaps for the very reason that I didn't know what it meant, the vision stayed with me and waited for my mind to catch up with my mind's eye.

I think I know now what the green lips would have said to me.

When one has a vision as archetypal as this, filled with so many symbols that seem drawn from the ancient religions despite one's personal ignorance of them, there is a temptation to think oneself somehow chosen, called upon to carry a special message. Naturally a skeptic should resist the temptation. It's too self-serving and it doesn't explain anything. For centuries men have been imagining themselves chosen by God to tell the rest of humanity what to do, and the results have been disastrous. Visions are not necessarily useful to the rest of the world. Like a dream, however, the vision is certainly a communication from one's inner self to one's outer self. If it contains archetypal material, one might theorize that such material actually is, in some mysterious way, inherited.

If this and other subsequent visions led me to make certain choices, to pursue certain directions in my life, it was always without conscious realization. My green tree woman was not beautiful, but I liked her and felt good about her. Why not, indeed, if she was a part of myself? I could never see any obvious connection, since I never became the type of woman usually described as an earth mother. Yet in some inexplicable way she gave me myself. Afterward I never doubted my own competence to decide for myself what was right or wrong, to follow my own conscience, to fear nothing except real physical dangers. The terrors of the mind could not move me. I would feel interested rather than uncomfortable in the darkness of my own depths.

Much later I wondered how many thousands of women throughout the patriarchal centuries had seen similar visions, responding to their own inherent archetypal mystery without a shred of book-learning about it. If such images arise naturally—and perhaps they are even genetically programmed—then surely there must have been many individuals in every generation who encountered some version of them.

Under ancient patriarchy, men who saw or heard their God were usually granted intense interest and attention, even if they seemed otherwise insane. Indeed, modern mental hospitals are still full of people who hobnob familiarly with deities. Yet no Christian seemed inclined to doubt the sanity of St. Paul, whose vocation was accepted on no better ground than his own claim to have seen a vision of Jesus. Similarly, all the Old Testament prophets were believed to have chatted with God in actual fact. This was the basis for the orthodox notion of biblical authority.

Before patriarchy, Goddess religions doubtless evolved from similar "revelations" recorded by the priestesses and prophetesses, who expected to encounter their Divine Mother just as medieval visionaries expected to encounter the Holy Virgin—and so, of course, did. Culturally instilled expectations inevitably influence visionary material. Yet there seem to be certain basic patterns, like my tree woman, that do not arise from learned standards and still recur again and again, in all centuries and all societies.

Was my vision just another in a series of unacknowledged, unrecorded images repeated by the minds of unknown women throughout the ages? How many thousands of women might have been burned as witches for having envisioned the wrong kind of deity? While the revelations of male mystics were being carefully copied and incorporated into orthodox dogmas, how many similarly visionary female mystics were ignored, silenced, or persecuted?

It took me many years to arrive at a state of enlightenment

sufficient even to wonder about these matters. Perhaps women of the future may know enough to skip some of the early stages.

Romance

In junior high school my girlfriends and I began to talk about Boys and to engage in a wide range of activities and endeavors that older women might have called Looking for a Man. Boys to us were symbolized by a half-formed wish image of a compatible male with whom to try out the unfamiliar modes of physical and mental interrelating with the opposite sex that were dinned into us by books, magazines, movies, advertisements, and other twentieth-century media of acculturization.

Unfortunately the boys had not yet absorbed their part of the message. Most boys were friendly enough, at least when isolated from their peer groups and therefore not constrained, at the moment, to show off by being nasty to girls. They were, however, still coping with an absurd schoolboy combination of fascination and fear. They seemed devoted to society's fiction that humanity consists of only the male sex, and the female sex is the Other. Besides, they were just local kids. None of them looked like lover material.

So, seeking further possibilities, I once went to a meeting of the Young People's Fellowship at the church. I had seen a poster promising Fun and Friends under the auspices of this Fellowship, with a picture of a boy and girl dancing together, smiling into each other's eyes, while stars and other sparkly things wheeled around them. This was attractive, but when I arrived on the appointed evening I found the reality rather less so.

The meeting was held in a cheerless basement room with pitiless overhead lighting, exposed steam pipes, and shiny paint in an objectionable shade of olive green. There were thirty or forty girls, mostly older than I, and perhaps half as many boys, listlessly setting up wooden folding chairs and spreading stale finger foods on a large table covered with flowered yellow plastic. After a while the minister called everyone to order by rapping his ring sharply on the punch bowl (ginger ale and cherry soda). He then offered up a sonorous prayer for the well-being and moral guidance of "these fine youngsters." After winding up his directive to God, he smiled and opened his arms with a shorter directive to his audience: "Now let's all have a good time!"

Well, not exactly. Boys and girls clumped up in diffident, separate groups even after some records were put on a turntable and the music began. A few couples started to dance under the glaring light. Most of the boys went to the table and began to eat. There was much scuffling, snickering, and shoving. Because I didn't know anybody and no one seemed to want to meet me, I soon regretted my decision to come alone, without any supportive friend with whom to make conversation.

Then a voice asked me if I would care to dance. I looked up and immediately knew that I would not care to dance, at least not with him. He was fat, sweating greasily, aflame with volcanic pustules and smelled bad. To my adolescent eyes, he might as well have been wearing a lapel pin reading CREEP. Nevertheless, I didn't know it was possible to refuse when asked to dance, so I allowed him to take hold of me and lead me forth.

He told me that his name was Ernest. He drew me up tight against his shoulder, laid his acned cheek against my hair, and began to hum off-key. He stepped on my toe and muttered "Sorry." Then he stepped on my instep and ignored it. He seldom moved on the beat. After enduring him to the end of the record, I disengaged myself and headed for the refreshment table. Ernest followed, talking.

"Are you new around this neighborhood?" he asked.

I said I had lived here since childhood.

"I never see you in church," said Ernest.

"I don't go to this church," I answered.

"Oh. What church do you go to?"

"None."

"What? You don't go to church at all?"

"No."

"What are you, Jewish?" Ernest cried. "You don't look Jewish."

"No, I'm not Jewish. I just don't like churches much."

"Well, say. That's something we have to do whether we like it or not, isn't it? Don't your parents make you go to church?"

"No."

"Some kind of weird parents," Ernest pronounced. I felt that I was becoming awfully tired of him. The music started again, and he seized my wrist to lead me back to the dance area. I was hanging back, trying to think of a believable excuse for not dancing anymore, when along came a rescuer.

This was an older and considerably handsomer fellow whom I had not seen before: all of 17 or 18, I judged, perhaps even 19—an Older Man! He cut in smoothly and elbowed Ernest out of the way with a bland smile. He introduced himself as Randy and took me twirling gracefully around the floor before I knew what was happening. He smelt a lot better than Ernest, though one component of the scent was the yeasty smell of beer.

Over the course of several dances and conversations I learned that Randy was out of school and working for an insurance company; also, he had his own car. He seemed a rare, privileged being. He flattered me by giving me nearly all of his attention, which no young man of comparable age and status had done before. Well before the Young People's Fellowship meeting was over, Randy offered to take me home after a ride in his car. I accepted at once, having walked the half-mile or so to the church. It was with gratitude that I sank into the blue plush upholstery of Randy's large, nearly new Buick—the kind with the ring-shaped radiator ornaments that kids used to collect. I was not sorry to leave the Young People behind in their dismal dance hall.

Randy immediately pulled two cans of beer from under the seat of his car, opened them, and handed one to me. I didn't like beer, but I sipped at it anyway, not wanting to seem backward. As the car purred along in the darkness, we chatted. Presently he asked, "How come I never see you in church?"

I went through the same I-don't-go-to-church routine that I had covered with Ernest. I thought Randy, being older, might understand. I said, pretentiously, "Basically, I'm just not a believer."

"You don't mean that," Randy stated flatly.

I felt a flicker of irritation. "If I didn't mean it, I wouldn't say it," I said. "How would you know what I mean or don't mean?"

"It's a dumb kid thing to say," Randy answered. "Dumb kids who don't know any better say things like that just for effect."

"I don't talk just for effect," I insisted. "I say what I mean."

"Well, if you're serious, then you're even dumber. Haven't you ever heard of the Bible?"

"Certainly. I even read it, several times."

"Yeah? Then tell me who wrote it."

"A lot of different people wrote it."

"Wrong. God wrote it."

"That's one of the things I don't believe," I said.

"So you know better than all the priests and ministers and bishops and popes and everybody for the past two thousand years, is that right?"

I felt the weakness of my position, but I wouldn't back down. "I don't know. I just don't agree with everything they say. It's a free country."

"Not *that* free. You have to believe in something. If not the Bible, then what do you believe in?"

"I don't know," I repeated. "I only know the way God seems in the Bible, he seems bad a lot of the time. I'd like another kind of deity, maybe a female one."

Randy snorted. "A female deity!" he sneered. "Yeah, there are some of those in the Bible. Know what they're called? They're called Abominations. They're devils. You want to be a devil worshiper?"

"I don't know what that means," I said.

"You don't know much, that's for damn sure," Randy told me. Stung, I subsided against the seat cushions and turned toward the window. Randy was looking a little less handsome each moment. He was giving me a series of odd, darting glances, which I was too inexperienced to recognize as speculative.

The joyride became less joyful. Eventually the car nosed into a dirt road that led to the local lovers' lane, a rough clearing in the woods. In my simplicity, I thought Randy was going to turn the car around in the clearing. Instead, he turned off the ignition and the headlights, seized me, and began to kiss me. Surprise, but not alarmed, I tried to respond. "Look at the moon," he hissed into my ear. "Isn't this romantic?" His fingers were probing my clothes.

I began to struggle. "It's not romantic to be so grabby," I protested. "Lay off. I'd like to go home now."

He only took a firmer hold me and yanked at my blouse. I tried to push him off. We wrestled. Apparently I was stronger than he had expected. After a time he sat back, panting and glaring at me. "What's wrong with you?" he demanded.

"Nothing; what's wrong with *you*?" I snapped. "You tore my sleeve. I've lost one of my buttons."

"Don't you like romance in the moonlight?"

"Is that what you call it?"

"You some kind of a tease or something?"

This was a conventional insult that I was not too young to have already heard: one of the two horns of every girl's dilemma. A girl who "put out" was a whore; a girl who didn't was a tease. There was no alternative except a boyless life, which amounted to female creephood.

Close to tears, I said miserably: "I don't like making out with anybody I haven't gotten to know yet."

Randy asked harshly, "Haven't we been getting acquainted here? What do you think this is all about, anyway?"

"It takes more than one evening," I said.

"Is that so? How much time do you think a guy has to fool around? Anyway, you believe in free love, don't you?"

"What makes you think that?"

"Well, you said you're not a Christian. So you're not one of the good girls. You can't have it both ways. You have to live up to your own ideas."

"I never said free love was one of my ideas. Just because I don't go to church, you think you can treat me like garbage? Take me home, like you promised."

In reply, Randy grabbed me harder than ever and shoved

his hand between my legs. I seized his wrist in both my hands and pushed it away. To release my grip, he bent my thumb back. It hurt. I screeched and kicked his shin. Scowling, he released me and sat rubbing his leg.

"All right, no more nonsense," he said. "You wanted to come here, now you stop playing games. Either you take off your clothes and get in the back seat or you walk."

"Walk?" I said. I was amazed at his brutal tone.

"Walk home. That's your choice. Don't give me any more coy baby crap. Make up your mind."

I calculated. Home was only a couple of miles away. Not bad. If I moved right along, I could be there before midnight. Without another word, I got out of the car and started to walk back along the dirt road, morosely trying to pull my torn sleeve together. The night was chilly, but when my eyes adjusted to the darkness the full moon showed me the way.

Before I reached the main road, Randy's headlights drew up alongside. He leaned out the car window. "What do you think you're doing?" he yelled. "Get back in here."

"Go to hell," I said.

"I thought you didn't believe in hell," he continued conversationally.

"I don't," I said. "But if you do, go. I'm just doing what you told me to do. Go away now, leave me alone."

"Come on," Randy said, a little more conciliatory. "I didn't mean it. I just thought you'd go for a little romance in the moonlight."

"I don't like being mauled."

"All right, I won't maul you. I won't even touch you, okay? I'll take you home, honest. You can't blame a guy for trying."

I paused. He sounded anxious, as if he thought matters over and had begun to worry about what I might tell. I was, after all, very young. I heard a note of desperation in his voice that told me he was not really the rapist type. I was hurt and embarrassed, and unwilling to trust him any further, but the car did look much more comfortable than a two-mile walk in my dress shoes.

"Come on," he urged. "I'll treat you just as nice as if you were a Christian virgin."

Why, I wondered, did an un-Christian virgin deserve no such consideration? But I relented and got back in the car, sitting as far away from Randy as possible. "Don't be mad," he said. "You know, some girls like a man to get a little rough with them."

"They do?" I couldn't envision such a girl.

"Sure," he said. "You're the one who's peculiar. You're peculiar in all kinds of ways, aren't you?"

I said nothing but remained bemused by the abrupt transition from desire to overt dislike, which I was later to observe again and again in male attitudes toward women. I couldn't understand it. How could one deliberately injure or insult a person one professed to like or love? I was growing angry at the way my feelings had been toyed with. When Randy stopped the car in front of my house, I got out and slammed the door as hard as I could.

He didn't respond with the hostility I expected. He hung his head and elbow out the window and asked, "You going to the next Fellowship meeting?"

"No."

"Want to give me another try sometime? Like a real date."

"No."

"Aw, come on, don't hold a grudge. I didn't mean to tear your sleeve." He thought the real injury was to a piece of cloth, instead of to my self-esteem!

I said, "That's not the point," and turned away.

"Hey," he called after me. "Want to go to a movie next weekend?"

"No."

"All right, then," he said, suddenly angry, "to hell with *you*." He gunned his Buick and drove off with screeching tires.

I never saw Randy again, but I have long remembered this encounter and what it taught me. It was my first inkling of what I was to observe often in later life: that men are most disturbed by women who deny their God and most disposed to punish such women. The reason is not far to seek. Father God is woman's internal fetter, more effective than any external chains.

As feminists have recently pointed out, authority relationships between the sexes depend largely on gender concepts of supernatural powers. "A woman can never have her full sexual identity affirmed as being the image and likeness of God, an experience freely available to every man and boy in her culture."[1] Only a God made in the image of man can successfully convince woman of her inferiority. Without God, woman might even see her own sex as the more significant one, the one that perpetuates the race and is intimately connected with the future; the one that generates all forms of love; the one that despises destructiveness.

No matter how unthinking they may be, sexist males understand on a gut level that God is their primary ally in the effort to control women. Without him, woman may simply laugh at male posturings of self-validation and assertiveness. The unforgotten all-powerful mother of the buried infant mind may come back to haunt her sons, indulgent but unimpressed by their frantic "Look at me, look at me!" She might respond with nothing more than her ancient, casual "Yes, dear, that's nice, run along now," and that would be the end of male self-importance.

Sexist males can't envision a better, happier society resulting from sexual equality. They like to pretend that God can take the place of the mother symbol, but in their theology, even on the crudest levels, they betray their own self-identification with God. It is their tragedy and the tragedy of their world that such identification can never be complete enough. Its basic falseness impels them to fill their emptiness with ever more destructive gestures. The woman who denies man and his attention-getting destructive gestures is the woman who must necessarily deny God also. As Matilda Joslyn Gage put it a century ago: "Woman's disobedience to man is regarded by both the church and the state as disobedience to God."[2] And vice versa.

NOTES

1. Peggy Reeves Sanday, *Female Power and Male Dominance: On the Origins of Sexual Inequality* (Cambridge: Cambridge University Press, 1981), 64, 215.
2. Matilda Joslyn Gage, *Woman, Church, and State* (New York: Arno Press, 1972), 314.

A Book Review

Leafing one day through a pile of papers that I had written in college and not perused since, I came across my review of that grand old gothic novel, *The Mysteries of Udolpho,* by Mrs. Ann Radcliffe (1764–1823), required reading for my long-ago course in romantic literature. I had not liked the book, and my professor, who had a certain rarefied enthusiasm for the genre, had not liked my review. Though he had grudgingly labeled it witty, he had thought it unnecessarily prejudiced against the book's heroine, the lovely and passive Emily St. Aubert. Here is what I had written of her and her adventures:

Emily is the daughter of gentlefolk in reduced circumstances. She grows up in the country, all "sweet innocence," as the author says. Her accomplishments are exactly three: she can draw pictures, play the lute, and write dreadful poetry.

She does these things for pages and pages of leisurely inanition, until she falls in love—more accurately, she is fallen in love with, for Emily doesn't deal in transitive verbs. Her lover is a squeaky-clean boy scout type named Valancourt, whose mind is almost as untroubled by any gleam of real intelligence as Emily's own.

Unfortunately, at this juncture both Emily's parents die. She is left in the care of a caricature of an aunt, rivaling Snow White's stepmother in her monumental vanity, bad temper, and selfishness. Then the villain enters the picture, and a sinister moustachio-twirler he is, too. He is Montoni, a fortune-hunting Italian (Mrs. Radcliffe's villains are frequently Italian). Under the impression that Emily's aunt is very rich, Montoni marries her, and plans to carry her off to Venice with Emily in tow.

Valancourt, shedding gallons of tears, now urges Emily to elope with him before she is removed to the Continent, for she has already had ample proof that her aunt and step-uncle mean her no good. However, Emily rejects his proposal, apparently for no better reason than that it might damage her reputation if she made up her own mind about anything without help. Yet she was tempted, just for a

minute there. "Her reason," says the author, "had suffered a tran-
sient suspension"—a not uncommon occurrence with Emily, who
had softening of the brain every few days or so. Still, "Duty and
good sense . . . at length triumphed over affection," though one
might doubt the good sense of Emily's non-decision. As a result, she
and her lover part, giving vent to a chorus of "convulsive sobs."

An interval in Venice ensues, with much feasting, slopping about
in gondolas, and dancing till dawn. Emily develops a "deep affection" for a charming Venetian lady, only to learn later that the lady's
virtue is not untarnished. Immediately and thereafter, Emily regards
her former friend "with terror."

Emily is almost choked with "fear and disgust" when an Italian
count proposes marriage to her. For a while, it seems Montoni might
force her to marry this fearful and disgusting aristocrat. But like
everyone else in the book, Montoni is only occasionally in touch with
his own mind. So, for no apparent reason, he suddenly spirits Emily
and her aunt away to his Castle Udolpho in the Apennines.

Now the stops are pulled out. Compared to Montoni's mountain
hideaway, Castle Dracula is a country day school. There are ghosts,
night noises, bloodthirsty banditti guarding the ramparts. In the
room next to her own, Emily looks behind a black curtain, and is
nearly prostrated by the sight of a horror so horrible that the author
declines to describe it. Emily's own room has a second door leading
to a secret staircase, which she sees, but is too timid to explore.
Suddenly the door is bolted on the staircase side by an unseen hand,
though Emily has no way to lock it on her own side. She protests
feebly to the master of the castle about this. She is summarily
brushed off, and thereafter spends her evenings in a dither of
dread, with a chair pushed against the mysterious door.

Montoni gets meaner. Because Emily's aunt refuses to sign over
to him all her estates in France, he locks her up in the east turret
until she sickens and dies. Now Emily inherits the estates, so Montoni begins to work on her. She also refuses him, thinking to give
her property to Valancourt if she ever finds him again. "Never, sir,"
she tells Montoni. "You may find, perhaps, signor, that the strength
of my mind is equal to the justice of my cause; and that I can endure
with fortitude, when it is in resistance of oppression." However, she
seriously overestimates her own fortitude. On the very next evening,
she meets one of Montoni's dissolute courtiers in a dark corridor.
Against her will, he tries to kiss her hand. The incident so unhinges
her that neither the strength of her mind nor the justice of her

cause can stand up to it; so she instantly changes her mind, and agrees to turn everything over to her sinister step uncle.

Through her tribulations in Castle Udolpho, Emily has one friend, a halfwitted maid named Annette, on whom Emily depends for food, firewood, light, information, and guidance. After living in the place for six months or so, Emily still can't find her way to her own room without Annette. On one occasion, when Annette fails to appear with her candle, Emily is forced to sit down alone on a dark stairway, leaking tears of "mingled terror and despondency . . . for she knew it would be impracticable to find her way through the intricacies of the galleries to her own chamber."

She is a marathon weeper. Both joy and pain elicit the same damp response from her. Physically, she is too feeble to run away from any threat, or even walk, or even "support herself." She is forever "sinking down" or "falling insensible." For all the necessities of life, she is reduced to "entreating" the servants.

Fortunately, Annette's peasant charms attract a manservant named Ludovico, a fine fellow, though Italian. After Emily, Annette, and a certain Monsieur Du Pont (Montoni's prisoner) have been languishing and futzing about for months without finding a way to escape from Castle Udolpho, Ludovico engineers the getaway in 10 minutes. Having carried his party of incompetents past Montoni's guards, Ludovico further proves himself by maintaining his correctly inferior status, "without forgetting the respectful distance which was due to his companions."

Monsieur Du Pont was placed in the castle dungeons by the long arm of coincidence, to serve as Emily's escort to France. Since his earliest youth, he has improbably languished with selfless love for Emily, who never knew of his existence. Having now conveyed her back to France (for she was naturally incapable of conveying herself anywhere), he fades out of the story, still languishing, and is forgotten by everyone, including the author.

Another series of coincidences lands Emily at a chateau in Languedoc, which turns out to be as riddled with hants as Castle Udolpho. Even worse, Valancourt reappears, a changed man. While in Paris, city of sin, the innocent lad fell into bad company and took to gaming. He says he is ruined, whereupon Emily, awash in tears, hands her former idol his walking papers. Though "agitated by convulsive sobs," she tells him primly, "Spare me the necessity of mentioning those circumstances of your conduct which oblige me to break our connection forever." "I am going, Emily," howls the poor wreck. "I am going to leave you—to leave you forever!" However, in the next breath he says, "I cannot now leave you—I cannot bid you an eternal farewell." After more backing and filling in the same vein, it is finally decided that because he is in debt, their eternal love has turned out to be a mistake. Practical Romantics! Their most forceful passions remain contingent on solvency.

Almost in the home stretch, with only a few hundred pages left to go, the author suddenly and unaccountably bolts off the track. A whole new set of characters is introduced, including a namby-pamby girl named Blanche, virtually indistinguishable from Emily. She also writes abominable poetry.

None of these characters have much to do with anything, except to get Emily into a new house of horrors, where the indomitable Ludovico mysteriously disappears from a haunted room, only to turn up later in a nest of banditti in the Pyrenees. A nun, dying of dementia in a nearby convent, somehow turns out to be the former owner of Castle Udolpho. She ran away from the unwanted advances of Montoni, and became the mistress of the former owner of the *other* haunted chateau, and the murderess of his wife, the marchioness, who turns out to have been Emily's real mother and Emily's father's sister. See? Everything is thus explained, at least to the satisfaction of the reader whose sanity is already reeling under the hammering of coincidence and who doesn't really care at this point whether all the loose ends are tied up or not.

The author wrings a few thousand more cubic centimeters of tears out of the love interest, before revealing that Valancourt was badly maligned; so Emily pronounces him "re-admitted to her esteem." A lesser man might have told Emily to get lost, and gone off to solace himself with some Parisian cookie whose esteem had fewer strings attached to it. Not this joker. He comes groveling back, watering Emily with his joyous tears, and Mrs. Radcliffe proceeds apace to the "divine bliss" of their nuptials. It's hard to imagine any ordinary mortal wishing to espouse either of them.

Concerning their long, soggy estrangement, an old peasant woman named Theresa makes the book's only sensible remarks: "Dear, dear! To see how some people fling away their happiness, and then cry and lament about it, just as if it was not their own doing, and as if there was more pleasure in wailing and weeping than in being at peace. Learning, to be sure, is a fine thing; but if it teaches folks no better than that, why I had rather be without it; if it would teach them to be happier, I would say something to it;

then it would be learning and wisdom too." But old Theresa is only a stage prop, and no one pays any attention to her.

My professor, an old-fashioned man, regretted the passing of such literary models of femininity as Emily was. He felt that it was not my place to criticize her, and he spoke to me regarding this. "Of course the novel is perfervid; that was the style of the times," he said. "But young women today might be better off with just a touch, at least, of Emily in their makeup. Perhaps you girls are making it too hard for men to feel protective toward you."

Judging from experience I wasn't at all sure that protective was the way men wanted to feel toward me. And I rather thought a person who imitated Emily's groveling ways would be more likely to provoke an attack. But I said nothing.

He continued, "It's a sharp, stylish review, even if you sometimes criticize the book for the wrong reasons. But I think you ought to remember how enormously popular this book was in its day—among women as well as men. What do you think all those women saw in it?"

"I don't know," I said, honestly puzzled.

I am still pondering the question. The gothic novel is still the most popular reading matter on the so-called women's market. Paperback clones, penned by dozens of Mrs. Radcliffe's spiritual descendants, still fill book racks in groceries and drugstores. You can always tell which ones they are. The covers show young women in white nighties, rolling their eyes nervously at sinister-looking dark castles or mansions in the background. The texts within are a little sexier, a little more briskly written, than Mrs. Radcliffe's opus. But, after all, she was blazing the trail. Her followers may have made improvements, but they have followed.

Later in the same course we studied two of Mrs. Radcliffe's far greater followers, the Brontë sisters. I had read both *Wuthering Heights* and *Jane Eyre* before, but enjoyed going through them again, taking better note of their subleties and refinements along the way. At the same time, studying the social background against which these brilliant women struggled to express themselves, I became more keenly aware of the magnitude of their achievements.

During a classroom discussion of *Jane Eyre,* I suddenly realized why this book had served as Charlotte Brontë's wish-fulfillment dream. "After all the troubles Jane goes through," I said, "the author finally rewards her with what was—from the viewpoint of a woman living in those times—the ideal husband."

"How so?" inquired my professor.

"He was blind, crippled, totally dependent on her, and rich." Everybody laughed except my professor.

Argument

College students of my generation seldom discussed controversial or sensitive subjects such as politics or religion. Having grown up with an interminable war, we were exposed to massive propaganda campaigns depicting citizens of enemy nations as uniformly demonic or subhuman creatures deserving of annihilation. Despite the irrationality of such a premise, few wanted to seem unpatriotic by challenging this or any other lie that Authority cared to perpetrate. War was one of the gloomy facts of life that intimidated us into becoming a Silent Generation.

Homecoming soldiers were rewarded with free college educations on the G.I. bill, so nearly every class had a few such veterans, who basked in the glamour of distant heroisms, real or imagined. Those who had lived through real horrors didn't talk much. Those who talked much usually were trying to add color to service experiences that were something short of dramatic.

One night at a party I got into an argument with one of these talkers, a veteran who had finished basic training in the army but was never sent out of the country. He told many stories about life in the service, firsthand and secondhand, and tended to monopolize conversations.

I never intended to argue with him. I kind of slid into it. He happened to repeat the epigram widely attributed to an unnamed chaplain that there were no atheists in foxholes. I couldn't help asking, "Are there Christians in foxholes?"

"You bet there are, girlie," he answered.

"Then I guess Christians must condone war."

"What do you mean, condone? Nobody condones a war. You fight a war because it's your duty to God and country."

"I can understand fighting a war as a duty to one or the other, but not both. God said, 'Thou shalt not kill.' The country says you shall. Don't they contradict each other?"

"Nobody believes that except conscientious objectors, and they're nothing but yellow-bellied cowards, afraid to go out on a battlefield."

"But weren't you just saying everybody's afraid on a battlefield?"

"Yeah, but they're *there*. The COs aren't."

"Didn't some of them serve as medical orderlies and go out on battlefields after all?"

"Maybe. But that was just to keep themselves out of jail, where they'd probably be killed for certain by other cons."

"Don't you think a person can be honestly opposed to killing other human beings in a war?"

"What human beings? Krauts and Japs? They're not human beings. They're vermin."

"That's just what Nazis said about the people they fed into gas chambers."

"Hey, you calling me a Nazi? You watch your mouth, girl."

"I'm not calling you anything. I'm saying that all prejudice against other groups is the same no matter who expresses it. Do you really think the God these foxhole soldiers are supposed to pray to intends them to hate and destroy whole nations of other people?"

"You mean yellow Jap heathen? Why should he care about them? He cares about people like us."

"Okay, aren't Germans and Italians people like us? Didn't their soldiers pray to the same God our soldiers prayed to?

Didn't their own home churches tell them that God was on their side just like our churches told us?"

"Maybe so, but they were wrong. That's why they lost the war."

"Is that how God lets people know they're wrong? By letting their towns be destroyed and millions of innocent people killed?"

"It's one way. Just who do you think you are anyway to question God's methods? Just be thankful you were on the winning side."

"I am, but not because I have any notion that God liked me better than some poor German girl who lost her family in the bombing, or a Japanese girl at Hiroshima, or a Jewish girl tortured to death in a concentration camp, or anybody else unlucky enough to live in the wrong place at the wrong time. Once men have decided that the thing they want to do right now is carry on a war, whether you survive is a matter of luck, not God."

"Maybe you don't deserve to be so lucky if that's the way you think. Like my old man always said, college education does women no good. It just gives them a lot of uppity ideas they don't need. It's God's own word in the Bible that women should stay home, raise kids, and shut up."

"That doesn't really suit me, however, and that's one reason why I don't pay attention to your kind of God."

"Is that so?" he sneered. "And just what kind of God do you pay attention to, Little Miss Smartass?"

"I don't know. I think maybe there isn't any clear concept around right now of the kind of God I would like."

"So you don't happen to like what God is, and you just decided all by yourself that you're not going to pay attention to him, or his Good Book, or his laws of right and wrong. All I have to say is, you've got some kind of nerve, lady. You better straighten up before you get into real trouble."

"What kind of trouble?"

"For one thing, you'll probably never find a decent man to marry if you go on with such craziness. You'll be a dried-up old maid, an unnatural freak, and what's more, God will punish you even into eternity."

"I don't think it's necessarily unnatural for a woman to stay unmarried. As a matter of fact, I don't intend to get married. I want to be independent and raise horses on my own farm, not kids in somebody else's house. Furthermore, I have paid attention to the Bible. I've read it all the way through, several times, and I know what it says. A lot of what it says is nasty. I don't think a good person would want to live by rules such as those. Nevertheless, I don't remember the Bible saying that it's a sin for a woman to stay single. And finally, I don't believe in that punishment-for-eternity nonsense."

"Next you'll be telling me you don't believe in God."

"That's right. I don't."

"If that's what college does for women, they'd better be thrown out of every college in the country right now."

"College didn't do it for me. I decided not to believe in the Bible's God years ago, when I was a child."

"Then you must be a child of the devil, that's all."

"Don't be silly. I don't believe in the devil either."

"Well, I do. And baby, you're as close to it as I want to get."

With that he rose and stalked away in high dudgeon: a warrior emerging victorious from the battle, leaving the enemy in ruins. I didn't feel ruined, but I did feel puzzled by the fervor of his hostility. I was left with the odd impression that neither of us really understood what the argument was about but that its subject matter was important.

Years later I figured it out. Even men without much reasoning ability can understand almost instinctively that the patriarchal God their fathers created for them is still their most powerful ally in the cultural subordination of women. That's why they think it essential that women be firmly convinced of this God's objective existence. A woman who denies him is seen as a threat to the entire structure. Her simple "No" could bring down what million of men's words have so carefully built up over centuries: the belief system of patriarchy, its tremendous financial investment in itself, its sexual and social privileges, its self-congratulatory sense of power.

I could almost smell the hatred and fear emanating from this man, but I'm sure he had no clear sense of its source. Probably he has remained ignorant of it. Yet I was ignorant for a long time also; I didn't realize how much inner freedom my antitheological opinions had already given me.

Arising from a generation of girls trained to revere the male (especially the male warrior), I was yet able to see how this man's orthodoxy made him a bigot and a fool, and to parry his attempts to intimidate me. I had unconsciously exorcised from myself the guilt and humility that orthodoxy forced upon women. When I decided that I would be commanded by no God, I took a first and perhaps most necessary step toward liberation.

But this is a curious thing: if my female intuition told me that God is only men's self-congratulation inflated to cosmic size, lo and behold, male intuition told men the same. Even the densest of men could understand, in a convoluted sort of way, that any woman's rejection of God was in some sense a rejection of himself. Two thousand years ago the shoe was on the other foot. Early Christians rejected the Goddess—destroying her temples, burning her scriptures, crushing her statues—and church fathers taught them to despise the alleged sinfulness of women. The sex of one's divinity does indeed matter.

On an occasion much later in my life, I was invited to address a group of Christian churchwomen on the subject of feminist theology. At one point in the discussion, a member of the group expressed her feeling of earnest gratitude that we, as women, should be "allowed" to speak together of such matters. "Just think how scandalized our mothers would have been!" she exclaimed. She further expressed her heartfelt thanks to her (male) minister, who was also present, for his unique liberalism and tolerance toward women's spiritual interests. He gave a complacent smirk.

I gazed from him to her in chagrin and pity. Inwardly I thought, how sad that she can't see herself as his moral equal at least, though she is probably his moral superior. After all, she has borne and raised children; he has not. She has given herself in loving and nurturing others without counting the cost; he has not. She has tried to tell the truth as she perceives it; he has not, because of the very nature of his profession. She belongs to the sex that does not make war, slaughter other groups, kill for enjoyment, rape, destroy, or exploit. He belongs to the sex that has initiated every evil known to humanity in the name of its God. He, not she, should be humble.

This woman, however, was still operating on a belief that patriarchal society thrusts upon women, a belief I had long ago abandoned: that is, the idea that women can get what they want by deferring to and flattering men. With this woman it had become an ingrained habit. She thought herself duty bound to admire, placate, and butter up male authority figures, to court their goodwill.

She had not learned the lesson that every feminist learns sooner or later: men don't respect deferential women any more than uppity ones. Men may like deferential women better just because they give less trouble, but men's chivalrous claim to respect womanhood in general is phony. It is just femaleness, rather than any particular female attitude, that triggers woman hatred in sexist males.

Elizabeth Cady Stanton noted long ago that man pretends to respect "womanliness," but man's idea of womanliness only means "a manner which pleases him—quiet, deferential, submissive." Let a woman step a little beyond the narrow confines imposed by man, and she soon finds herself most disrespectfully insulted, threatened, or abused. Absurdly enough, even female sexuality is open to the charge of "unwomanliness" if it seems to be more than man can comfortably handle. The men of Stanton's day often described promiscuous women as "unsexed"!

Women risk punitive treatment whenever they disagree with male myths or call men to account for such myths by the rules of reason, which men like to claim is uniquely characteristic of their own thought processes. Such a call is usually answered by unreasonable and emotional outbursts and by appeals to untenable, if widely accepted, hypotheses. Patriotism (never matriotism), heroism, God worship, and the necessity of war figure largely among such hypotheses. To do away with these and replace them with female values and priorities would create a new world indeed. Herein, perhaps, lies the real meaning of the "battle" of the sexes.

Holy Hell

It was in the university library that I first became aware of the fathomless depths of hatred that Christian men could hold for women.

I was doing research for a term paper in history. I happened to pick off the shelf an obscure treatise that was on no one's reading list. Leafing through it, I saw that it had some interesting woodcuts, so I carried it back to the table with my other books.

This was my introduction to the church's medieval Inquisition, which no history teacher had ever mentioned, as far as I could remember. There had been a holy organization that had terrorized all of Europe for nearly five centuries; had murdered multiple millions of human beings, nearly all of them women, for imaginary crimes; had formally instituted and codified atrocities of incredible cruelty—and no history course I had attended had touched upon it! Perhaps it was mentioned to history majors at the college level. I was not a history major. I was only interested in finding out, in a general sort of way, about my civilization's past. From this library book I found out more than I wanted to know.

There were official transcripts of witch burnings and witch torturings, so horrible that if they had been luridly written, I would have dismissed them as the ravings of a dreadfully deformed mind. Alas, these were real. They were dry, matter-of-fact reports by ecclesiastical clerks who were on the scene, recording what happened without any emotional response. In itself, this was perhaps the most horrible part.

In a typical day of torture in Prossneck, Germany, in 1629, the head torturer tied a woman up and burned her hair off with flaming alcohol. Then strips of sulfur were laid under her arms and around her back and set afire. Then she was put up in strappado, a device for dislocating the shoulders: her hands were tied behind her back with a rope that jerked her up to the ceiling. She was left hanging like that for three hours while the torturers went out for a bite to eat. On their return she was jerked up and down a few more times with heavy weights attached to her body. Then her thumbs and big toes were crushed in a vise, and then the same was done to the calves of her legs. Then she was whipped bloody with a rawhide whip and revived and questioned each time she fainted. Again the torturers went out to eat, leaving their victim on the torture stool for another three hours with her toes and fingers pressed in the vise. Later she was whipped again and then finally put away for the night so the torture could begin all over again the next day.

As I read what this seventeenth-century scribe had written, I felt my knees getting watery and a churning in my stomach. I kept wondering, how could one human being even *watch* such pain inflicted on another human being, without wanting to stop it instantly, without feeling either sympathy or outrage? Instead the dry words of the clerk seemed to suggest no more than a certain sickly smug enjoyment of her screams. The scene came before my eyes so vividly that I could almost observe the pitiless, twisted half-smiles on the faces of those depraved men, gathered around their victim, making her confess the impossible devil-copulations and storm-raisings that their own imaginations had suggested. I could see and smell the blood, the urine, the oozing blisters, the terrible red puffed-up tissues, the anguished eyes that searched for mercy and found none.

Shakily, I put the book down and tottered off to the bathroom, because I was sure I was going to throw up. I leaned over the toilet for 15 minutes, swallowing my nausea until it passed away. Never before had I been made to feel sick like that from a nonphysical cause.

I was still a little wobbly when I returned to my pile of books on the table. Nothing had really happened. The scene was the same as before. Afternoon sunlight slanted in through the high windows, warmly gilding the already golden oak tables and desks and the bent heads of students, and the subdued rustlings of their paper shuffling could be heard. The walls of the big room were bright with multicolored book spines. All was peaceful. It was a quiet day in the library.

Yet something had happened. I had discovered that righteous men were capable of what seemed to me unbelievable depravity, all in the name of their God, an accomplished torturer himself, if one listened to what was told about his hell. Still, hell was only a sick fancy, a nightmare of the ignorant. The Inquisition and its doings had been all too real, a literal hell on earth. What I found unthinkable had been actually done, not once, but millions of times over. There had been recommended ways of doing it, instruction books for the torturers, and official records of the proceedings, which never referred to the agony and terror of the victims.

I left the library and walked across the campus in the gathering dusk. Mellow stone pseudo-Gothic towers, decently clothed in their canonical ivy, gazed down on students strolling among the trees. Another peaceful scene. I thought, on what horrors had the real Gothic towers gazed down in those witch-hunting centuries? Would the sonorous pieties of the all-male church choirs have drowned out the screams of women burning alive in the public square before the church?

I passed the chapel. Its door stood open. Within, a large crucifix invited contemplation. I contemplated it.

In how many ways throughout the centuries, through how many endless, careful, graphic descriptions, had people been pressed to imagine the pain Jesus must have suffered on his cross! To have thus tortured him was considered a crime so dreadful—even though his loving Father had ordained it—that human beings were still being punished for allegedly having done this Father's dirty work. Millions of innocent Jewish men, women, and children had been mistreated, robbed, and slaughtered century after century on the specious ground that their remote ancestors were Christ-killers.

The horrors induced by that ancient prejudice were not over yet. They still occurred in our own century, worse than ever. And yet not one voice or finger was lifted against the men whose ancestors had been responsible for torments astronomically greater than Jesus' alleged suffering.

I thought the unspeakable martyrdom of 9 million women

ought to have been remembered more clearly than that of one man, who may or may not have existed, innumerable mythical martyrs who certainly did not exist, but were invented for profit by ecclesiastical relic mongers in the eighth and ninth centuries. I thought the woman hatred that fueled those real martyrdoms ought to be comprehended and dealt with, instead of being buried out of sight. It occurred to me that something has been dreadfully wrong in the collective psyche of this male-dominated world for a long time, and that men should be called to account for it—though surely not by their God, who was obviously an accomplice.

This was a revelation that produced no outwardly visible effect on me. I never even talked about it. Yet inwardly I had been shaken to my foundations. Once again my feeling was confirmed that, in the ultimate analysis, I was really much too tenderhearted to be a Christian.

Let it be said to the eternal shame of our species: not only have our major religions countenanced, approved, and even invented ever more refined tortures, but despite our vaunted "progress," such activities still exist in our allegedly civilized world. In some places political prisoners are routinely tortured. It is taken for granted that criminal organizations and even some law enforcement organizations consider torture a legitimate tool in their repertoire of coercion. There is even an enormous and profitable body of torture pornography based on the assumption—apparently justifiable—that many men are sexually gratified by scenes of women or children enduring physical abuse (and yes, the inquisitors did torture children, whom they considered basically demonic).

Some have assumed that this taste for giving pain, either in fantasy or in reality, is a natural if regrettable development of male aggressiveness. Other mammalian species, however, show that male aggressiveness tending to damage the female or the young is neither natural nor biologically sound. Such behavior would hardly conduce to preservation of the species, because females are not expendable in that context, whereas the majority of weaker males are. Such males never mate, anyway, because they cannot win their rutting battles.

Torture pornography leaves most women puzzled and revolted, falling back on the feminists' perennial question, "Why do they hate us so much?" It's impossible for most women to understand how anyone could be sexually turned on by a picture of a woman bound and gagged and looking terrified while a man threatens her with a whip, knife, or gun. What has this nastiness got to do with sex? The only possible connection winds through labyrinthine ways of ascetic religions that considered sexual pleasure nasty in itself and demanded that women be punished just for being capable of providing that pleasure. Thus the pleasure might become permissible only when accompanied by the punishment—a sick confusion of good and bad feelings, where such simple, obvious distinctions never should have become confused in the first place.

The majority of women have a natural morality that tells them it is good to give or receive comfort and evil to give or receive pain. Whatever became of this simple, clear, natural feminine morality in the society that literally gave its blessing to the kind of horror I was reading about, where self-styled moral leaders had instruments of torture inscribed with the motto Glory to God Almighty?

The books on witchcraft agreed that the one crime with which all these unfortunate women were charged was that of worshiping the devil. The books didn't say what I was to discover much later: that the "devil" women worshiped often had names such as Juno, Minerva, Aphrodite, Freya, Ashtoreth, Astarte, or Isis. In other words, the he-devil seemed to be a she, the same Great Goddess adored by women throughout classical civilization.

This may explain why so many medieval pictures of the devil gave "him" round breasts or a pregnant-looking belly. Certainly he was a composite of the ancient horned and goat-footed gods, but he also carried elements of the Mother of the Gods, whom medieval women remembered long after Jehovah's priests usurped her moral and spiritual leadership. Again and again European peasants paid with their lives for following the example of their ancestors and preferring the counsel of "wise women" to that of priests.

I found early church fathers bitterly denouncing women for invoking the blessing of "the foul devil Venus" at weddings; for asking Minerva's protection when they walked the highway; for offering cakes to Ceres for her gift of grain or to Terra Mater for her gift of a child; for making pilgrimages to the old Goddess's sacred springs or for praying to Mother Moon in her megalithic stone circles. I found that the real reason for the church's hostility to women was its fear of the few surviving remnants of women's religion, wherein pre-Christian Europeans had frankly acknowledged a female principle of supreme divinity.

Nowadays, in an attempt to recoup some of their losses, churches have begun to maintain that deity is neither male nor female or else that it is both: a "Father-Mother God." Such concessions, however, are grudging and tentative. Father still comes first. The pronoun of choice is still *he*. Women are still barred from the upper ranks of ecclesiastical decision-makers. A cleric is still supposed to provide a Jesus image. Mary is still denied her ancient pagan birthright as the universal creatress Mari-Anna. The Holy Ghost is still called male even though its (her? his?) symbol is still Aphrodite's sacred dove. Christianity buries woman and Goddess along with historical truth. It always has.

Significantly, the cautious hints of nonsexist or androgynous divinity are never permitted to reach the ears of children. Christian instructors of children mention only a Father and a Son. No little girl in Sunday school ever hears the word *Goddess* as an equal counterpart of God. Sexist inequality is the essence of Western religion. This can't be changed without changing the entire character of the myth as well as its derivative meanings. Western theology is locked into the fatherhood equals power, motherhood equals nurturance mindset, the reverse of those Oriental sects such as Tantrism that viewed femininity as active and creative, masculinity as passive and deathlike.

In view of the profoundly injurious, death-centured manifestations of Christianity in history, it is realistic to regard this religion as antilife. To torture and kill women, sacred vessels of human love and future generations, is surely more sacrilegious than any witch could ever be in her appeals to a nonorthodox deity. In the final analysis, history shows that the only criminals of the Inquisition were the inquisitors.

Once I had discovered this well-nigh incredible criminality in the system that purported to embody all that was good, my course was firmly set in the opposite direction. If I had to find any inkling of the divine in my life, it certainly would not be in a church. Perhaps the object of such a quest might lie far beyond the so-called Age of Faith, in times and places that orthodox scholars prefer not to reveal to female students. Like nearly every other woman who ever approached this subject, from any angle, I proceeded alone into territory that was, if not precisely uncharted, then at least thinly furnished with charts that were out of date and long since forced out of print.

One finds the female archetype not only in the dark well of the unconscious, but also at the bottom of an artificially created well of forgetfulness, like one of the Inquisition's oubliettes.

PART TWO

The Mother:
Revelations

The Archetypal Mother

Modern psychologists refer to mother and father archetypes as images in the collective mind resembling the images of mythologies and religions, which may be regarded as graphic forms of the archetype. Differing only in minor details, true archetypes represent universal human experience.

The father archetype is likened to numerous mythological versions of the Sky Father or King-of-Gods, known to most ancient cultures by such names as Dyaus Pitar, Jupiter, Zeus, Ra, Shang-Te, Ahura Mazda, Anu, El, Yahweh, Wotan, Odin, the Dagda, and so on. The archetypal father image is supposed to embody not only the power of begetting, which makes him technically a father, but also temporal authority, law, force, retribution, stern judgment, and aggressive leadership. He wields the thunderbolt. He commands armies. He smiles only on those who prostrate themselves and obey his orders. Though given to merciless punishment of the disobedient, he exchanges favors for offerings and sacrifices, including even the favor of salvation. The Christian version of him, however, condemned the whole human race to eternal torture in the afterworld, mitigating this sentence only upon the bloody sacrifice of his "dearly beloved" son. So abject was the fear this god inspired that none of his faithful followers dared proclaim his methods unduly harsh. All men who considered themselves his dearly beloved sons could feel understandably uneasy about his possible chastisement.

Father God is clearly a projection into collective adulthood of the young child's perception of father: a giant-sized male with a loud voice and the power to hurt, sometimes making unreasonable or unpredictable demands, which must not be questioned. The religions of father gods typically kept the faithful off balance and apprehensive, instilled a lively sense of sin, and fostered a puritanical mistrust of sexuality. Instead of a shared pleasure, sex was seen as a somehow unwholesome female entrapment calculated to endanger men's souls. Fear tended to be presented as virtue. To be God-fearing was to be good.

Mere mortals could seldom relax in the presence of such gods, yet men insisted on endowing their patriarchal deities with these characterisitics. Father God reflects the power men would like to have for themselves.

Father God is now "perceived" in some form nearly everywhere. One may doubt, however, whether he is a true psychological archetype. By strict definition, an archetype is present in the unconscious of every individual throughout the history of the race. And the human race is much older than its idea of fatherhood.

Fathers did not even become full-fledged family members until the most recent three or four thousand of humanity's several million years on this planet. Mother's brother used to be the usual male authority figure, because he was seen as a "real" relative, via the all-important maternal blood bond. Matrilineal kinship groups have been the rule, both in remote antiquity and in many preliterate societies recently studied. Biological paternity was simply unknown, because it's not easy to see.

Marriages were of little account, forming only frail, temporary bonds. Spouses often lived apart, with their own mother-descended families. In early root-planting cultures, the oldest woman headed the family, which was composed of her brothers, children, and grandchildren. Daughters inherited the property. Husbands would visit their wives secretly at night in the mother-in-law's house.[1] In Japan, where marriage remained matrilocal until A.D. 1400, the old word for *marriage* also meant "to slip into the house by night."[2]

"The custom of tracing descent and transmitting property through women instead of through men is common among uncivilized races. . . . The women are the only lifelong members of the household."[3] Neolithic societies similarly were dominated by the mother. Despite the absurd modern myth of the club-wielding caveman, Neolithic women were not subject to coercion by men.[4] "That societies in the past have arranged themselves on the principle that woman is the superior sex, we know well: in fact, it seems likely that until men found out their power of fertilization, woman was always regarded as superior." Society was shaped according to female priorities and judgments; the social order was founded on authority passing from mother to daughter. "It was a natural state of affairs arising from a primitive ignorance of the part played in procreation by the male."[5]

To comprehend even dimly the general mindset of prepatriarchal cultures, we must shed ingrained patriarchal attitudes, such as the modern belief that a father is at least as significant a parent as a mother. Our more remote ancestors did not believe this. Indeed, the pagan tribes of northern Europe still did not believe it in the early centuries of the Christian era. The first missionaries to pagan Britain complained of the "great sin" of matriliny that they found there; biological fathers and sons paid no attention to one another.[6] The primary loyalty of all men was to the maternal clan.

Today we are taught unquestioning acceptance of such verbal conventions as our paternal surnames, the generic description of the human race as man, and fathers being blood relatives—though this concept was stolen from the women who, according to ancient belief, actually produced the blood that made the generations. We accept the concept of the universal creator as a divine father, and such phrases as "fathers of our country," "fathers of the church," "founding (or town) fathers," and Abraham Lincoln's much-admired statement that "our fathers brought forth upon this continent a new nation, conceived in liberty and dedicated to the proposition that all men are created equal."

Lincoln said nothing about women, whom the fathers did not consider equal. His mellifluous declaration was also inaccurate on several other counts. His nation was not conceived altogether in liberty, but at least partly in slavery (for blacks) and massacre (for Indians). Moreover, fathers may beget but they don't bring forth. As personified by its people, any nation is brought forth only by mothers.

This was understood by *all nations of the human race* during the earlier 95 percent or so of its existence, when the fact of biological paternity was as unknown to human beings as it is to any other mammal. Yet any mammal knows about motherhood from its very first breath. It is born hungry for the nourishment and comforting warmth of the mother's body, for the stimulation of the mother's touch. However weak, blind, helpless, or ignorant of the environment it may be, the infant mammal knows one fact with clarity: Mother alone means survival.

Therefore the infant mammal cries, crawls, clutches, and clings to Mother alone; knows her by smell, touch, and sound; wants her constantly close; watches her every move whenever it can; and feels safe only in her presence. In a very real sense, Mother is life.

The impact of this singleminded, all-consuming need upon the young organism can hardly be overemphasized. Never in adult life, except perhaps under extreme duress or in moments of sexual coupling, will there again be such an intense focus of attention. In animals and humans alike, normal development of the intelligence, body awareness, social bonding, and successful mature sexuality are all rooted in the interaction between mother and infant. Here we have something that seems to fit the strict definition of an archetype far beyond the scope of any paternal image.

In most species, females control the reproductive cycle, making use of the males only on the limited basis required by fertilization. The most powerful bonds between individuals are those of mother and offspring. It is for the sake of this vital relationship that nests and communities are established, work is done, problems solved, food procured and stored. "The single-parent family is the rule in nature and that parent is almost always female. . . . When one looks at females in nature one sees industry, progenitiveness, and efficiency; when one looks at males one sees the most amazingly elaborate forms of wastefulness."[7]

Because the process of growing up takes so much longer for humans than for other animals, the period of dependence on maternal imprinting is correspondingly longer and more complex in humans. During this lengthy apprenticeship in living, the young human learns mostly from Mother all the fundamental cultural skills, including language. In their intense envy of—and hence concentration on—the merely physical aspects of motherhood such as birthing and nursing, men seldom realize that by far the greater part of motherhood is made up of the long years of patient teaching and socialization of the young.

Through the most subtle, complicated psychophysiological mechanisms, which we do not even begin to understand, the postparturient female is programmed to think constantly of the care and instruction of her child, just as the child is programmed to pay attention to her with a prodigious alertness and concentration that it will never duplicate in later years, even if it grows up to be a genius. We all learn more in our first year than in any subsequent year, and only a little less in the second year, and a little less in the third, and so on. Our attentiveness to our primary teacher is probably the most tenacious mental effort we will ever make.

Observing this complex interaction of teaching and learning, the unquestioned authority of the mother-teacher, the prestige and power of parenthood, men probably desired parenthood thousands of years before they understood that they could be parents. Mythology is full of stories depicting men's (or gods') attempts to produce their own children by some crude magic, usually an imitation of the birth process, showing that birthing was the only kind of parenthood they could comprehend.

Father Ra, Father Uranus (Heaven), and the Babylonians' god Kingu, firstborn of the Great Mother, all gave birth to living creatures by castration: a radical redesigning of the male body to replace projecting genitalia with a womanlike bleeding orifice. It has been shown that male envy of the female body has led to countless rituals of transvestism, imitation birth such as couvade, and mutilation of male genitals ranging from circumcision to full amputation. Egyptians were the first to circumcise, making it clear that the operation was symbolic of feminization. Among some primitives male genital mutilation at puberty was labeled menstruation and the wound was known as a vagina.[8]

When male priests were first permitted to join priestesses of the Mother Goddess, and gods of the Sky Father type were first added to formerly female-dominated pantheons, the priests apparently underwent castration in order to become more like priestesses. So we are told by myths from many places: Greece, Scandinavia, India, Phrygia, Phoenicia, Canaan, and Syria. The gods permitted themselves to be castrated to serve as models for their priesthoods, it seems. For instance, Father Odin received the title of Jalkr, "Eunuch," following his theft of the mysterious magic called *seidr* from the Earth Goddess or All-Mother, a kind of magic that used to be the province of women only. It was said that early priests of Odin were required to attain a high degree of "effeminization."[9]

From similar traditions came the extraordinary number of castrated heroes or sacred kings associated with the Holy Grail myths, which were only loosely Christianized versions of the pagan stories centering on the ancient womb symbol of the Cauldron of Regeneration. As a rule Christian translators euphemized the elder heroes' wounds as between or through the thighs, but it was clearly castration that was meant. Grail heroes so treated included Joseph of Arimathea, his successor Josephe, Bron and the Fisher Kings, King Evelake of Sarras, Galaphes, Lambor, Pellehan, and Pelles.[10]

Female-imitative devices were necessary to all men (and their gods) in early civilizations when they were just beginning to aspire to a social significance comparable to that of the tribal mothers. Before the facts of fatherhood became generally known, men seem to have gone through many absurd theories about conception, all of which prove that men didn't understand their own reproductive role until the beginnings of civilization were well established. Even some of the higher civilizations such as Phoenicia and Egypt preserved written traditions of a recent past when fatherhood was unknown.[11] The same confusion has been found frequently among modern primitives. Arunta tribesmen of Australia insisted that sexual intercourse does not beget children. Conception is caused by totemic spirits that may live in a "child stone" with a hole in it, where the spirits can peek out and select a mother among the women who visit the stone, hoping to conceive thereby.[12] A similar explanation may apply to the famous "holed stones" of northern Europe and the British Isles, which are known to have been sacred places in pre-Christian times.

One of the clearest indications of former male envy and mystification about the female magic of parenthood is the vast number of mythological and symbolic male imitations of birthing used to solemnize nearly all rites of passage, initiations, baptisms, investitures, and other ceremonies representing a new phase of life. In the Hindu ceremony of Abhishekaniya, a king is consecrated by an enactment of his pseudobirth from beneath a robe known as "the womb of knighthood" (*kshatra*). The officiating priest is said to cause the king to be born—that is, to become his surrogate mother.[13] In other versions of the born-again ceremony, devout Hindus were dragged bodily through a huge artificial yoni (vulva) and then called twiceborn.[14] Male pseudomothers often figure in boys' puberty rites.

Even the Father Gods of classical antiquity resorted to mother-imitative devices to establish a position of authority over other, chronologically older deities. Father Zeus' peculiar birthing of Athene from his head and Dionysus from his thigh present well-known examples. Even the biblical Yahweh had to use a crude imitation of birth to make man (Adam) the mother and therefore superior of woman (Eve). Actually the story of Adam's rib was stolen from the story about the earlier Sumerian Mother Goddess, Nin-Ti, "Lady of the Rib," who used mothers' rib bones in forming the children in their wombs.[15]

Yahweh himself did not beget, so his title of Father was not wholly deserved. He manufactured. Making his children out of clay with his hands, he copied the ancient magic of the Sumerian and Babylonian Mother Goddess, who had titles such as Ninhursag, Mami, Aruru, and Nana, and who taught women her secret birth charm: clay figurines may be brought to life as future babies if they are properly inoculated with menstrual blood.[16] The mystic name of this popular female magic was *adamah* or "bloody clay" in Hebrew, which biblical scholars delicately translate as "red earth," taking care to avoid the suggestion that Adam's name makes him a child of the ancient blood mother.[17]

Lacking the essential magic of menstrual blood, the biblical

God who later claimed to have manufactured Adam used breath to animate his clay, "and breathed into his nostrils the breath of life" (Gen. 2:7). This was a common device among gods of the time, when men were identifying breath with soul and pretending to give souls to newborn children by breathing on them, so as to claim parenthood.[18] God used the same device in other biblical stories, notably Ezekiel's magic restoration of life (or soul) to an army of dry bones (Ezek. 37:10). Nevertheless the Bible also inconsistently maintained the earlier opinion of the life essence derived from the Mother: "The life of all flesh is the blood thereof" (Lev. 17:14).

Now that men have overcome the ignorance that so plagued their sex in ancient times, there are some who claim that men have always known about fatherhood. They are vague about just how far back in time this "always" is supposed to extend. Obviously male animals don't know they can be fathers, and a couple million years into the past, the line between animal and human was blurry indeed. At what point were primitive humans or protohumans supposed to have received their information?

The clue could hardly have come out of the way of life of primitive groups, with their matrilineal clans, lack of records, and loose, temporary sexual affiliations. It has been amply shown that few primitives know exactly how long a pregnancy lasts.[19] Even those who had come to believe that sexual intercourse might have some sort of effect on it still couldn't identify any given sexual encounter as the start of a pregnancy. Most of the time it was thought that conception was due to magic, not sex. Many ancient conception charms depended on (menstrual) blood, the "fluid of life."

If men had always understood fatherhood, the ties of relationship would never have centered on blood. Prehistoric myths of male parenthood would never have been made the crude female-imitative devices that they are. The world's creation would never have been so commonly envisioned as a cosmic birth. There would never have evolved the matricentric, matrilineal systems of tribal descent and property inheritance so common in the ancient world. Mothers used to rule that world, not by fear or intimidation as the fathers would eventually rule, but by natural right as givers of life and bearers of the culture, the traditional wisdom, and the all-important blood bond.

Before man ever dreamed of colonizing other planets, conquering the earth, ruling nature, winning fame and fortune, or making himself immortal, he yearned to produce life and to be honored as the source of other human beings. Some psychologists have even attributed man's more grandiose yearnings to his fundamental envy of woman's ability to give life.

With the material help of his Father god, man has finally colonized woman's eternal miracle of parenthood. He has created a society in which he can demand even more respect for his momentary, unconscious act of begetting than a mother can expect for her nine-month hosting, effortful delivery, unremitting nurturance, and lifelong concern for her children. Even neglectful, punitive, cruel, or destructive fathers can legally claim the right to control children.

Man's domination can hardly go further than to usurp the parental role that not even a female animal will allow her mate. In fact, mothers of most mammalian species will fight to the death to keep adult males from interfering with their young. If males tend or play with the offspring, it is usually under the mother's watchful eye and subject to her approval.

Although no one would deny that many human fathers are good people and good parents, yet there is something not altogether reassuring about the way patriarchal males often claim the rewards of parenting without having earned them. So common is man's tendency to neglect the real demands of parenting that it is reflected even in our words. "To mother" and "to father" have very different meanings. "To mother" implies deep caring, hands-on nurturing and comforting, love, watchfulness, compassion. "To father" means to simply beget. That has never been quite enough.

Ancestor worship is a natural response of human beings to the realization that one's existence is due to others who have existed before. In prehistoric times reverence for the mother, giver of life, was naturally extended to the mother's mother and the mother's mother's mother, and so on back to the original foundress of the clan, all of whose members came to regard themselves as her children. Inevitably then, the foundress began to assume the status and meaning of a goddess.

Though she might be long departed from the earth, it was believed that her spirit continued to look after the welfare of her descendants, as all mothers were trusted to do. Her images and relics were carefully preserved to act as tribal guardians. Her name was often invoked so she would hear what her children needed. Her advice was sought through prayer or trance. Probably such was the earliest beginning of each Goddess name or title in mythology's worldwide horde of Holy Mothers and Creatresses.

No doubt postmortem deification of the clan mother was another cause of male jealousy. Therefore when male gods began to gain acceptance, it was primarily in the role of tribal culture hero and begetter of many descendants, who would honor the god as author of their being. Even the Bible mentions the perennial desire of men to beget whole nations of descendants (Gen. 17:6). The more descendants a man had to keep his cult, build temples to his memory, and offer his spirit sacrificial meats, the more divine the status he would attain in the afterlife.

Copying their patriarchal forerunners in India, Old Testament writers kept interminable lists of male ancestors, mostly mythical (the "begats"), to be invoked by name on every solemn occasion and thus honored in the spirit world. The names of corresponding foremothers were significantly omitted, although the "begats" contain many female names left over from Israel's matriarchal period, which were simply redefined as male.

Biblical writers seem to have been influenced by the older patriarchal ancestor worship of Vedic sages, who said every man needed sons, because sons are useful to make oblations to the fathers.[20] Men without father-worshiping male descendants would wander alone, cold and hungry, in the waste spaces of the afterworld. Therefore one of the blessings men craved from their new paternal gods was a plenitude of sons to deify them, as the clan mothers had been deified.

The Old Testament God won adherents by promising men that he would make their progeny as numerous as the stars or the sands of the sea, so they would be revered as founding fathers of rich, populous nations, able to sustain their holy ghosts with many fat offerings (Gen. 12:2). Then as now, it was thought that deities needed to be constantly fed and flattered, sung to with great praises, and "magnified" (in the biblical term) to keep them benevolent. Even in the Christian heaven this became the daily duty of all the angels and blessed spirits. Thus God was represented as a kind of Oriental pasha whose outsize conceit required a never-ending chorus of sycophantic acclaim.

Such extravagant reassurances of worth and virtue were typically demanded by male gods and by the gods' representatives or embodiments on earth: kings, emperors, pharaohs, sultans, prophets, priests, popes. One might suspect that this insistence on ceaseless adulation owed much to man's paternal insecurity and womb envy. The universal parenthood and creativity of the god were repeatedly emphasized (he never tired of hearing about it). Men seemed to find no inconsistency in their notion of an all-powerful deity who invented the entire cosmos, yet needed constant, abject reassurances from mere mortals. This particular projection of male uneasiness has always hinted that the real nature of God is nothing more than man writ large.

Similarly, the Goddess was woman writ large, but she was a truer archetype, representing a perception shared by every individual member of the human race forever. As the ancient writers pointed out, a mother is the only parent every child knows of itself, without needing to be told.[21] Children must be told about their fathers, but Mother is a direct experience from the moment of birth and even before, when she is the living environment.

So it was with the entire cosmos, the ancients thought. The Greek "cosmos" itself was Diakosmos, the universal order imposed by the Goddess (Dia) at the beginning of time. She created the world by bringing order out of a primal chaos, which was herself. All women's bodies retained the spirit of her divine wisdom, with their ability to make order in the form of a perfected child out of the mass of mysterious Goddess-given lunar blood within their wombs.

Judging from the multitude of their taboos, men regarded this blood as the most sacred and most dangerous substance in the world, so full of life-and-death magic that it was shunned with "holy dread." Words with the double meaning of "sacred" and "taboo" applied universally to this blood. The idea translated "unclean," used for menstrual blood in the Bible, also meant "holy."[22] In their patriarchal dread of that female essence, however, later translators chose the more pejorative meaning.

Other scriptures revealed more about this substance of creation. Hindus said there was a sea or ocean of blood at the beginning of the world; this ocean was also the essence of Kali-Maya the Creatress. According to the Orphics and others, the Creatress Eurynome (Universal One) performed a magic dance to cause her primordial sea to clot or curdle, like blood, to form living solid matter and the substance of all things in the world.[23] Babylonians said the primal Goddess Tiamat menstruated for three years and three days (by her lunar calendar) to provide the same essence of creation: the "Red Sea." The Bible called this mysterious sea the Deep (*tehom*), but the original Spirit brooding over it was female, often represented by that Aphroditean totem the dove.

Sometimes the vast creative reservoir of maternal blood was referred to as a cauldron. In many religious traditions the cauldron symbolized the Goddess's all-producing womb, not only at the original creation, but also as the vessel of ongoing creation as long as the universe continued. Every plant and animal, from the gnat to the whale, took its life force from the same source, the Mother's ever-churning cauldron. Again, the same mighty vessel took back the life force of everything that died and recycled it to make new combinations.

Thus the ancient pagans evolved a holistic view of the universe. All things were part of the Mother and therefore part of each other as well, united in her cauldron-womb as water drops were united in the sea. The universe was her clan, and all creatures were her children. The universe itself was related to one of her ancient names, Uni, the Sabine/Etruscan Goddess who eventually became Juno, mother of the Roman pantheon. Eve's biblical title, Mother of All Living, was taken from older traditions in which the Goddess was regarded literally as progenitress of the world and everything in it.

By contrast, followers of father gods tended to chop up the universe into categories, especially dualisms: good and evil, we and they, chosen people and infidels, soulless animal and soulful human, virtuous man and sinful woman (the original meaning of *virtue* was "manliness"). Things for which father gods disclaimed responsibility had to be assigned to evil spirits, or human wickedness, or some of the newly invented superdevils; although the biblical God also said he was himself the creator of evil (Isa. 45:7). Probably this biblical lapse was copied from some older scripture of the Goddess, who blended death and destruction in her cauldron as well as birth and creativity. The holistic view was fundamentally repugnant to patriarchy, as it would naturally assert universal kinship among all creatures and thus prevent men from seeing themselves as superior beings. Wars, for example, were best fought when men could manage to convince themselves that all the enemy were subhuman monsters or devils in human form.

Warfare has been the province of men in most societies, excepting those the ancient writers called Amazonian, where women fought either in all-female companies or in armies composed of both sexes. When women accompanied men into war, it was usually because their magic was considered essential to the casting of victory spells and the invocation of helpful deities. No ancient army would stir without first taking omens and setting up the right charms. This was woman's work. Even material from Israel's matriarchal period in the Bible relates how Barak refused to lead his army to battle unless the high priestess Deborah went with him to ensure victory by her magical presence (Judg. 4:8).

A favorite male myth about war views it as a natural and inevitable expression of man's innate aggressiveness. The myth says all real men like to fight and find it exciting to risk their lives in combat. The same male aggressiveness, coupled with superior physical strength, is often cited as the root cause of patriarchy: that is, men dominate women because men can win physical fights with women. The myth claims that men have always been able to intimidate women because they are stronger and fiercer, and so men have always made themselves the dominant sex.

This widespread myth needs to be re-examined. We know that men have not always dominated women, and that physical strength alone has never been the determining factor in social relationships. Moreover, it is absurd to argue that every woman feels intimidated by another person's greater size or strength. This is a habit of men only, to be constantly measuring themselves against others in terms of the likely outcome of a physical fight. The I'd-hate-to-meet-him-in-a-dark-alley response to another's physical presence is a result of masculine conditioning. Women don't think that way. Instead women are conditioned to view bigger, stronger people—that is, men—as potential lovers, not potential rivals. Therefore women are not as intimidated by physical size as men are.

Furthermore, even the strongest man is puny compared with many other animals whose size, strength, and speed vastly exceed his own. There never has been a Samson able to kill a healthy lion with his bare hands. Even wild animals much smaller than a man can easily defeat him in one-on-one combat. Nevertheless, man can enslave many kinds of big, strong animals, such as cattle, horses, mules, camels, and other beasts of burden, not because he is stronger than they, but because he is smarter.

Thus one can hardly maintain that superior strength necessarily means dominance. The prerequisite is not strength but intelligence. And there has never been any valid evidence that females are less intelligent than males. On the contrary: the statistical edge seems to belong to the females.

Despite centuries of patriarchal insistence on feminine stupidity, recent studies have indicated that women may be generally better thinkers than men. Men used to point with pride to their larger brains, conveniently ignoring the fact that elephants and whales have much larger brains than men, yet are not inevitably smarter. Actually, the crucial factor is not mere brain size but the proportion of brain to body weight. In this respect women have the advantage. Also, women's frontal lobes show more development than those of men.[24]

Women also seem to have keener hearing (especially in the

higher ranges), better visual perception, more sensitive touch, more retentive memories, superior verbal skills, and quicker wits than men. Perhaps it is only to be expected that the sex responsible for the continuation of the race would be provided by nature with such advantages. Maximum alertness and learning ability in females would naturally ensure better protection for the young.

It's hard to see how the myth of male dominance by strength could be upheld in the face of anthropological studies showing that dominant individuals in primitive societies are by no means those of greatest muscular strength. More often they are simply the cleverest ones. Successful warriors and war heroes may have their place of honor, but this is not the same as the place of rulership. In a fair number of uncivilized groups women wield the real social power because they represent the sacred principle of motherhood, hence of all fertility magic affecting such vital issues as population, health, the food supply, and communication with spiritual forces.

Societies where women are degraded and abused evidently represent degeneration of the social bond following male usurpation of female life-magic. Men dominate not because of their muscular strength, but because they have come to believe themselves somehow holier than women. This should not be difficult for a member of our own patriarchal society to understand, because this was the primary means of female oppression in Western Europe for nearly two thousand years.

Our own complex civilization presents ample evidence of this kind of social degeneration, in itself a powerful contributing factor to the perpetuation of the male myth. For centuries the Judeo-Christian system has incessantly proclaimed the innate sinfulness, weakness, and mental frivolity of women. Within this system women have been commended not for achievement but for self-sacrifice and self-effacement. Accordingly, the system encouraged physical coercion and chastisement of women who showed any sign of self-assertion. Women's verbal protests against their oppression, that is, "scolding," have even been defined as a crime, punishable by torture and imprisonment.[25]

Judeo-Christian authorities depended heavily on enforced

monogamy (enforced for wives, that is) to keep each woman in subjection to her own personal male guardian, who was responsible for her obedience. Husbands were given virtually unlimited authority over wives and children. Up to the nineteenth century, husbands could even get away with causing wives to die of marital chastisement.[26]

This is not, however, attributable to biologically inherent aggressiveness in males. Animals show that the real purpose of male aggressiveness is to establish mating priorities. The aggression is directed against other rival males, not against females or their young. Displacement of male hostility toward the female sex is not a natural phenomenon but a culturally conditioned one.

Therefore patriarchy can't be explained as the result of superior muscular strength or fighting spirit in males. It is a result of assiduous social training of both sexes from early childhood. Especially in the crucial adolescent years, when relationships between the sexes assume new importance, we learn that masculinity implies muscularity and readiness to fight, and femininity means physical delicacy, indolence, helplessness, and constant deference to males. Big, strong, assertive girls are considered sexually unattractive, because males feel threatened by them. Similarly, girls of obviously gifted intellect are also unattractive, because males feel threatened by them too. Boys receive unequivocal praise for physical and mental accomplishments, but girls pay a stiff price for them in terms of social acceptance.

There have also been severe prices to be paid for such basic female functions as sexuality and motherhood. Far from being celebrated as holy, as they were in pre-Christian religions, these functions were directly tied to Christian concepts of original sin, ritual uncleanness, and the danger of damnation. Early Christian authorities said such hard things as women do not deserve to live, and every woman should feel ashamed of her womanhood.[27] Women's genitals were described no longer as the gate of life, but as the gate of hell. Even men's perpetual desire to enter that gate was blamed on women and turned against them. Men's capacity for sexual love was converted into frustration or self-disgust, which could be expressed only in an abusive attitude toward women.

Were it not for our society's relentless training of both males and females to accept such distortions as normal, women would not tolerate physical abuse. Wife-beating, child abuse, incest, and rape are symptoms of our social sickness. Wives don't tolerate brutal husbands just because they are physically incapable of fighting back. Any battered wife could catch her tormentor off guard or asleep and take an effective revenge. The real reason wives tolerate abusive husbands is that women are brainwashed into trying to love their oppressors, in addition to religious and social training that tells them they are fundamentally inferior, hence deserve contemptuous treatment.

Actually, physical aggression is not a preferred occupation of the average man. Even in highly aggressive societies such as our own, males must undergo extensive conditioning from their earliest years to accept the risks of fighting and the role of the warrior, to believe in the glory of war, and to go willingly into battle. Boys must be taught to play with toy weapons. Their sports should imitate warlike rivalry, team against team, even when the activity aims at individual self-improvement, such as gymnastics, swimming, or weight lifting. Boys' entertainments should feature violence and the triumph of hero figures. Even when all these training aids are abundant, as they are among us, there are yet some males who resist them. These may grow up to prefer peace; to envision their God as a gentle sort of deity evincing the "feminine" qualities of compassion, forgiveness, nurture, self-sacrifice, and love; and even—the ultimate betrayal of patriarchy—to genuinely like women, not as sex objects but as people.

We have seen in our own generation how collective ideas of deity are constantly evolving to suit changes in social attitudes—despite fundamentalists' contention that deity is changeless. The modern Zeitgeist has forced extensive renovation of the ferocious Old Testament warlord, who now seems unnecessarily barbaric as well as a late derivative from various Canaanite, Midianite, Phoenician, and Syrian "Baals." Even the pseudo-feminine, pseudomaternal Jesus is less credible than he used to be, before contemporary scholars discovered the fraudulent nature of his scriptures.[28]

This generation, however, faces a world crisis in human relations and moral ideas, which may call for changes more sweeping than any others have been since the course of civilization was permanently altered by the revelation of fatherhood. That long-ago revelation set humanity into a patriarchal mold that suppressed the sense of maternity as a primary motive power in society, and produced "an attitude of distrust, contempt, disgust, or hostility towards the human body, the Earth, and the whole material Universe."[29] Ironically, it was probably women themselves who gave that revelation to men, because women were the first to invent calendars and to keep temporal records, based on their own body cycles in harmony with the phases of the moon.[30]

Now the next phase of revelation must pass in the other direction through men's rediscovery of the Mother archetype, which lies deep within the unconscious of every woman-born human being.

Some theologians tentatively grope toward the hidden Mother archetype with notions such as "God is love," or "God is both (or neither) male/female." These notions, however, are never realized in Western thought with the same boldness that symbolizes the divine duality in Eastern images of an eternally copulating couple such as Shiva and Shakti, representing the principle of love in terms perfectly comprehensible to mortals, or in androgynous divinities such as Ardhanarisvara, or the ancient world's Primal Androgyne, neither the male half nor the female half able to exist without the other.[31] Western religion is afraid of the female principle and certainly reluctant to grant it any vivid graphic representation.

The reason for this fear is buried in still another secret that Western religion dares not face: the secret admission that any graphic representation of a deity is not just an imitation of a reality but the reality itself. In other words, man has created God in his own image, and he knows it, but is afraid of knowing it.

For centuries the Western world has been torn by the question of its God's literal existence. At one extreme stand the atheists, who find any God-belief irrelevant to their emotional stability, moral integrity, or social functioning. At the other extreme stand the fanatics, who defy objective evidence to insist on the Bible's verbatim truthfulness, the direct intervention of God in human affairs, and the everlasting life after death of the elect (that is, themselves). Most people fall somewhere in between, along a spectrum of uncertainty or confusion. The majority just don't think much about it.

It is a disgrace to our allegedly advanced civilization that such issues are considered beyond the understanding of the ordinary person, especially when the ordinary person's ethical and moral behavior is tied to them. We are not told to treat other people decently because it is the best way to get along in life. We are told the rules must not be questioned because they are direct orders from a Father God.

When the more perceptive look at the character of that Father God as he is presented by conventional sources, they see him repeatedly violating his own rules. The God who says "Thou shalt not kill" ordains one massacre after another. The God who lays down "unbreakable" laws of nature lets them be broken again and again to impress the ignorant who want something unbelievable to believe. The God who professes to love his children demands the torture and death of his son; this is supposed to save the rest of his children from eternal torture in hell. Yet, somehow, it doesn't.

Largely as a result of such theological ambivalence, the moral character of our civilization has advanced hardly an inch beyond that of ancient Sumeria. In fact, thanks to nearly complete suppression of the Mother image and the ancient laws of mother right, we have even regressed into a hostile polarity of the sexes and routine mishandling of the young, of which the ancient world was innocent. Our violent society has not evolved a workable ethic to stamp out weaponry and war. We are encouraged to feel guilty about making love, but not about making guns, bombs, and environmental poisons.

A different theological attitude is sorely needed to counteract the doubt and naïveté that make many of us moral cripples in a world that cries out for moral strength. Insistence on the literal reality of a Father God is not an intelligent course when all we have so far discovered of the real cosmos has yielded not a shred of objective evidence for a real deity. Fundamentalist belief is forced to deny or ignore the incontrovertible findings of science, a denial that can only bring on eventual embarrassment, as it did throughout the Age of Enlightenment.

Western God-seekers have not searched in the one place where deities have their only obviously "real" existence: in the human mind. Eastern thinkers dealt with the problem rather better through their numerous ways of perceiving identity between God and Self. The pagans of classical antiquity also founded their sacred Mysteries on the idea that a man or woman could be literally God or Goddess, merging with the divinity. Early Christians copied this idea from Mithraic, Hermetic, Orphic, and Osirian Mysteries, basing their whole system of salvation on self-identification with an immortal God. In later centuries, though, this idea was anathematized as Antinomian heresy, and the Judeo-Christian deity was set forever in outer—as opposed to inner—space.[32]

Yet there is always an implicit denial of God's external reality in the belief that he must be perpetually described and explained so his image is built up in human minds. The same theologians who call God incomprehensible are always busy telling the rest of us about God's thoughts, desires, and actions. Consequently any visions of God, Jesus, Mary, angels, saints, and so on, are usually perceived with exactly the same lineaments that the visionary has learned by looking at statues or pictures or by listening to descriptive words. The deliberate creation of God through human words is the original root of the Logos doctrine, which Christianity long ago stole from its pagan predecessors.[33]

The female half of the human race created the earliest images of divinity, which naturally assumed female characteristics. The male half of the human race modeled its gods on the ancient goddesses, then gradually eliminated the female image by declaring it false, frivolous, or devilish.

Images of deity must be reassessed from the ground up if we are ever to achieve a new balance or to comprehend the original archetype, the Mother who encouraged peaceful human existence. It is high time for women to reclaim their own deity, the Goddess who took on her first reality in their hearts when they worshiped the spirit within themselves and their ancestresses and equated motherhood with the motivating energy of the universe.

For many centuries after the initial establishment of father gods, both sexes were represented in divine pantheons. Like people, the deities also had fathers and mothers who headed their families. Goddesses and their gods represented a celestial paradigm of the coexistence of women and men.

Asian gods were once said to be powerless without their female counterparts, who embodied their true vitality.[34] Even the biblical Jehovah used to have his all-important spouse, the real source of his power or wisdom. She appears in the Bible as the Queen of Heaven, long considered by the people of Jerusalem to be God's superior (Jer. 44:17–19).

This Hebraic Queen of Heaven had many other names, such as Mari, Anath, Asherah, Hokmah, Sophia, Malkuth, Matronit, Virgin Zion, or the Shekina; her splendor feeds the angels, her body measures millions of miles, she can punish God for his excessive vengefulness. It was said her spirit dwelt in the two stone tablets carried by the Israelites in the wilderness. Joseph Gikatilla claimed she was named Sarah in the days of Abraham, Rebekah in the days of Isaac, and Rachel in the days of Jacob. She was also known as Moon, Pearl, Sea, Garden, Earth, Discarded Cornerstone, and Supernal Woman.[35]

Goddesses of the ancient world had many similar titles, often reinterpreted by patriarchal writers as separate names for different divinities governing different departments of nature. Later some of these names were even adopted into the Christian canon as saints, and fictitious lives were invented for them.[36] Such a compartmentalized view, however, was opposed to the holistic mindset of earlier matriarchies.

Though each tribe may have had its own Great Mother in the beginning, all Great Mothers sprang from the same archetypal foundation: the image of the human mother, laid down in the mind's core by actual experience before any other experience in life. She could be culturally suppressed, but never annihilated. Like the later Father god, the Mother figure assimilated all the attributes that various peoples had emphasized in their own cultures through thousands of years, so she was easily seen as a monolithic, monotheistic, all-encompassing deity.

Even when paired with a Father God, the Great Mother long continued to control the basic cycles of life and death. She governed the eternal alternations of God the father and God the son, each a perpetual seasonal reincarnation of the other. The old god often grew like vegetation, as a child from the maternal earth, then reentered her in an annual love-death as both spouse and corpse (buried seed), in anticipation of his resurrection. Symbols of the god included the sun, the crop, a sacrificial animal, the turning year, or the dying and resurrected Savior. All partook of the holy mystery and its continually reenacted sacred dramas.

The sacred drama typically demonstrated the necessity of death and the subsequent cyclic renewal of life. Objects or living forms were personified by the god, who was mutable. Son became father, father became son. New Aeon grew old and gave way to the new again. Rising sun became setting sun, and vice versa. The process, eternal becoming, was personified by the Mother, herself everlasting. Egyptians sometimes called her Isis, the Oldest of the Old, who existed in the beginning. "She was the Goddess from whom all becoming arose."[37]

Even Christian iconography retained the same basic alignment of God the father, God the son, and the Queen of Heaven as the mother/bride of both. Unlike the male deity, she was shown neither as a baby nor as an elder. She appeared only in her eternal young matron phase—the one men liked best, implying both sexual and maternal caretaking of the male.

In earlier times natural cycles of feminine life had their own image in the Goddess's trinity of Virgin, Mother, and Crone (or Creator, Preserver, Destroyer). Human minds seem to have an affinity for triads, especially as connected with the Great Mother figure. The triadic Goddess was often represented by three figures at the apexes of a downward-pointing triangle, perhaps derived from the shape of feminine pubic demarcation or the female body reduced to essential points of nipples and pubis. The name of Demeter meant Mother De (D) or delta, a vulva symbol in the sacred alphabet of archaic Greece. Similarly, the Hebrew letter *D* was daleth, the door, another reference to the gate of birth. In India the triangle was "the yantra of the vulva," or Yoni Yantra.[38]

A further possible reason for the triangle's use as a true archetypal glyph of the feminine is that it may show the essential points of the mother's face as seen by the newborn infant: eyes and mouth. Experiments have shown that newborns will smile and respond to any three spots arranged in a downward triangle, whereas other arrangements of spots elicit no interest. Human beings don't see very clearly in the earliest days of life, but they do come equipped with the necessary reflexes to engage the attention of the one person who can ensure their survival.

Hindus represented the female trinity by a triangle pointing down and the male trinity by a triangle pointing up. Their sexual merging created the famous hexagram, now accepted as the emblem of Judaism.[39] The hexagram was really a Tantric sex sign, which first appeared in Jewish tradition by way of Cabalistic sexual mysticism in the A.D. thirteenth century. Cabalists claimed the world had become evil because God had been separated from his Shekina—the Great Mother. In secret rites of the conjugal bedroom, they sought to reempower the feminine spirit that medieval patriarchy in general had so vilely slandered.[40]

Naturally, medieval clergy condemned as heresy any attempt at reactivation of the feminine spirit. Many clergy still do so today, though they no longer have the rack and the stake to help reinforce their views. The virulence of the Christian fathers' attack on the ancients' Goddess figures, from the latter days of the Roman empire all the way up to the present, shows how powerfully the Mother archetype affected men. Even when most of her magnetism was bled off into the deliberately mortalized, sanitized image of Mary, the Mother archetype still threatened to upstage both Father and Son. Without her ageless appeal, the patriarchal church itself would not have survived.[41]

Christianity's bitter thousand-year war on paganism was largely an attempt to eliminate the Mother archetype altogether, to replace it with the purely masculine images of Father and Son. The third member of the triad, the original Holy

Spirit, was another attenuated form of the Mother in whom both Father and Son were anciently united—as shown by her dove symbol and some of her Gnostic names. She too, however, was first neutered and eventually masculinized.

Throughout the Roman empire women worshiped their Goddess in her own temples, and men worshiped their God, with joint rites at certain crucial seasons such as the resurrection feast in March, fertility festivals in May, the rites of Vesta, first-fruits, harvest home, and the feast of the dead (which later became Halloween). Pagan women had a deity with whom they could identify; who understood women's problems; who supported women at all important stages of their life cycle: birth, menarche, marriage, motherhood, menopause, death. Juno, Queen of Heaven, embodied feminine wisdom and morality. She was also the female interior soul called *juno* that dwelt within every living woman.[42] The corresponding male soul had the Latin name of *genius,* meaning "begetter." The latter word was carefully preserved and its meaning expanded by patriarchal authorities who also carefuly erased every reference to the female *juno.* Consequently, the world has forgotten the Goddess spirit once said to dwell in women.

Paganism had room for both male and female deities, who demonstrated their interdependence in frank presentations of sexuality and motherhood. It was once thought that their creative power was best invoked through bonds of physical love. Christians regarded this as the epitome of evil. Equating the Goddess and all her works with the Christianized devil (a composite of the elder gods), they taught men to call their own impulses of sexual or filial love dangerous to the "pure" masculine soul. Christian theologians maintained that love should be directed only to God.[43] The fact that most men persisted in wanting to love women was a perpetual thorn in the side of Europe's moral arbiters, who never gave up trying to poison sexual relationships—even within marriage—with the taint of original sin. As long as the fable of Adam and Eve was generally accepted as history, the sin was said to be primarily Eve's, and all her female descendants were to be blamed forever.[44]

It is instructive to imagine what might have happened if this fable had never been believed; if the Christian church had not succeeded in destroying the temples of the Goddess; and if women had continued to take an active part in both the ritual and the theology of Western religion. What might have been made of the Mother archetype if our civilization had continued to develop it over the centuries instead of trying to erase it from human consciousness?

What if all the music, art, literature, and legend poured forth to the glory of the Father for the past two thousand years had been devoted to the Mother instead? What if the great cathedrals had been built in honor of the full archetypal Goddess instead of her desexed Christian shadow, Mary? What if the hymns, liturgies, invocations, prayers, creeds, and sacraments had been addressed to her instead of him? What if the many scriptures of the Goddess had not been burned early in the Christian era but rather had been as assiduously copied as the canonical books of the Bible? What if her statues had not been broken up by Christian fanatics but rather had been preserved as holy treasures, with the same reverence later accorded the church's fake relics?

In short, what if women still had a deity of their own, aproachable through visible works of the finest talents, intellects, and spiritual leaders in history? Suppose every modern church in every city, town, and village was understood to house a spirit of the Mother instead of the Father—a house of the Goddess instead of a house of God? In what ways might our present morality, our ethics, or our rules of social behavior differ from present patterns? How would our notion of gender roles change if it were generally recognized that the divine Father image—which many women now perceive as inadequate to their spiritual needs—was only a Johnny-come-lately on the scene of civilization? In primitive hunting-gathering societies, after all, a male god would not even have been seen as a significant food provider, in view of the fact that men's hunting activities provided only about 20 percent of the total food supply, the other 80 percent being gathered by women.

In the light of modern scholarship that reveals the specious nature of the origins of the patriarchal god, the unreliability of texts formerly regarded as sacred, and the historical propensity of male clergy to dissemble, women have every reason to distrust traditional religious structures. Therefore some women have been delving into older sources, seeking the Goddess image at a time in history or prehistory when it was still intact. Some look into their own hearts, seeking the female version of what used to be called the divine self, like Rome's *juno*, the spirit said to dance out its life in "the Cave of the Heart."[45]

Men are not likely to understand very easily what women find within their own hearts. It will take some effort, of a kind most men are not used to making. Men still like to talk of the mystery of woman. She is sometimes compared to a locked box with its key hidden inside. Men conveniently forget that it was men themselves who snapped the lock shut and insisted that the key remain hidden.

Women are still the core of the family, the primary nurturers, caregivers, and acculturizers of the children they bear. Their vital role as mothers, however, is increasingly usurped by male-controlled symbolism, most perniciously at present in the fantasy world of television, to which the average American family exposes itself for more than seven hours each day. It is a cold, violence-ridden, spectator world almost guaranteed to induce alienation in place of cozy old-fashioned story-telling, when a child could nestle beside a reassuring adult presence and receive a real human response to questions and could grow into literacy by watching the storybook's pages as they were read.

Instead, television fosters illiteracy and gives the child frightening, sadistic images, with no time to talk about them. In isolation and loneliness before the flickering tube, today's child is a passive spectator who hardly even knows how to invent games anymore. Television is a sinister fantasy world indeed, where women are usually portrayed as helpless victims of male violence and sexual exploitation, and the socialization of an entire culture is turned over to a soulless medium whose only real purpose is to sell consumer products.

With increasing frequency women turn against the male-dominated culture of consumption and exploitation in order to find their own roots. Many are beginning to say bluntly that they have had enough of the father-oriented ideologies of guilt, sin, pain, and punishment. Women seek a renewal of their self-confidence without the pernicious Judeo-Christian doctrine of inborn sin (usually attributed to female influence). They seek a new version of the intergenerational connectedness that joined daughters with mothers, mothers with grandmothers, and all ancestresses with the Goddess in prehistoric times.

A resurrection of the feminine archetype that all women still keep somewhere deep inside themselves, even if they don't know it, may be the only ideological possibility for rehumanizing and reuniting the world that now sets generation against generation, nation against nation in endless cycles of pointless aggression. The final results of patriarchal ideologies have been so disastrous that almost any shift toward feminine imagery in the spiritual realm would be beneficial. Reinstatement of the Goddess in the hearts and minds of her earthly daughters— and sons as well—may turn out to be the only practical salvation from the final chaos with which man in his vast cultural imbalance now flirts. Sometime in the not too distant future, the world's newest religion might take shape as an updated version of the world's oldest one.

We must now, however, recognize the fact that this religion has been struggling to take shape for more than a century out of archaeological and anthropological revelations, not to mention many centuries before that, when women's folk memories, fairy tales, and old wives' rituals based on Mother-religion were condemned as witchcraft. Women have had to reinvent the wheel of their faith in every generation, because the insights and research of their foremothers are persistently buried by the fathers again and again.

Women's mouths have been stopped, often by violence; their books have been removed from libraries or even burned; their histories have been slanted and falsified; even the very language they use has undergone sexist revisions. References to prominent female rulers, philosophers, artists, inventors, or religious leaders have been extensively edited or omitted from textbooks. The accomplishments of ancient queens have been derogated and those of kings have been glorified. Even now most of us know almost nothing about such names as Semiramis, Zenobia, Livia, Boudicca, Aethelflaed, Hroswitha, Matilda, Olga of Kiev, Hildegard of Bingen, or dozens of others.

Scriptural references to the Goddess or to the holy women who represented her on earth were dropped or diabolized in patriarchal revisions. Gnostic books referring to Sophia as the Mother of God and the source of all God's knowledge were destroyed early in the Christian era. Great Mother Astarte-Ashtoreth, one name for the Goddess who once ruled all the Middle East, survives in the Bible only as an "abomination." Men learned to define only themselves as humanity, their line passing from father to son without any apparent passage through mothers. The Old Testament word translated "people" does not mean "men and women" in the original Hebrew. It means only "men."[46]

Yet many pieces of the sexist jigsaw puzzle were already in place as much as a hundred years ago, plain to be seen by those who wanted to look. Matilda Joslyn Gage wrote in 1893:

> So slight a hold have historical facts upon the mind when contrary to pre-conceived ideas, that we find people still expressing the opinion that man's place has always been first. . . . Where woman was undisputed head of the family, its very existence due to her, descent entirely in the female line, we still hear assertion that his must have been the controlling political power. But at that early period to which we trace the formation of the family, it was also the political unit.[47]

Gage also remarked, tartly for a woman of the Victorian era, "The most grievous wrong ever inflicted upon woman has been in the Christian teaching that she was not created equal with man, and the consequent denial of her rightful place."[48] She went even further and declared in her fine book *Woman, Church and State* (a classic, but hard to find today): "The most stupendous system of organized robbery known has been that of the church towards woman, a robbery that has not only taken her self-respect but all rights of person; the fruits of her own industry; her opportunities of education; the exercise of her judgment, her own conscience, her own will."[49]

The process still continues today in a culture that has only begun to dimly understand what a terrible price man has paid for his vaunted supremacy and how far out of balance his society has gone. The obsession is unquenchable, as if men still remember the time when "Men were the original other; long before philosophers had begun to speculate on the uselessness of women save, in Napoleon's words, as a machine to produce babies, it was man who was useless."[50] A civilization rife with callous cruelty, exploitation, alienation, and war is only a part of that obsession.

Our culture's runaway masculinization might be seen as a collective lunacy. We now take for granted the prevalence of war, rape, and murder in our real world as well as in its model and reflection, our fantasy world of so-called entertainment. We have long since forgotten the collective mindset of past matriarchal societies, where such behaviors were as rare and restricted as cannibalism is for us. Even among the strongest of our women, there are some who still think all important decisions should be made by men and who bow down to an exclusively male God.

Nevertheless, times change. More people now express concern about the cultural sickness of male-dominated society, the unscrupulous greed of its leaders, the moral poverty of its religion. New religious ideas drift in from the East, from Native American traditions, from new knowledge about European paganism, and from the ancient and primitive sources of both myth and mind: the unchanging archetypes. Women can find the Goddess within, where she has always been, even if they were taught to call her God. She has a new name now, and there are more and more groups of women every day who know what it is.

If men could give birth, the names of the Goddess would never have been forgotten. If men could give birth, then birth would be seen still as the most important, dramatic, meaningful, quintessentially human of all acts, deserving even more attention than men now pay to their own sexuality. If men could give birth, then birth would now be an even more prestigious affair than it was in the ancient matriarchies, attended by the same cultural huzzahs that now accompany reaching the top of a mountain, crossing the North Pole, or wiping out an enemy machine gun nest. If men could give birth, they wouldn't need to steal women's creativity for themselves.

140 / THE SKEPTICAL FEMINIST

But men don't give birth. Patriarchal cultures teach them to compensate for this not only by belittling the birthing sex but also by learning how to give death instead. One good reason for the return of the Goddess is that men must be taught what a poor substitute this is before it's too late.

NOTES

1. Elise Boulding, *The Underside of History* (Boulder, Colo.: Westview Press, 1976), 145, 151.
2. Robert Briffault, *The Mothers* (New York: Macmillan, 1927), 1:369. C. Gasquoine Hartley, *The Truth About Woman* (New York: Dodd, Mead & Co., 1913), 159.
3. Sir James G. Frazer, *Folk-Lore in the Old Testament* (New York: Macmillan, 1927), 191.
4. Marija Gimbutas, *The Goddesses and Gods of Old Europe: Myths and Cult Images* (Berkeley and Los Angeles: University of California Press, 1974), 237.
5. Brian Branston, *The Lost Gods of England* (London: Thames & Hudson, 1957), 130.
6. Sir Thomas Malory, *Le Morte d'Arthur* (London: J. M. Dent & Sons, 1961), 2:179.
7. Fred Hapgood, *Why Males Exist* (New York: William Morrow & Co., 1979), 16–19.
8. Barbara G. Walker, *The Woman's Encyclopedia of Myths and Secrets* (San Francisco and New York: Harper & Row, 1983), 142–46.
9. Georges Dumézil, *From Myth to Fiction: The Saga of Hadingus* (Chicago: University of Chicago Press, 1973), 68.
10. John Darrah, *The Real Camelot: Paganism and the Arthurian Romance* (London: Thames & Hudson, 1981), 107.
11. *Larousse Encyclopedia of Mythology* (London: Hamlyn Publishing Group, 1968), 83. Walker, *Woman's Encyclopedia*, 107.
12. Ernest Crawley, *The Mystic Rose* (New York: Meridian Boooks, 1960), 222.
13. John Weir Perry, *Lord of the Four Quarters* (New York: Collier Books, Macmillan, 1966), 129.
14. Sir James G. Frazer, *The Golden Bough* (New York: Macmillan, 1922), 229.
15. S. H. Hooke, *Middle Eastern Mythology* (Harmondsworth, England: Penguin Books, 1963), 115.
16. Erich Neumann, *The Great Mother: An Analysis of the Archetype* (Princeton, N.J.: Princeton University Press, 1963), 136. Walker, *Woman's Encyclopedia*, 635.
17. Hooke, *Middle Eastern Mythology*, 110.
18. Walker, *Woman's Encyclopedia*, 954.
19. Briffault, *The Mothers*, 2:445--47.
20. Wendy Doniger O'Flaherty, *Hindu Myths* (Harmondsworth, England: Penguin Books, 1975), 263.
21. J. J. Bachofen, *Myth, Religion and Mother Right* (Princeton, N.J.: Princeton University Press, 1967), 133.
22. Briffault, *The Mothers*, 2:412.
23. Robert Graves, *The Greek Myths* (New York: Penguin Books, 1955), 1:27.

24. Ann Oakley, *Subject Women* (New York: Pantheon Books, Random House, 1981), 122.
25. W. Carew Hazlitt, *Faiths and Folklore of the British Isles* (New York: Benjamin Blom, 1965), 158.
26. Walker, *Woman's Encyclopedia*, 593.
27. Marjorie Malvern, *Venus in Sackcloth* (Carbondale, Ill.: Southern Illinois University Press, 1975), 1. Wolfgang Lederer, *The Fear of Women* (New York: Harcourt Brace Jovanovich, 1968), 162.
28. Homer Smith, *Man and His Gods* (Boston: Little, Brown & Co., 1952), 181.
29. Joseph Campbell, *The Hero With a Thousand Faces* (Princeton, N.J.: Bollingen/Princeton, 1949), 113.
30. Walker, *Woman's Encyclopedia*, 645–48.
31. *Larousse Encyclopedia of Mythology*, 371.
32. Walker, *Woman's Encyclopedia*, 41–42.
33. Ibid., 545–48.
34. Heinrich Zimmer, *Myths and Symbols in Indian Art and Civilization* (Princeton, N.J.: Princeton University Press, 1946), 25.
35. Raphael Patai, *The Hebrew Goddess* (Ktav Publishing House, 1967), 141–45, 147–49, 161, 177–78.
36. Walker, *Woman's Encyclopedia*, 879–83.
37. Merlin Stone, *When God Was A Woman* (New York: Dial Press, 1976), 219.
38. *Mahanirvanatantra*, trans. Sir John Woodroffe (New York: Dover Publications, 1972), 127.
39. Zimmer, *Myths and Symbols*, 147.
40. Lederer, *The Fear of Women*, 188.
41. Geoffrey Ashe, *The Virgin* (London: Routledge & Kegan Paul, 1976), 236.
42. Salomon Reinach, *Orpheus* (New York: Horace Liveright, 1930), 102. H. J. Rose, *Religion in Greece and Rome* (New York: Harper & Bros., 1959), 193.
43. Briffault, *The Mothers*, 3:490–94.
44. Malvern, *Venus in Sackcloth*, 30.
45. Zimmer, *Myths and Symbols*, 205.
46. Elizabeth Fisher, *Woman's Creation: Sexual Evolution and the Shaping of Society* (New York: Doubleday & Co., 1979), 345.
47. Matilda Joslyn Gage, *Woman, Church and State* (New York: Arno Press, 1972), 15.
48. Gage, *Woman, Church and State*, 12.
49. Dale Spender, ed., *Feminist Theorists: Three Centuries of Key Women Thinkers* (New York: Pantheon, 1983), 144.
50. Fisher, *Woman's Creation*, 214.

The Strength Myth and
the Intellect Fable

The question is often asked, if the natural primitive social condition of humankind is one of matriarchy, how did patriarchal societies get started in the first place? What was the original cause and mechanism of men's assumption of ascendancy over women?

The most popular answer is the least thoughtful one, that it boils down to men's superior physical strength and its implied capacity to hurt women. By professing this doctrine, men give away the secret of their real morality, which is that might makes right. All religious cant about loving one's enemies or turning the other cheek is shown up as pure sham in a sex that not only worships fighting but also believes in a God-given right to rule the other sex by violence or the threat of violence.

Aside from the questionable morality of the might-makes-right doctrine, however, one may doubt whether this is the true basis of patriarchy. Among primitive people rulers are by no means always physically strongest. Certainly they are not so among the civilized, either—not even in a macho society that reveres physical strength.

To attribute sexism to superior musculature and physical aggression alone, one must make the highly improbable assumption that women were stronger and more aggressive than men during all the long millennia of matriarchy, up to a mere three or four thousand years ago, when the great changeover was taking place. Obviously, this is nonsense.

It is true that prehistoric human females were probably not much inferior to males in physical strength. Prehistoric skeletons show less gender differences in height and size of joints or muscle attachments than modern skeletons. The earliest known artworks depict both sexes about the same size. Most prehistoric women undoubtedly worked as hard at physical labor as the men, if not harder, and developed their muscles accordingly. Many primitive peoples of the present have told anthropologists that women do heavy work and carry the camp baggage not because they are oppressed, but because they have more endurance than men, and the property belongs to them anyway. Nevertheless, it would be foolish to assume that there ever was a time when women as a group were appreciably stronger than men as a group and used their superior strength to dominate by physical intimidation.

Of course not all women are necessarily weaker than all men. A young, healthy, athletic woman is stronger than an old, sickly, or out-of-shape man. A big woman is probably stronger than a small man. A woman who has learned fighting techniques can probably overcome a man who hasn't. Women can also gang up on a man and overwhelm him by sheer numbers.

Moreover, every man has an Achilles heel, located not on his foot but in his crotch. The vulnerability of male genitals led the early patriarchs to make anxiously rigid rules against women taking advantage of it, as shown by the biblical taboo: a woman who twists a man's testicles in a fight must have her hand cut off, even if she has done it to her husband's enemy to help her husband defeat him—one of the more outstandingly unfair commands of the Bible's sexist God (Deut. 25:11–12).

Patriarchal strictures against women's possible attacks on men were thought essential to keep women from effective retaliation against male oppressors. Given time, almost any woman could plot an appropriate vengeance to incapacitate or kill an abusive husband, say, or an abductor who carried her off as a spoil of war. Even to go to sleep in the presence of abused and resentful women, men needed controls provided by their God to convince women that they must not strike back. The intense patriarchal fear of female "guile" was actually a recognition of women's potential for revenge in the form of spells, calumny, poison, property destruction, or other clandestine attacks.

The same kind of passivity training for women can be seen

today in the entertainment media (magazines, films, television) that have so largely taken over the socialization process in our society. One sees women threatened, struck, raped, mutilated, or killed so often in these media that it almost begins to look like a social norm. Almost never do female victims strike back. In a movie or television drama, a woman punched or slapped by a man never seems to become angry as a result. She never tries to kick him in the groin, or throw something at him, or pick up a weapon and bash him. She doesn't even snarl or curse him. She just stands there and takes it. The message is clear: women don't retaliate, and therefore men can attack women with impunity.

This is one of our modern methods for upholding the strength myth, which depends on convincing women that they have no choice but to forestall male aggression by their obedience or else suffer physical harm. Yet it may seem that the real harm is more mental than physical, for this surely is a process of brainwashing. Women are thereby convinced that neither law nor religion will countenance their personal retaliation, which must be left up to some other male in a rescuer role (father, police officer, hero, God), even when experience has demonstrated that such rescuers do nothing really effective.

A recent television documentary on the Yanomamo Indians, one of the few wholly patriarchal tribes of the Amazon basin, showed a graphic example of the strength myth in operation. Significantly, not a single word of the commentator's script suggested what was really going on.

A group of young Yanomamo boys began teasing, shoving, and slapping a girl. She grew angry and fought back energetically, chasing the boys' ringleader, who retreated before her onslaught although he was bigger than she was. The other boys kept tormenting her, pushing, kicking, or trying to trip her. Eventually, they all ganged up on her and forced her to the ground. They tied her arms behind her back, and then took turns beating and kicking her.

Both male and female adults were looking on (including the civilized camera operator), but no one tried to help the girl. Not even the other female children showed any inclination to interfere on her behalf, though there were enough of them to teach the boys a sharp lesson if they had made a concerted effort. Women, too, could have interfered, as mothers normally put a stop to children's fights. But Yanomamo women are trained by just such youthful experiences to accept male violence in their adult lives.

This is the real secret of male dominance: not just superior strength, one-on-one, but techniques of collective bullying and of convincing women that they must not resist. Certain biblical passages demonstrate the use of gang rape in early Middle-Eastern patriarchy (Gen. 19:8; Judg. 19:24–29), but in former societies, such as the Goddess-worshiping pre-Hellenic Aegean cultures, rape was a capital crime.

Freud had the peculiar notion that the true original sin, leading to collective guilt and compensatory deification of the father image, was the sons' aggression against fathers in what he liked to call the primitive horde. He believed the ensuing murder and cannibalization of the father was reenacted in sacred sacrificial dramas ever since. Characteristically, he ignored the vital significance of women and motherhood in primitive culture. He overlooked the many examples of primitive matrilineal societies where fathers were of little or no account.

Later, better informed thinkers recognized the basic patterns of aggression in primitive society as adult male jealousy of the children who held first claim on women's attention, just as a female animal ignores her mate after the birth of her offspring. Obviously, it would make no sense for adult males to kill the children outright, because their tribe would then become extinct. Men learned to disguise their jealousy as painful or frightening puberty rites that their gods directed them to inflict on the young, or else as rituals of ordeal, sacrifice, and battle, where younger, more virile and attractive males could be sent to face injury or death—for no better recompense than a promise of postmortem heroship or godhood. Promises, of course, cost nothing. To make a man into a saint, boddhisattva, or god after his decease is the cheapest kind of death benefit ever paid.

Another target for adult male jealousy of the powerful bond between mother and child was the mother herself. In societies where the absolute authority of mothers began to be undermined by the discovery of fatherhood, men began to assume the right to give the orders, to coerce women's attention to themselves, and to punish women for infractions of the male-serving rules supposedly laid down by their new begetter/creator gods.

This, not superior male strength, is the real basis of patriarchal sexism. The root of sexism is not physical but psychological and religious. Religions provide the original hints that men may be permitted to use their strength against women and children to enforce their obedience.

Matriarchal religions insisted that men should pattern their behavior after that of the tribal mothers, give loving attention to children, help women in their work, and become caring, responsible custodians of the collective resources. Patriarchal religions advocated the taking of private property—including multiple wives and concubines—the accumulation of personal wealth and power, aggrandizement by warfare, and the shedding of blood for forgiveness of sins and the glory of God. Their deities (including the biblical God) became as jealous as the men themselves; they also became accusatory, fear-inspiring, vengeful, puritanical, and cruel.

The turning point was not the improbable scenario that envisions men suddenly finding a way to increase their physical strength above that of women. Rather, the turning point was their discovery of fatherhood, with its new proliferation of male ancestor gods, placed in a position to give any divine commands their prophets and priests might think desirable. This process goes on still.

Women are still coerced by the commands of an allegedly paternal God, who makes use of motherhood but does not participate in it. Like the Yanomamo girl, the females of Western civilization are subjected to various kinds of male bullying. It can be as brutal as the abusive father who beats his little girl and her mother, because he thinks he has the right to control their behavior; or it can be as subtle as the cleric who kindly tells a naïve young bride that God wants her to obey her husband's orders as if they were divine edicts. Every woman has encountered thousands of such incidents in the process of growing up in a patriarchal society. To this day, many Christian authorities insist that a woman can lead a true Christian life only by submitting to masculine will and accepting all masculine decisions, even when results are disadvantageous to herself or her children.

From its inception, the Judeo-Christian belief system has been committed to antifeminist doctrines. For example, the Bible's lists of "begats" show sexism in a formative stage. As in the similar Brahman lists, the names of ancestral mothers are conspicuous by their absence. The litany of descent, intended for recitation on all important occasions, traces the male line only, as if men had given birth to their sons all by themselves. Priestly authors of this material tried to combat the ancient matrilineal clan system that took notice of the obvious parent (mother) only. They were overturning a whole social structure dating from humanity's earliest beginnings. They were instituting a new form of marriage, where only one man could have sexual access to each woman, so her children could only be his.

Naturally, this meant rigid policing of women to prevent extraneous fertilizations. It was essential that a girl be a virgin at the time of marriage. If she was not, men stoned her to death by God's order (Deut. 22:20–21). It was also essential that a wife remain sexually faithful to one husband. If she was not, men stoned her to death by God's order (John 8:4–5).

In such ways motherhood was colonized by males and maintained for their exclusive use as the only significant parents. The rules were always attributable to God, without whom patriarchy would never have gained its first foothold. With God's blessing men felt empowered to gang up on each offending woman in turn, for their notion of superior strength originally meant collective strength, the power of a group to overwhelm an individual.

To keep women in an enslaved condition, patriarchal rules have often insisted on their physical weakness to the point of making it a self-fulfilling prophecy. A notable example is the Chinese custom of footbinding, which aimed to cripple women by making their feet useless for walking (let alone running away). Naturally, the extreme indolence imposed by the constant pain of bound feet caused all the muscles of the body to atrophy.

A usual method of forcing women's acceptance of such torments is to present them as esthetic necessities, the epitome of sexual attractiveness. Men were taught to adore the weak, crippled woman as a sex object. Women were taught to view feminine strength as ugly and unsexy, a characteristic of peasants, to be scorned by the beautiful women of fashion.

Although we may display horror at the idea of Chinese footbinding, consider the many ways of weakening the female body that have been declared fashionable in the Western world and how abjectly women have conformed to them on pain of being labeled unattractive.

There was the custom of tight corseting, which prevailed during roughly the same thousand-year time span as the Chinese bound feet, up to the present century. Severe corseting seriously interfered with the functions of internal organs, atrophied the abdominal muscles, increased the hazards of childbirth, and made almost all natural movements uncomfortable.

There was the dainty high-heeled shoe, still with us today, which makes running difficult, throws the spine out of balance, and leads to various afflictions of the feet, knees, and back. Hobble skirts, hoopskirts, farthingales, bustles, heavy and elaborate hats or coiffures that immobilize the neck: feminine clothing in nearly all periods of patriarchal history has been apparently designed for maximum inconvenience, to hamper and restrict body movement as much as possible or else to expose so much of the body to cold weather as to become a health hazard, as in the recent case of the miniskirt. Almost never have women's clothes been designed primarily for comfort. When women wanted to be comfortable, they had to adopt men's styles.

Moreover, strong, active women have often been penalized by male disapproval, and weak, sickly women admired. It used to be mandatory for a "lady" never to be seen exercising at anything more strenuous than a sedate walk. Women with obvious muscles were considered ugly: consider the cartoon character Powerful Katrinka, who was funny just because she was strong. Female athletes were virtually unknown in Christian civilization prior to our own century. Except for peasants and slaves, who had to do farm work, women were expected to lead a wholly indoor life.

If women were really so much weaker than men, it would hardly have been necessary to impose so many physical handicaps on them. It almost seems as if the slight statistical edge that men do have was never thought to be enough.

All the physical handicaps imposed on women may have arisen from men's secret fear that women might be the stronger sex after all, in ways not directly related to musculature. The ancient Hindu gods were considered weak and helpless as babes without their corresponding goddesses, or shaktis, whose title meant "power" and who embodied all the gods' creativity or spiritual force in female forms. Similarly, central Asian and Native American shamans and Roman and Jewish priests all had to have wives in order to maintain their spiritual preeminence, for women were considered the true source of their powers. Even the biblical Jehovah once had his essential Goddess, embodiment of the Wisdom that he needed. She was variously named Sophia or Hokmah or Shekina or sometimes Matronit or even Mary (Mari); certain Gnostic sectaries believed that God could do nothing without his Queen.

It must be remembered that the earliest, deepest-rooted experience of the female in the life of every male is the caretaking mother, an all-powerful giantess in the eyes of her infant. She lifts him, carries him about, manipulates his body, provides for all his wants, and does the things his muscles are yet too weak to do. Of course the mother is just as immensely strong in a girl's infantile experience, but the girl may become Mother herself. Apart from this innate archetype of female strength, it has been found that the female body is more durable than the male body, with extra reserves to withstand diseases, chronic afflictions, and the somatic and neural stresses of motherhood. Men usually surpass women in the strength of shoulders, arms, and upper back, but women may surpass the average man in the strength of hips, legs, and pelvic structures. And no muscle in a man's body ever contracts as fully as do female abdominal muscles during childbirth.

Women should not be deterred from developing their physical strength by men's mockery of female muscles, any more than women should forego education because men call educated women unattractive. The label of unattractiveness is a last-ditch attempt to keep women from doing what men claim women can't do. As long ago as 1825 philosopher William Thompson said physical strength is called unfeminine only because it might enable women "to approach too nearly to those high prerogatives in your masters, with whom to aim at equality is the summit of female audacity if not wickedness." In 1857 Barbara Bodichon wrote: "To think a woman is more feminine because she is frivolous, ignorant, weak or sickly, is absurd: the larger-natured a woman is, the more decidedly feminine she will be; the stronger she is, the more strongly feminine."[1] She added that one does not call a lioness unfeminine.

When women were trying to strengthen themselves and their position in nineteenth-century America, many of the clergy bitterly opposed their efforts, insisting that women must remain completely dependent on men instead of working for self-determining citizenship in their own right. The famous Pastoral Letter of 1837 said, "The power of woman is in her dependence, flowing from a consciousness of that weakness which God has given her for protection."[2] Only the clergy, perhaps, could have been sufficiently trained in doubletalk to define dependence as power and weakness as protection.

Some men have tried to place the primitive origin of male dominance in a notion of protective aggressiveness aimed at defending tribal mothers and children from danger—meaning, of course, from other men. Adrienne Rich saw through this fiction, pointing out that men's historical attitudes toward women have been far more self-defensive and hostile than protective, all the way from earliest patriarchal mythology through the ecclesiastical slaughter of witches, female infant gynocide, "modern rape laws, mother-in-law jokes, and sadistic pornography of our time."[3]

History shows considerable male circular reasoning in putting down women's power of mind as well as power of body, and such putting down reveals a hope of keeping it minimal. Women couldn't learn about important issues, men claimed, because women were too frivolous; conversely, women were frivolous because they knew little about important issues. Women were ignorant because they weren't educated; women couldn't be educated because they were too ignorant.

Many were the male experts who, frightened by the numerous women craving to enter schools and participate in the Enlightenment, worked up "scientific" proofs that educated girls would suffer nervous breakdowns, atrophy of the uterus, sterility, or milkless breasts. A male authority wrote in the 1850s: "Some loose notions have been thrown out of women's intellectual equality with men, and of their consequently equal right to all the advantages of society . . . these are speculative, extravagant, and almost unnatural opinions."[4]

Unnatural was a word often used to belittle women's political, religious, or intellectual curiosity. Men thought it natural for women to do all the boring, repetitive, or onerous chores that they themselves didn't want to do; but for women to do something interesting or intellectually stimulating was viewed as a violation of the divine order. In 1876 the Rev. Dr. Craven of the Presbytery of Newark, New Jersey, forbade women to speak in church because "it is base in the sight of Jehovah. The whole question is one of subordination." So it was. Rev. Morgan Dix of Trinity Church, New York, told women that any intellectual activity on their part would destroy men's respect for them, and they would be "thrust away with loathing and disgust."[5] This was perhaps an ineffectual deterrent, because the women already knew that men's alleged respect for their ignorance was nonexistent.

Even modern scholars reveal sexist bias in more subtle implications that female minds are inferior. Discussing a description of corpse animation by the Roman author Lucan, Georg Luck states that Shelley admired Lucan's work, and "must have read this passage with his wife, Mary," to account for her own story of corpse animation, *Frankenstein.*[6] Luck apparently supposes that Mary Shelley could not study classical authors on her own or form any ideas without her husband's guidance.

Actually, the borrowing went the other way more often than not. Feminist scholars have found over and over that male authors appropriated the work of their wives or sisters, publishing it under their own names. Over and over it has been shown that men really believed women could surpass them, judging by the extreme measures that were taken to keep women out of schools and professional organizations in medicine, law, theology, science, engineering, and other technological fields, so as to preserve men's favorite myth that women cannot think rationally.

Women themselves sometimes support this invidious notion, to the detriment of their clearer-minded sisters, by adopting the bipolar model of masculine logic versus feminine intuition. In fact, the number of people who think more rationally than emotionally is probably about equal in both sexes; reasoning powers might even be a bit greater in the female. After all, it is woman who "puts two and two together" while man is still wondering what happened. Of course he would prefer to think her mental acuity a lower, animallike quality, rather than admit that it betters his own performance, but women should never minimize their own potential for clear, rational thought.

When women gather together and seriously exchange ideas, they often find themselves in agreement about male irrationality, not only on the individual level but also on the collective level of leadership or authority. A sharing of feminine insights can lead to the realization that "we are right not to accept the universe . . . as it has been presented to us by male authority, in terms corrupted by a greed-based civilization." Elizabeth Fisher speaks of a pressing need to "get at the causes, the oppressive principle growing out of the relation between man and woman which has mushroomed to be the greatest danger to the world's survival. . . . The dominance hierarchy is the underlying problem."[7]

After two thousand years of leading their world through rivers of blood, centuries of war, incessant exploitation, and spiritual dissimulation of the most shameless sort, the patriarchs may find that their loss of feminine understanding and creativity is their true original sin. By destroying the spirit of their Mothers they may have brought about the destruction of themselves.

NOTES

1. Dale Spender, *Women of Ideas (and What Men Have Done to Them)* (London: Routledge & Kegan Paul, 1982), 394, 410.
2. Spender, *Women of Ideas*, 222.
3. Adrienne Rich, *Of Woman Born: Motherhood as Experience and Institution* (New York: W. W. Norton, 1976), 113.
4. Spender, *Women of Ideas*, 443, 448.
5. Matilda Joslyn Gage, *Woman, Church and State* (New York: Arno Press, 1972), 479-483.
6. Georg Luck, *Arcana Mundi* (Baltimore, Md.: Johns Hopkins University Press, 1985), 194.
7. Elizabeth Fisher, *Woman's Creation: Sexual Evolution and the Shaping of Society* (New York: Doubleday & Co., 1979), 398–405.

The Battered

In her book *Alone of All her Sex*, Marina Warner pointed out that in Catholic countries there was a direct relationship between piety and the degree of submission and self-effacement expected of women. The more fervent the religion, the more the men swagger and command. Christian women were defined by humility, forbearance, gentleness, and obedience to the lordly male, and such supposedly feminine qualities could readily degenerate into irresolution, cringing docility, and the victimization syndrome.

I received hints of such a connection between women's victimization and religious notions of the feminine ideal during years when I served as a hotline volunteer. Women callers who seemed immobilized by their problems, unable to take any remedial action, were the same ones who talked a lot about their dependence on God. They thought nothing could sustain them in their troubles except their faith, which actually seemed to drain them of initiative. Several battered wives told of seeking the help of clerics, who almost invariably counseled submission, patience, and more careful avoidance of whatever behavior might arouse the wrath of violent husbands. Apparently these clerics knew nothing of the psychology of victimization.

I became curious. I began to read the new outpouring of literature that was shedding a little light into the dark corners of the violent home. I was astonished by the official estimates that slightly more than half of all married women were physically abused by their husbands in some way, sooner or later, and that abusive husbands could be found at all levels of education, profession, income, age, and ethnic background.

Case histories of battered women recounted in this literature touched me so deeply that I felt enraged on their behalf. I wondered how my society could have allowed such a terrible way of life for so many women and their children, especially in view of its dire effects upon the latter, perpetuating emotional disabilities for generations to come. I wanted to discover the roots of this problem and, if possible, do something about it.

I learned that the official records must be only the tip of the iceberg, for obviously the courts, police, and medical profession become involved in only the worst cases. The volume of these was horrifying enough. New York police estimated that "husband-wife disputes"—their euphemism for wife beating—accounted for 40 percent of their calls. Atlanta police said 60 percent of their night calls were for "domestic disturbances"—*their* euphemism for wife beating. Boston police reported in 1975 an average of 45 calls per day for "husband-wife disputes" or "domestic disturbances." A Boston hospital reported in 1977 that 70 percent of the assault victims admitted to its emergency room were wives who had been beaten by their husbands. In 1971 approximately one third of female homicide victims in California were wives murdered by violent husbands. An Advisory Commission in Bergen County, New Jersey, found in 1977 that physical abuse of women in their homes occurs more frequently than all other violent crimes combined.

Police seemed virtually useless as defenders of husband-battered women. In an address to the American Bar Association Convention in 1975, James Bannon, Ph.D., executive deputy chief of the Detroit police department, remarked that most police officers are socialized to regard all females as naturally subordinate; many think they deserve to be—to use more of the hypocritical euphemisms—slapped around, straightened up, given what for, taught some respect, shown who's boss, knocked about, and so on. "Family violence"—another euphemism for wife beating—was not usually perceived as a serious problem. Because so many battered wives failed to prosecute, Dr. Bannon reported, police tended to view their complaints as frivolous even when they were badly hurt. The fact that such women were usually threatened with even further abuse if they didn't drop charges seemed not to enter into consideration. One beaten wife told how she had called the police repeatedly but received no help until her husband made the mistake of slapping one of the officers. Then they had him up on charges of assault and battery.

I read guidelines published in a report of the Bergen County, New Jersey, Advisory Commission on the Status of Women for the benefit of battered women. The victim was advised to insist on signing a complaint, "even if the police officer is discouraging," and to refuse to back down afterward, because that might discourage the police from helping her again. In other words, a beaten individual was told to summon the strength to withstand both the authority figure (police officer) and the husband, who might well be threatening to kill her, for the sake of not "discouraging" her purported rescuer. The point was made that involvement in "family disputes"—another euphemism for wife beating—was "a high-risk duty for policemen." Therefore they are "understandably reluctant, and the woman's behavior should be reassuring with regard to the officer's safety." Nothing was said about the real source of the officer's risk, the violent husband. Even in a bedraggled, wounded, and terrorized condition, the woman was expected to play mother to two little boys fearful of each other's temper and to reassure the cop who was supposed to be reassuring her.

The medical profession, apparently, was no more helpful. A woman whose skull had been fractured during a little husbandly "discipline" was told by her doctor to go back to him because he seemed remorseful. Doctors long followed an unwritten rule that battered wives' injuries were to be reported as accidental. Physically abused women who gave way to despair were given antidepressants or shock treatment to bring them out of their depressed state. Few attempts were made to recognize, let alone treat, the real cause of their condition: incessant fear and physical torture.

Social workers and psychologists made similar mistakes, according to Beverly Nichol's "The Abused Wife Problem," published in *Social Casework*, because they still operated according to the Freudian theory of passivity and masochism as basic female personality traits. Social workers usually advised beaten women to be more placatory toward their husbands, though psychologists now have recognized that placatory behavior only makes the situation worse. The battering husband is a bully, and bullies attack even more savagely when the victim looks less able or willing to fight back. Battered wives experience the opposite of what used to be called the ideal of manliness: to defend the weak and never attack any individual whose strength was less than one's own, no matter what the provocation.

My husband and I had arguments, but without physical violence. Therefore the extent of this problem in the United States came as a shocking revelation to me. Too many other nonbattered women, I thought, must be ignoring this problem that really affects all women, just as the horrors of Hitler's regime affected all Jews or Ku Klux Klan lynchings affected all blacks. One of the battered wives told me that she had been afraid to speak to other women about her troubles, even her mother. She felt paralyzed by her isolation and loneliness. She said, "I knew other women wouldn't be able to understand what I was going through." Poor thing, poor thing, I thought. Can she really have believed that we have so little empathy with our sisters? "Try me," I told her. "I have a vivid imagination."

No imagination, however, could have conjured up some of the things battered women told me when I arranged some interviews, with the aim of collecting their stories for a book. I never wrote the book, because a half dozen or so excellent books on the same subject were published within the following year, most of them having researched the matter more thoroughly than I could have done, with my limited time and resources. Yet tapes and transcripts that I made did contain some enlightening material. These ex-wives' character studies of their abusive husbands showed many common patterns, such as abusive fathers, a pathological need to feel in control, a love of hierarchy, authority, success, and money, a distaste for children and for mutuality in sexual relationships, and a religious background of the rigid, authoritarian, guilt-inducing sort. For example:

My husband's family was severely Greek Orthodox, very traditional. There was no warmth in the home. When a family member was hurt, the others tried to make him feel worse. The Greek religion is a brutal, sadistic religion. My husband never really gave up his orthodox religious training, which was a brainwashing, done with such ferocity through his church and through his family. The church's idea of the man-woman relationship, the woman being evil, influenced a lot of his thinking. It was pounded into him as a child.

He was highly intelligent but never intuitive or spontaneous. Every situation had to be rigidly structured and precise. He had an insatiable need to control other people's existence. In obedience-training our weimaraner he would keep at it for hours at a time until the dog became so nervous that it would just shake. He behaved in a sycophantic manner toward older men in his business, men in authority. He needed male approval.

He liked to control money. He made me account for every penny that was spent. He did all the buying of major items. He spent a lot of money on status-symbol purchases. He collected sports cars, cameras, and fancy stereo equipment.

Sexually he was very cold, he had little sex drive. He would never initiate sexual activity. It was difficult to arouse him. I had to be careful in everything I did. He was not impotent, but he was a cold, indifferent lover. Sometimes he accused me of being lascivious or wanting too much sex. He thought I was immoral. He avoided me completely during menstrual periods. He wasn't interested in looking at my body. He made love to me in the dark. I could have been anybody.

When he decided that the children must learn about the Bible, he would force them to read it with him, punishing them for errors, as usual. I was forbidden to read the Bible to the children. I was too immoral in his opinion, too guilty, but I never found out what the guilt was.

He wanted absolute control of every thought. He would put me down in front of other people. I found myself being blamed for every idea that came from a feminist group, like NOW. He thought of all women as basically evil temptresses.

When I was nursing the baby, he would give me orders about other things I had to do. He never held, fed, changed, or cared for any of the babies in any way. If I went to the doctor or the dentist, I had to take the children with me, because he would not look after them at home. Even if I prepared their food beforehand, he would not give it to them. They would not be fed until I came home. Yet he thought he was qualified to tell me how to take care of children.

Every evening our son would have his father standing over him while he did his homework, hitting him when he made mistakes. Our son's marks never improved, though. At last he had to spend several years in a special school. He was a nervous wreck. Sometimes I would run away from the house to escape a beating, but I was afraid to leave my husband alone with the children.

Holidays and vacations were horror stories. He spent every minute of his spare time controlling his family. Every one of his "suggestions" had to be carried out exactly. I was so constantly on guard against him that my stomach was always tight. He would deliberately tantalize me, hoping to goad me into talking back so he could hit me. On a picnic in a crowded park, he took exception to something I said and beat me in the face with a heavy thermos bottle. The children were all screaming. People around us heard it all, but nobody interfered.

Other people seldom gave me any help. Police are on the husband's side. Psychologists, social agencies, counselors, and police were not very helpful. The doctors too were on my husband's side. Doctors didn't sympathize. They asked me what I had done to cause the problem. They refused to release my hospital records to me, but my husband was able to get those records within 12 hours.

Like this woman, others also told me of battering husbands aided and abetted—perhaps even created—by the social and religious training that our society considers normal. Another example:

I was brought up a Catholic. They make you feel guilty, or sinful. My family gave me no help. Coming from a European background, they figured it was my problem that I was being abused. Once I sought help from a priest. I had the door slammed in my face. I said, "I have a problem, Monsignor." He said, "I have problems too. Go away." The only people who first gave me any real help were other women.

My husband wanted to control everything absolutely. I had to be like a puppet. There was constant stress. You never knew what would precipitate a scene of violence. He spent vacations working, or rather seeing that I and the kids did the work under his direction. The kids called our vacation house the work farm. He had little to do with bringing up or educating the children. He never resolved any problems for them. He abused them a great deal. The strap used to come out quite a bit. It was "parental admonishment." A father was primarily a disciplinarian. A mother was a scut-girl. The night I got a broken collarbone, one of my daughters intervened and got a broken jaw.

At times I'm overwhelmed at the breakup of my marriage. I think, "Why couldn't it have been different?" I'm a giving person. If he had ever treated me decently he could have had it all, freely. He didn't have to force me or control me.

This woman's ex-husband was a wealthy man, but he was careful to keep his money concealed from her in bank accounts and investments she was not allowed to know about. The house-wife-and-mother job that she performed received no wage in terms of money and of course lacked also the less tangible reward she expected when she married: love, appreciation, emotional support. Our money-oriented society not only denigrates the unpaid labor of a wife, it also isolates her in her nuclear family home, which a violent man can turn into his private torture chamber. Patriarchal systems make a husband his wife's sole judge. If he doesn't value her, she may find it impossible to value herself.

A guilt-inducing religion may make it even harder for a woman to value herself if she truly believes the myths of primary female sinfulness and God's hostility toward her sex. One battered wife said her husband once told her that "he was very upset that I was not a Catholic. Catholics are even easier to manipulate, in terms of causing the person to feel guilty about everything." Another woman said her Catholicism was one of the reasons she tried for many years to preserve a really horrible marriage in which she and her children were actively tortured by a husband who showed the typical characteristics:

> I was a southern Catholic. I went to church every Sunday. It used to be that for women, especially Catholic women, clergymen would try to talk them into making the marriage work even when they were mistreated. One of the priests I went to advised me to get out of the situation, but I received no material help. No one helped me.

My husband's mother was abused by his father. There was no affection in their home. His father did a lot of slapping and pushing the mother around. My husband's feelings toward his mother were also disrespectful.

My husband was in the Navy, and loved it. When we married, he went into the Coast Guard. He liked it very much. He loved violent entertainment, crime dramas, cowboys and Indians. He said he always wanted to be a policeman. He seemed to want to be in with law-enforcement officers. Uniforms meant an awful lot to him. He had no hobbies, no personal interests. He was never a reader. Television was his only entertainment.

He resented anything that I enjoyed. I can't tell you how many times he took books out of my hand and threw them across the room, or hit me for reading. He resented my knitting; he resented anything creative that I liked.

I have a lot of fear of men, left over from my marriage. I think some of it will never leave me. I used to dislike going into a supermarket, having people behind me. My husband had a habit of attacking from behind, when I wasn't looking. Me, a person who loves people, I couldn't even bear to be in crowds.

After listening to a number of these victims, I also found myself looking at the people in stores and streets with somewhat different eyes. I would wonder which of the men I saw were wife beaters. Any woman who looked downtrodden or dispirited or who showed signs of injury on her face or limbs led me to suspect she might have been husband battered. I wanted to reach out to such women, to find out the truth, to give them the name and telephone number of the local shelter, to let them know there were ways of finding help, somehow to draw them out of the paralysis of fear that I knew battered wives suffered. While doing this investigation I was in a strange state of paranoia on other people's behalf.

One of my interviewees, lucky enough to have found a second and much more acceptable husband, had achieved enough psychological distance from her experience to analyze the violent husband's patterns quite accurately. She said:

A battering husband is highly insecure and can take no stress—absolutely none. He needs a wife, children, and possessions to hold him to the world; he needs a focus for his hatred. When he has someone to abuse, he feels righteous, more comfortable with his life.

He has no core. He wants all the appearances, the externals, all kinds of artificial frameworks to keep him directed. He has no understanding of other people's feelings, no empathy, no ability to comprehend or relate to his environment on his own. He's often obsessed with rank and hierarchy. Money is life to him. Battering husbands often use money as a control, to keep the wife imprisoned and controlled, unable to escape.

The typical obsession with money came out clearly in an interview of a convicted wife beater published in *The Village Voice* in 1977. He said: "My wife always told me that I didn't own her. Like hell I didn't! I did own her. That was part of the deal and she knew it. . . . I put her in the hospital a couple of times. Broke her nose and arm. No, an arm and a wrist. I divorced her; she didn't divorce me. And she didn't get a penny. . . . I can tell you, she's not living the high life she was living with me. My wife took it for seven years because, though she didn't like the pain, she liked the charge cards."

The idea that women should put up with any sort of torment for the sake of charge cards is not unrelated to the general philosophy of the industrialized society, which men impose on each other as well as on women. (The difference, however, is that men may freely consent to do whatever it is they will do for money and to stop doing it if the find it too onerous.) Battered women have no such freedom. Though they are nominally citizens of a free country, their country's laws give too much economic power to their husbands, making it possible for them to exist in abject slavery in fear for their lives and the lives of their children.

The effects of male domestic violence on children are equally terrible. As one director of a shelter said, "It is painful to see the new children flinch when they see a man in the corridor or in their playroom" Some run screaming from any adult man. Richard Gelles of the University of Rhode Island reported a nationwide survey showing that between 10 and 14 million of the 67 million children under 18 in American homes were physically abused. Human Services Commissioner Ann Klein commented, "Thousands of children are living in the most perilous circumstances you can imagine. We are breeding a future that is frightening."

From many such sources, written and verbal, I concluded that our society, which has been so concerned about identifying "unfit mothers," has never noticed the large number of unfit fathers that emerge from patriarchal socialization. Social, legal, and religious controls too often force women to live with men who terrorize them and their children, because in practice they require nothing more than biological fatherhood to give a man total control of a child's life. Because parenting is a functional activity, to beget a child is not really its definition but only its prerequisite. Most mothers would be inclined to choose only men capable of sucessful parenting behavior if they could make informed decisions to provide their children with true, rather than merely biological, fathers. The animal kingdom shows us that a begetter is only a stud, not necessarily fatherly in the human sense at all. A human father should be capable of copying and supporting the natural behavior of mothers.

Our morality doesn't have precedents for codifying women's right to pick and choose husbands on the basis of their qualifications as human beings, husbands, or fathers. Men aren't asked to measure up to the things that are important. In fact, their moral training may push them in precisely the opposite direction. In an address at Fairleigh Dickinson University, Dr. James Prescott said our current moral and religious structures promote "pain, punishment, repression and suffering over physical—sexual and sensual-pleasures," and that recent studies have shown brain cells actually destroyed and pleasure-related nerve endings stunted by lack of body pleasure in childhood. People thus treated will become insensitive to the feelings of others in direct proportion to the degree of abuse they have suffered themselves. The little boy terrorized by a "spare the rod and spoil the child" type of father may well grow up to become the same type himself.

On the basis of what I learned, then, I offer the following rules of thumb to young women contemplating marriage who may have been fooled into thinking that love alone will solve all problems or that a man need only be a good provider in order to be a successful husband. There are danger signs that a woman can see beforehand; if she heeds them she will spare herself and her future children a life of unmitigated horror.

First and foremost, little sister, don't consider marrying a man who hits you, even once, for any reason whatsoever. Don't accept subsequent apologies. Don't believe any remorseful promises. A man who hits is probably not enough in control of himself to keep any such promises. He will do it again and will be increasingly less remorseful in the future. Don't make excuses for him or tell yourself that you had it coming. No matter how much you love him, don't let yourself think you can't live without this man. It's far more probable that you can't live with him.

Don't marry a man who experienced severe repeated physical abuse in his childhood. He is a bad risk. To him, violence is normal. He already sees marital and parental roles as a license to hurt. His personality defects are deep-rooted, in ways that he himself will not understand.

Don't marry a man who rejects his mother or women in general. You may think this a good sign—that you won't have mother-in-law problems or he considers you a miraculous exception to the average, unacceptable female. Don't be fooled. It isn't a good sign. The mother relationship colors his attitude toward all women, including you. If his father didn't teach him to respect his mother, when he steps into that role he will not know how to respect you. A man who is genuinely affectionate toward his mother is most likely to be a loving husband.

Be wary of a man who has had a severe, repressive religious background, especially if his sense of righteousness makes him intolerant of others. Be wary of a man who thinks he knows what God wants.

Avoid a man who seems overly jealous, who wants to control you or call you to account for your every move, who becomes violently angry when you act independently. You may feel flattered that he wants to keep you all to himself—but beware. Such possessiveness doesn't respect your individuality. When a man thinks he has a right to possess you completely, he may think he also has a right to punish you for stepping out of line, as he sees it.

Avoid a man who is too insistent on conformity, hierarchy, or military discipline outside the military context. Beware of a man who believes a show of wealth essential to his self-image.

Beware of a man who seems obsequious toward richer or more powerful men. Beware of a man who lacks a sense of humor.

Don't kid yourself that your love has the power to change a man who has been abusive toward women or children. Battered second wives sometimes say they knew their husbands' first wives had been beaten, but they felt sure the earlier wives somehow deserved it, and their own marriages would be different. They were wrong. Never think you can reform a man by marrying him, even if he seems to change; everyone is on best behavior during the courting period.

Watch your man's reaction to minor accidents. If he flies into a rage and tries to fix blame on someone right away, he is probably not fit to be a father. All children have accidents for the reason that they are children. If a man can't handle the inevitable ineptitude of a young child, he will hurt the child emotionally and perhaps physically.

Finally, don't believe you have no right to sit in judgment on the personality and other qualifications of a male because he is "superior" to you. He is not. If you are choosing a mate for yourself and a father for your children, you have more important matters at stake than he has, and your judgment should prevail. Your moral sense is probably clearer, kinder, and more certain than his, and one of the advantages of marriage for him may be the possibility of his learning from you how to be a more complete human being. If he can't or won't understand this possibility, he's not for you. If he treats you unfairly, don't think you have to placate him and give in. You must retain respect for yourself if you expect a man to respect you.

One of the great problems for women socialized in the kind of morality that patriarchal religion dispenses is that their own natural morality has been concealed from them and from their husbands as well. One battered wife said, "Once, my husband actually tried to explain when I asked him why he was so hostile to me. He said women are no good by nature. He said man was made in the image of God—that's in the Bible—and God punished woman. So every man should be like God and punish woman for being no good and sinful. He said that was God's law in the Bible. When I asked him to point out where it said that in the Bible, he just hit me."

As long as these myths remain extant among the general population, persecution of women will continue. Sadism will masquerade as righteousness. As one of my informants said, a battering husband feels righteous when committing violence, not when refraining from violence. He uses religion to support his habit, not to break it.

Backed by its patriarchal religion, our society still clings to medieval ideas about women's sinfulness and need for punishment (which also underlay Freud's theory of female masochism). In England, a century after courts had declared it unlawful to keep slaves in the house by physical force, lawyers were still insisting that it was legal for a man to keep his wife in the house by physical force.[1] In the eighteenth century the law gave a man permission to enslave his wife, rape her, beat her, starve her, rob her of all her possessions, and threaten to lock her up for life in a madhouse if she didn't behave: a threat easily and simply carried out, because a wife could be committed on only her husband's word.[2] Not even the concurrence of a doctor was needed.

In the Middle Ages priests often heard the complaints of battered women in the confessional, but their superiors directed them to ignore such complaints, because "women are inclined to lie." In 1880 an Anglican clergyman named Knox-Little proclaimed that every wife owes her husband unqualified obedience. "It is her duty to subject herself to him always, and no crime that he can commit can justify her lack of obedience. If he be a bad or wicked man, she may gently remonstrate with him, but refuse him never."[3] One may well imagine just how much effect gentle remonstration might have on such a man.

In contrast to these Christian laws, Cato the Censor wrote in pagan Rome in 300 B.C. that men who beat wives or children "lay sacrilegious hands on the most sacred things in the world." To strike a pregnant woman was a capital crime; even to "disturb her mind" was illegal. Christian authorities, however, saw no harm in tormenting pregnant women. The earliest Christian laws in Iceland, A.D. 1119, recommended torture especially for pregnant women.[4]

Most of the time, then, clerics are useless to the battered wife in search of help. Neither religion nor law, as currently created and administered by males, can effectively stamp out wife abuse. But women can unite to combat the crimes of abusive men. Women must realize that what hurts one of their number can hurt all, in unforeseeable ways. Too often women have turned away from a battered sister with a secret contempt mingled in their pity, the I'm-glad-it's-not-my-problem reaction. But it is the problem of all. Women must become vigilantes to protect one another.

Shelters for battered women and children are a beginning, but they're not enough. They don't bear down on the real problem, the abusive man. There are ways to do this. When neighbors become aware of a wife beater in their neighborhood, they should organize to punish him. Only punishment is comprehensible to such a man. He should be harassed. Spray paint his car with the words WIFE BEATER or CHILD ABUSER. Telephone his boss anonymously and tell what he did to his wife. Hang labeled photographs of her bruises on the bulletin board at his workplace. Tell everyone about his nasty secret. Call a meeting of all neighborhood women and discuss what to do about him. Remember the primitive matriarchal village, where women worked together to defend any one of their number from male aggression.

Wife beating wouldn't happen if a group of women would gather immediately outside the house, yell their protests, take the woman into their protection, and follow up. That means being willing to serve as witnesses in court, supporting the wife in the presence of police, seeing that she receives proper medical care, taking charge of her children when necessary, and never letting the abusive man pass by without a needling remark about his habits. Women must help each other. Keep in mind how men first gained the upper hand: they organized and ganged up on isolated women. To deal with violent men as they deserve to be dealt with, women must now do the same. Don't let your sisters remain isolated with their pain. One woman's abusive spouse is every woman's problem.

Marriage is sold to women almost as aggressively as any other consumer product, but the claims made for it are often fraudulent. "Women are encouraged to believe that they will find lifelong happiness in monogamous unions with men, but what they are in fact likely to find is that it is precisely marriage that oppresses, suppresses and depresses them."[5] A major reason for this is that men don't sufficiently value the wife's role as a voluntary contribution, because they need not directly pay her. Thus they come to believe that marriage gives them the right to keep a female slave.

Cicely Hamilton noted that the arrangement called marriage is amazingly useful to men but less so to women, because women's part of the bargain includes all the more distasteful jobs. Still, men insist that this division of labor is natural. "One wonders why it should be 'natural' in woman to do so many disagreeable things," she remarked. "Does the average man really believe that she has an instinctive and unquenchable craving for all the unpleasant and unremunerative jobs?"[6] The real reason women undertake the demanding and demeaning tasks in a violent, nightmarish household is hardly that they find it natural, but rather that they feel trapped. The average woman's socialization in patriarchal society points her toward wifehood as the only job she is fit to do. Often a violent husband can convince her that she does it so badly that no other man would want to salvage her for himself.

These trivializing attitudes must be changed by a shift in women's attitudes toward their loves and their labors. Women themselves know that nothing in the world is more useful than a wife. How many women have said with bitter humor that they longed for a wife of their own? Yet this literally priceless gift comes to a man for free, provided he knows how to appreciate it. He can have it for the asking, but it is not to be bought at the price of terror. A husband's behavior must be worthy of his wife. She is not a household appliance. She is not a breeding machine. She is not a slave. She is not a punching bag. She, and she alone, is the rightful judge of whether her services are properly and adequately appreciated. Just as a working man must be able to leave any job he finds too onerous, so also a wife must be able to leave a marriage that she finds painful.

Perhaps, after all, the fair half-and-half sharing of financial rewards will prove the only workable way to make men value their wives. Men who can't understand love can at least be made to understand money.

NOTES

1. Ann Oakley, *Subject Women* (New York: Pantheon Books, 1981), 3.
2. Marilyn French, *Beyond Power: On Women, Men, and Morals* (New York: Simon and Schuster, 1985), 372.
3. Matilda Joslyn Gage, *Woman, Church and State* (New York: Arno Press, 1972), 493, 518.
4. Gage, *Woman, Church and State*, 223, 332.
5. Oakley, *Subject Women*, 241.
6. Dale Spender, *Women of Ideas (And What Men Have Done to Them)*, (London: Routledge & Kegan Paul, 1982), 615.

Managing Motherhood

One of the most profoundly patriarchal images we are given to contemplate at Christmas is the picture of the Virgin Mother piously kneeling before her baby's cradle like any other worshiper, her eyes upturned, her hands joined together in homage to him, her whole attitude humbly adoring of the prodigy which, presumably, she has just brought into the world. With godlike serenity and complacency, the infant gestures a blessing toward his mother or else gazes out of the picture toward a vision of his own apotheosis. The mother may be a special favorite among his servants, but she still seems evidently servile, overwhelmed by the honor of waiting on him.

Of course, new mothers do adore their babies. Of course they may sit by the crib in a trance of love to watch the infant sleep or gaze upon it constantly with an inner sense of having created a miracle. The creater and caretaker, however, is the mother, not the child. An infant's utter dependence and helplessness rivet the mother's attention upon it. The secret of infantile charm is a great weakness, not an illusion of power. In this human dyad the approximation of divinity lies with the mother and not with her offspring.

Thus the typically patriarchal denial of biological realities extends through Christmas imagery not only to the absurdity of virgin motherhood—incorrigibly attractive to men deeply

afraid of female sexuality but also insistent on female nurturance—but additionally to a fundamental perversion of the
mother-child relationship, upon which, after all, the physical
and cultural creation of every human being originally rests.
Perhaps the most essential characteristic of this relationship is
body contact. A baby must have hands-on care or it may simply
die. Typically, however, the Divine Mother of Christianity
doesn't touch her child. She worships him from a little distance,
as if to show that the relationship between them will never be
so intensely physical as to offend the sensibilities of grown-up
men (or god).

Man has always been jealous of the sensual bond between
mother and child, wishing to keep woman's attention focused
on himself and resenting the small interloper who comes along
to preempt it. Among other animals, adult males instinctively
avoid interfering with females' all-important maternal functions. As a rule, a male will accept his mate's rejection of himself
in favor of her offspring. He goes away and leaves her in peace.
Human males, however, can't seem to comprehend the natural,
biological priorities of the mother, which inevitably decrease
her interest in themselves.

Ever since patriarchal religions obtained their foothold in
human society, men have been inventing ways to obscure the
fact that mothers, not gods, make humanity. The Christian image suggests the opposite, that God makes his own mother and
controls her with a noninfantile power even in his helplessness.
This contradicts the older pagan concept of the total authority
in heaven and on earth of the Mother of the Gods.

Mary was traditionally called the second Eve, a purified
reincarnation of her sinful ancestress, whose mythic origin was
yet another patriarchal denial of biological truth. Eve was
"born" out of a male body, another one of many ancient male
imitations of maternity devised out of men's archetypal envy of
motherhood. Male-engendered myths are replete with birthing
gods, nursing fathers (Num. 11:12), transvestite priests enact-
ing childbirth, and obviously birth-symbolic rites of passage and
initiation for men. Some peoples still practice couvade, the
mock labor and delivery pantomimed by a father during the
real birth in order to claim the child. There is perhaps a similar

motivation behind the modern enthusiasm for admitting a father to the birth chamber in home or hospital, even encouraging him to help the mother "manage" her labor according to the lessons of the prenatal class, and to claim a part of the credit for the delivery. Concerning such classes, it is generally assumed that whereas every other female animal knows how to give birth and take care of her newborn, no human mother knows anything unless she is taught the technique devised by males.

Managing is a favorite medical term, implying that the (usually male) doctor is in complete control. Illness, dying, and birthing all take place under his management. A laboring woman is often viewed as a mindless biomechanism subject to man's management, rather than as a sentient person engaged in a strenuous physical feat. Instead of maintaining a decent humility in return for the privilege of assisting at the miracle of birth, doctors too often work against both woman and nature in their eagerness to usurp credit for the whole process and consider themselves the masters of motherhood.

Dozens of medical customs foster male control of birth, ranging from the campaign to drive midwives out of practice around the turn of the century to the modern performance of excessive numbers of Caesarian deliveries. Many women today have been indoctrinated with the false idea that normal childbirth is a medical emergency that only a physician can "cure." A baby born naturally, before the mother can be brought under medical management in a hospital, is often considered a kind of accidental disaster that must be medically repaired as soon as possible. Even when the baby born at home is perfectly healthy, needing no further attention but warmth, cuddling, and mother's milk, and the mother's body is intact—not having been subjected to "preventive" episiotomy or any other mutilation—still she is encouraged to rush to the hospital, where her baby will be taken away from her and placed under observation in a separate room to wail out its frustrations, while she is made nervous and depressed by what feels like an unbearable loss.

Doctors eagerly adopted the drugs that would induce or retard labor, bending nature's timing to their own convenience and ignoring the fact that most parturient women hated the sensation of having their labor suddenly accelerated or interrupted. Until it was shown to endanger their success record, doctors also liked total anesthesia for the laboring woman, depriving her of participation in the birth process. As an added convenience, she would remain unaware of any doctor's mistakes.

If the laboring woman remained partially or fully awake, doctors liked to convince her that she was being permitted to serve as the doctor's helper, not that he was serving as hers. Usually, her participation was made as passive as possible; she was laid on her back and tied down, her pelvis and legs elevated to a position unnatural and embarrassing for her, but convenient for the doctor, who did not wish to stoop.

In addition, the mother's concentration may be deliberately dissipated by peremptory orders from her male manager. A woman doctor writes of male obstetricians yelling at their patients in the delivery room: "Push! Push! You lazy female, push!" When a woman answered, "I'm trying," her doctor snapped, "You're not trying hard enough." Later he explained, "When people are in a subservient position, sometimes you just have to tell them what to do." Of course, the woman's subservient position was arranged by the doctor himself.

Sometimes doctors were sneeringly jocular, saying to the laboring mother, "You didn't scream like that when it went in" or "You should have thought about this nine months ago"— continued examples of the Judeo-Christian theological contention that painful childbirth is God's curse on all women and a punishment for their sexuality. The woman doctor who witnessed such deliveries said birth is "a sacred act that has been turned into an ugly ritual. . . . The medical birth is pornographic. The woman is degraded. The physician intimidates her and forcefully takes from her both the act of birth and that which she herself has nurtured. All day long I watch women who have been violated and don't even know it."[1]

Although some women may need help delivering their babies, most women in the normal birth process need only emotional support, encouragement, and comforting while they and nature take charge of what their bodies are doing. A society with true reverence for motherhood would see to it that women are gently encouraged to do their own managing of their bodies' miracle. Certainly no woman needs to be insulted or roughly treated at this crucial moment. As much self-management as possible not only allows the mother to gain a sense of her own competence to take care of the new life; it is also a more natural response to the subtle, complex, mysterious inner forces that impel her to love her child—forces that men do not even begin to understand, because for all their intense power, the only means of comprehending them to date are wholly subjective. Yet it really ought to say something to the medical profession that postpartum depression is so common in the modern world where postpartum separation is considered routine, where mothers and newborns can't even see, let alone touch, one another. No other mammalian species has ever devised so many ways to keep mothers and babies apart. In fact, the one virtually unbreakable rule of mammalian life is that every infant remains in close physical contact with the mother from the moment of birth, because this is essential to the well-being of both mother and offspring.

The roots of postpartum depression certainly lie in the modern American hospital's forced separation of a woman and her infant. Even the subtle yet profound sense of alienation that plagues modern society may be based on the same custom. Too often, new mothers emerge from the hospital with a constellation of anxieties and unnecessarily traumatic feelings left over from impersonal or even cruel techniques of medical control and a depleted empathy left over from the experience of separation.

Lying alone in a barred labor crib, where no one pays attention to her except to give injections or perform pelvic examinations, a woman feels "the loneliness, the sense of abandonment, of being imprisoned, powerless, and depersonalized."[2] Patriarchal thinking has imposed this depersonalization on what should be a woman's most intimate and rewarding experience and the tender introduction of a new life into the basic sense of human love. Instead, in a modern technological version of couvade, man has taken this experience away from woman and tried to put himself in her place by making himself a child's birth manager, handler, name giver, supplier of artificial suckling, ruler and disciplinarian: doctor, priest, father, God. Man can take charge because the child is helpless by nature and the mother has been made so by artifice. He often, however, makes a mess of the responsibility.

"The birthing woman plays in an orchestra of her body, her soul, her baby, her loved ones, her past and her future. And we do not know who leads the orchestra. Doctors cannot lead the orchestra, because they are not within the process. Unable to hear the music, trained only in modalities of power and control, they can only interfere with the music being played."[3]

The patriarchal view of the miracle of birth treats the real giver of birth as a more or less passive assistant to the doctor. Even the baby—the one truly passive character in the drama—is verbally accorded a more active part than the mother. The baby "arrives" or "decides to be born." Doctors say the baby "wants" this or that position. Pregnant women even grant the baby more autonomy than themselves by verbal convention. They say "when my baby comes," not "when I bring my baby." Sometimes the baby is even spoken of as a gift for the husband. By implication, mothers renounce their own inalienable right to what comes out of their bodies, just as they are frequently brainwashed into relinquishing control of their physical or emotional natures to male doctors, whose arrogance may even exceed that of male priests.

An especially nasty example of male medical meddling in the motherhood process was rife two generations ago, when male experts forbade mothers to pick up and comfort their babies when they cried. Mothers were given rigid schedules for holding and feeding their infants at set times during each 24-hour period. At any other time, the doctors said, the baby must be left alone to "cry it out," because excessive handling would only produce a spoiled child. Even though we know better now, many people were emotionally spoiled by this cruel theory, and many a mother was frustrated almost to insanity by the war between her natural mammalian instinct and her desire to obey doctor's orders. The fear of being considered a bad mother has driven many women to deny their own sense of what an infant really needs, severed as they are by the patriarchal culture from their true selves.

Male experts seldom admitted that female instincts alone had birthed, nurtured, and socialized every individual for millions of years, long before there were any male experts to instruct mothers in proper mothering. More recent experts have now overthrown the authority of earlier ones, as experts will. Now it is claimed that every baby needs to be kept as close as possible to the mother's body in the first hours and days of life. Any primitive mother could have explained this to our modern pediatric specialists as the only commonsense procedure. Among primitive people who automatically obey this command of nature, babies are generally quieter, more contented, less fussy or nervous, and eventually better able to cope with the new experiences of growth.[4]

In many primitive societies women also took the initiative in limiting the number of children they would have, so that each child would receive its proper share of mother's attention and mother's milk. Precivilized women the world over would have sneered at the habit of Western civilized man of keeping a wife continually pregnant until she reached the end of her childbearing years or fell dead of exhaustion and a mass of "female complaints" brought on by reproductive traumas. Savages often suckled their children to the age of 3 or 4 or even longer, and refused sexual relations meanwhile or used alternative sexual practices that would not produce impregnation. By contrast, medieval Europeans instituted the immediate farming out of a newborn to a wet nurse, so the mother could conceive again as soon as possible—for it was believed from antiquity that a woman couldn't become pregnant as long as she was lactating. Ancient methods of family limitation known to the Greeks and Romans—contraceptive sponges, abortifacient drugs—were outlawed by the clergy and retained only in some secret traditions of witchcraft.

Nevertheless, it is significant that Western civilization considered abortion legal up to the middle of the nineteenth century, when abortion procedures finally began to attain greater success and lower mortality rate. Although surgical abortions were more often lethal than otherwise, male authorities paid little attention to them previously, on the theory that if a woman died of a botched abortion, she only got what she deserved. This was an extension of the curse-on-Eve idea, which led nineteenth-century clergy and doctors to insist that God wanted women to suffer in childbirth, and it was a sin to relieve their pains.[5] Even up to the present, doctors may withhold pain medication from abortion patients, maintaining that the pain is not as severe as patients say it is.[6] How would they know?

Of course the real issue in any abortion controversy is not whether a fetus has the right to life, but whether a woman has a right to make her own choices. Male doctors have always had the right to choose abortion on a woman's behalf. When a man is making the decision, somehow the rights of the fetus seem to evaporate. But when a woman decides to relieve herself of an unworkable commitment to motherhood, no matter how compelling her reasons she faces patriarchal punishment.

Around the turn of the century, when medical abortions became relatively safer under the proper conditions, stern measures were taken against making them available "on demand," as the phrase has it, a subtle but telling use of verbal connotations. Naturally, back street abortions always remained available. The fact that they frequently killed their patients was not considered important. Men simply assumed that if women feared the risks, then they should renounce sexuality or take the consequence, an unwanted baby. Nice single women were not supposed to get pregnant; nice married ones were not supposed to refuse to get pregnant. There were few extenuating circumstances. It made no difference if the fetus was conceived by rape or incest, if the mother-to-be was in her early teens, if she was a tired, ill, middle-aged mother of too many already, if she was too poor to care for a child without extreme hardship, or too overworked to do anything but neglect it. It may be well said that our shortsighted abortion laws have flooded our society with unloved children who, unless fortunately adopted, often grow up to be unworthy citizens. An infant improperly mothered stands a good chance of becoming, in adulthood, one who will always have great difficulty with interpersonal relations.

Difficulty of this kind is actually fostered by patriarchal

training of boys, who are often given to understand that they must renounce Mother and all females when they are quite young, eschew touching, stroking, hugging, and other physical kindnesses as sissy stuff, and learn to be hard, tough, and physically aggressive. Such training does much damage. Not only does it make men poor lovers of women (for in adulthood they will never be able to understand what a woman wants); it also makes them partial persons, who may respond to their own feelings of loss and inadequacy with any of several varieties of mental illness.

What used to be worshiped in India as the sacred principle of *karuna*, mother love, covered all forms of sensual connection and caring: tenderness, compassion, romance, sympathy, kinship, and sex play were all intertwined. Sensuality is fundamental to all loves. The capacity for sensual expression is laid down by the mother-child bond. A thousand times a day, in essential ways that a man may not even notice, the bond of *karuna* is established between a mother and her child in touches that feel good and other attentions. Mature lovers repeat the same patterns of intimacy.

What men often fail to realize about motherhood is that birth is only its first, toe-in-the-water approach. Motherhood is a 20 year commitment to the raising of each child and a lifetime commitment of emotional energy and empathy. To impose this responsibility on an unformed, ignorant teenage girl, willy-nilly, is an outrageous error. Such personal commitment and responsibility as a mother assumes toward her child can't be ordained by any third person, least of all a person unable to feel such commitment, such as a celibate priest. Men usually remain just as unaware of the complex of maternal emotions as they are of the internal physical sensation of pregnancy and birthing. Therefore no man can tell a woman when she is ready to bear, nurture, and raise a child. Because unwilling mothers produce ill-adjusted citizens, forced reproduction can only harm our future society.

A chief reason why men presume to control women's pregnancies is that men identify with the child, not with the mother. Christian iconography amply shows that man's image, God, constantly appears in his infant aspect, nurtured by a perfect, perpetually attentive mother. Woman's image, however, the mother, has no child form. She is always grown up enough to be capable of caring. The implication is that man can see himself as a baby, because this is part of his memory, but not as a woman or a mother. He doesn't empathize with woman's problems. He sees abortion from the fetal point of view, not from the maternal one. He perceives a woman's decision to reject her fetus as a rejection of himself, a lack of proper respect toward his precious seed.

Patriarchal theology strongly reinforced man's primitive fear for the safety of his seed by maintaining that semen contains a portion of the father's soul, which passes into the child. Church fathers even claimed that children's souls always came from their fathers, whereas a mother was only passive soil to nourish the planted seed. Church fathers were, of course, ignorant of the huge and complex ovum, whose many functions are still relatively unknown.

According to the old-age principle of sympathetic magic, any harm done to something that had once been part of a man's body would harm the man himself. Hence the nervous care throughout the ages in disposing of fingernail cuttings, hair clippings, spittle, blood, and all other body effluvia. Sometimes men insisted that witches could work evil spells with nothing more than the dust of a man's footprint. How much danger might be incurred by killing the product of his semen? Men were so worried about this, in fact, that it was a primary cause of their aversion to sex. Patriarchal priesthoods always maintained that men lost some of their store of vital energy through ejaculation. Essenic and early Christian ascetics claimed that a godlike immortality could be achieved only by celibacy, even by self-castration, so that no semen/soul would ever be lost to the dark, mysterious, threatening interior of a woman.[7]

Even further absurdities remain in Islam, left over from primitive ignorance of physiology. The period of pregnancy is officially supposed to last from six months to two years (Hanafi theological school) or four years (Shafei and Maliki schools).[8] Moreover, Islam still remains officially unaware that the sex-determining chromosome comes from a paternal spermatozoon. Moslem mothers can be beaten or divorced by their husbands for bearing female children instead of sons, as if the sex of the children were under their mothers' voluntary control. In denying the real powers of women, patriarchal men credit them with ridiculously great powers.

It is time for women to reclaim that miracle of which they are the sole proprietors; to throw off the male management that treats them like inert soil, subject to the manipulations of a "husbandman"; and to reassume the same authority over their offspring that every animal mother assumes as a matter of course.

It has been customary in our culture to say every child needs a father, which is only partly true. Many fathers don't deserve the title. Every child should have a *good* father, who conscientiously devotes himself to learning the skills of parenting and acts as the mother's willing assistant, not as a family tyrant. Like the designations of mother or doctor, that of father should be earned by honest performance.

A man can't become worthy of so vital a role in the making of posterity by doing nothing but ejaculating a teaspoonful of fluid, then afterward ignoring—or worse yet, mistreating—his child. To be a begetter isn't good enough. Men who want to partake in the miracle should earn the privilege, bearing in mind the law of nature that the primary parent is Mother.

For women, the decision to be a mother is a serious one. The responsibility is enormous, the commitment hardly imaginable before the fact. Such a demanding choice must never be forced on anyone, least of all the immature and ignorant.

One might suggest as a solution to the abortion controversy that every time the right-to-lifers succeed in forcing a woman to bear a child she doesn't want, let them be compelled to adopt and raise it, guaranteeing that it will have sufficient love, care, and material well-being to become a useful citizen. Under a rule such as this, the abortion controversy would fade away like morning mist.

As Sir Richard Burton sagely remarked, man has never worshiped anything but himself. Thus he has always thought it necessary to assimilate to himself everything he perceived as awesome or holy: motherhood first and foremost, because it holds the real power of life. Women should see to it that this archetypal power will never again be made the property of men.

Of all the male experts seeking to manage motherhood for their own purposes, perhaps the most pernicious are the mental health experts, Freud-guided into blaming mothers for all the emotional and social ills of patriarchal civilization. Psychiatrists even have the temerity to declare themselves most competent to train mothers to love their children.[9] Patriarchal arrogance thus manages to ignore the fact that the human race has survived this long only because mothers have loved their children for several million years—without the assistance of psychiatrists.

Psychiatrists have unfailingly pejorative labels for every function of motherhood and every type of mothering behavior, so Mother can always serve as a scapegoat for whatever goes wrong with her children. If a mother is selflessly devoted to her children, nurturant and careful as she is expected to be, she can be called overprotective or overanxious. If a mother is casual, easygoing, and unfussy, as she is also expected to be, she can be called neglectful. If a mother needs to support her family by "working"—that is, working for money, because mothering is unpaid and thus not regarded as work—she is still expected to do the mother job well in addition, or she is called unmotherly. If a mother expects the reward that society implicitly promises her, the love and gratitude of her offspring, she can be called demanding and manipulative. "Mothers have nearly all the work and receive nearly all the blame," a woman psychoanalyst admits. Yet "when women have had some success in the work of mothering, they have rarely been given any credit."[10]

One factor that contributes to this state of affairs is patriarchal society's insistence on the vital importance of fatherhood without, however, imposing a corresponding responsibility on fathers. As is well known, the new poor in American society are mostly divorced mothers struggling to support their children without even financial assistance from the men who begot them. A majority of divorced fathers get away with ignoring court-ordered child support payments, and alimony is rare these days.

Divorced men tend to become more affluent after separating from their families, while their ex-wives become decidedly less so. Such women bear the quadruple burden of (1) having to work outside the home, at a job that usually pays them poorly because they are female; (2) having to deprive their children of their attention because of (1) and bearing guilt feelings because of this; (3) having to raise their children under less than optimal conditions out of economic necessity; and (4) having to shoulder the blame of male-dominated society if their children turn out badly as a result of (3).

Fathers bear much less blame when children turn out badly—even when they have indulged in the most blatant wrongdoing in their paternal role, such as incest or child beating. Fathers may be cold, harsh, abusive, overly demanding, irresponsible, or neglectful to a much greater degree than mothers without incurring much censure. Indeed, mental health workers and family counselors have been known to call abusive fathers normal and shift the responsibility for a family's difficulties onto an already abused mother, regarding her as masochistic if she tolerates an emotionally or physically violent home atmosphere even though she sees no possibility of escape.

Patriarchal society usually rewards men for taking even a minimal interest in their children. Divorced fathers now routinely win custody battles if they want to, even when it is evident that their only purpose is to hurt the mother or when they are shown to be unfit parents. Though most men prefer to be relieved of day-to-day responsibility for their children, those who insist on keeping parental control are generally given it by law. This is described as equality. Today's society shows no hint of what ancient societies believed: namely, that the bearing, nursing, feeding, training, constant attention, love, and responsibility that makes a mother's contribution to her child's life so much greater than a father's should also carry correspondingly greater authority.

If authority really is shared equally between two parents, family therapists tend to view that family as automatically flawed. They say the father is too passive and the mother too assertive. Even the kind of earth mother who genuinely loves producing and caring for children is negatively described as a woman who deals with that mythical Freudian absurdity, penis envy, by overinvesting in vicarious achievement through her children. There is a pejorative label in the mental health profession for every type and degree of mothering behavior. Mothers can never win.[11]

Patriarchal society even presumes to decide whether mothering behavior is to be allowed at all. Throughout the history of Western civilizations, millions of babies have been taken away from their natural mothers because those mothers failed to provide them with "legitimate" fathers. Being so used to this idea, we can hardly perceive the perverted artificiality of thinking that maternity must be validated by a man, or else it is a crime and a disgrace, to be forgotten as soon as possible. Can we imagine any animal mother rejecting her young because an adult male wouldn't claim them? Of course the truth is the contrary: the animal mother rejects the adult male because her young are more important to her. Nothing is allowed to stand in the way of her maternity.

Because the human patriarchal ideal is that no woman should have the right to reject a man, our religious and ethical systems conspire to convince women that not even that most powerful of connections, the mother-child bond, can supersede the purely social bond of wifely servitude blessed by a paternal God. A curious culture indeed, to insist that within legal marriage motherhood must be pushed to such extremes as to endanger a woman's health or emotional stability, whereas outside of marriage it is a sin for her to bring even one new life into the world and a scandal for her to love it.

Patriarchal society tended also to deprive mothers of the natural mutual-aid networks they had in ancient tribal matriarchies, when a woman's home remained her matrilineal property, and the stripped-down male-headed nuclear family was still unheard of. The normal primitive extended family or clan gave each child the advantage of many adult caretakers: aunts, uncles, grandparents, elder siblings, and cousins. At the same time each mother had plenty of help. She could sometimes lay aside the cares of mothering altogether, trusting others to take over for a while.

In stark contrast to this, modern civilization usually isolates each woman in one house with her husband and children (or perhaps children only), forcing her to buy extra child care unless she has a friend or relative willing to trade mothering duties. The patriarchal idea is that a wife is installed in the home to minister to her husband. As he sees it, the home exists to nurture him, to do for him the same things that his mother did for him when he was a little boy. If the home produces children, then the wife looks after them too, but the patriarchal home is not primarily a nest for the raising of the young. Children tend to be an afterthought in the male mind.

Corporations, those mechanical models of patriarchal utopia, periodically uproot the nuclear families from their homes and send them off to establish new homes in distant places, where the burden of trying to put down new roots also falls upon the wife. The ill effects of this corporate habit have been often noted. Women and children must part from friends or congenial kinfolk in their neighborhood. Many children fail to adapt to the emotional trauma of being, over and over, the new kid in school. It's hard enough to form solid friendships at certain stages of growing up without having to start afresh every few years. Uprooted children may feel uncomfortable enough to vandalize the unfamiliar surroundings where they know no one and feel no ties with the neighbors, no responsibility to the community.

Increased stress within the nuclear household is another common symptom of the alienation and friendlessness thus imposed on the family by the corporate hierarchy. And if the stripped-down family collapses under the stress, it is again the woman who bears most of the blame. Trained to believe it's up to her to hold the family together, to be the unfailing nurturer for the children as well as an adult man, she may exhaust herself in heroic efforts to maintain the model family ideal against the disruptive forces of modern living. Then, when it falls apart anyway, she is tormented by guilt.

Patriarchal civilization provides virtually no support system for the wife and mother. On the contrary, she is expected to become the basic support system for all the rest of it: husband, children, school, church, community, business, even the economy in general, which depends on her function as consumer.

Patriarchal society traps women in an insoluble dilemma. On the one hand they are expected to be superpeople, juggling all necessary roles and jobs with more aplomb than is demanded of any average man. On the other hand they are still expected to behave as inferior people, deferring and submitting to male management even in their most vital, biological, species-perpetuating role. This paradox of feminine life has brought unhappiness to many. The mothers of humanity must reclaim their natural powers and ancient rights. As the true creators of the future, they should be free to give it a truly human and humane direction.

A significant bit of patriarchal incongruity appears in our popular culture in the arts, literature, and music created by men. Far and away the most ubiquitous theme of all the arts is sexual love, in all possible permutations and combinations. If there were no such thing as love between man and woman, four fifths of the world's art and music would be meaningless. Countrywide, radio stations daily flood the airwaves with songs about some aspect of man-woman love, one after another, by the thousands.

But not one song ever celebrates the most fundamental love of them all, the bond between mother and child: the true wellspring of human life.

We are familiar with a large number of songs that celebrate the macho model of man, the war songs intended to be stirring, to glorify the warrior and encourage young men to take up arms on behalf of the old men (their country's leaders) to feed the elder males' insatiable appetite for ever more power. As a social device for fathers to demand the supreme sacrifice from their sons, war neatly parallels the religious image of Father God and his sacrificed son. One of men's favorite methods for coping with their envy of the female power to give life was to claim for themselves an equal and opposite power to take life. Thus male-dominated societies are characterized by war and violence, opposing the will and instincts of the mothers, who must submit to management as the machines that produce more fodder for the wars that occur in each generation.

Despite its lip service to the principle of peace, Christianity has proved itself history's most warlike religion, from its very beginning, when church fathers asserted their God-given right to slaughter pagans and dissenters "by the sword." St. Augustine said Christians were duty bound to wage any war as long as God commanded it. Hence every war Christians ever fought has had the divine sanction, even when God seemed to have issued the same command to both sides. The Jesuits officially advocated war as a legitimate weapon against heresy, and churches of all denominations have equated Christianity with patriotism in wartime.[12]

Several wars have occurred within the memories of this generation, including World War II, also known as the War to Make the World Safe for Democracy, which did no such thing, of course, so the slogan has been shamefacedly dropped. In this most recent of the ever-recurrent "war to end all wars," the initial aggressor was Christian Germany, whose Third Reich was eagerly supported by the churches. They were on Hitler's payroll, the largest nongovernmental landowners in Germany. Hitler contemptuously said of them, "They will swallow everything in order to keep their material advantages." They did. German bishops never discussed the moral implications of Hitler's policies but ordered young people to serve the Nazi regime with all their might. The German government easily purchased the papacy's promise not to criticize its activities during the war. Pope Pius XII finally denounced Nazism in June 1945—after Germany had surrendered and Hitler was safely dead. World War II "exposed the emptiness of the churches in Germany, the cradle of the Reformation, and the cowardice and selfishness of the Holy See."[13]

But let us not judge only Germany and the papacy guilty of pusillanimous behavior. Churches conveniently forget their alleged commitment to peace when it is politically expedient. Nearly every church in America also supported the war. Few even hinted that men might follow the mothers' morality of aversion and express their disapproval of war by boycotting it.

Perhaps the ultimate gesture of contempt for motherhood was carried out by the United States government in presenting gold star window stickers to women whose sons had been killed in the war. Grown-up women, suffering perhaps the deepest grief a woman ever knows, were given the same emblem that was pasted on their first-grade school papers when they spelled all the words right. Gold star mothers were told that they should be proud of that emblem, which in effect declared them good little girls who willingly gave up their life work to the patriarchal cause. No mention was made of the bad little girls who might have torn the silly gold stars to shreds in their rage against the old men who deprived them of the lives they brought to birth and tended with concern day and night for two decades or more.

Men may "possess" their own life work under the law, even patenting a useful invention so that its usefulness is denied to anyone who does not pay for it. Yet women are made to think themselves evil for trying to "possess" (that is, preserve) their own living life works, their children, whose lives are seen as belonging to the state rather than to the mother who birthed and raised them. That the state may feel a certain shame about its callous use of the mother's production is implicit in its offer of a compensatory token. But what a token—a childish piece of paper to replace a warm, strong body, a living mind, a beloved face, and an affectionate interaction dating back to her labor and lactation.

Perhaps, while tenderly handling her new baby, every mother should give some thought to what her country's male leaders might be planning to do with that human being in 20 years' time. Men make their wars, and women are told that they must helplessly lament the terrible waste of life instead of rising up and seizing the power to make government behave with the mature responsibility and solicitude for others that women are expected to show as a matter of course.

Patriarchal society generally keeps elder women out of the seats of power for various reasons not unrelated to women's maternal tendency to value ordinary life above patriotic death. In ancient times elder women stepped naturally into positions of leadership in their communities, because their clans honored motherhood as a divine principle, the basis of all cooperative bonds. Considered the wisest of beings in consequence of their life experience, female elders governed with the kindly but sure authority of mothers, aided by a keen comprehension developed after years of seeing through men's masks. Indeed, what patriarchal society called the old woman's evil eye seems to have been the eye of undeceived perception.[14] Fear of her wisdom may be the real reason why patriarchal males so strongly dislike an old woman:

> It would seem as though the man is afraid of her because of her capacity to understand him and see through his failures, or weaknesses, if necessary. She knows very well that his masculinity is not real, not an essential truth, but only an external shell, built up and imposed on women by societies based on class and sexual discrimination. The experience and intelligence of women are a menace to the false position in which man is placed. . . . That is essentially why most men fear and even hate intelligent and experienced women.[15]

Our culture has circulated much slander against old women, ranging from the notion that they are physically repulsive (but men of the same age are not) to the notion that they are incapable of thought (but men of the same age are authorities on everything). Even in the twentieth century doctors have routinely advised postmenopausal women to avoid mental activity, and then medical literature has often castigated such women for being dull.[16]

Denigration and insult have been the Western male's customary methods of managing motherhood even as a potential, in the young woman, or as a past accomplishment, in the old woman. If a woman is heard to doubt the intelligence of men, she can be hated for contentiousness, but men may insult the intelligence of women more or less constantly in ordinary conversation, expecting women not to show resentment. Buried beneath all such manifestations of sexism is the secret jealousy of motherhood that men have harbored ever since they learned to worship the unknown power that made only women the carriers of humanity's future.

Not only jealousy of that power becomes evident among men, but also a concealed dread or fear of it: the same "holy dread" that patriarchal males demonstrated in the presence of menstrual blood, which was the world's primary taboo when it was thought to contain all female magic of life and death. There is a similar undercurrent of male dread in the presence of a pregnant belly. Many men seem to feel uncomfortable or embarrassed when faced with a visibly pregnant woman. Her protruding abdomen inescapably reminds them that gut level comprehension of life's mystery is hers alone, mocking their inflated self-congratulatory words as sheer babble in the face of her silent reality.

It should be remembered that Western male doctors left the mysteries of birth to midwives for many centuries, even as they usurped all other aspects of medicine for themselves and forbade women to practice them anymore, and Western clergymen made parturient women taboo as spiritually dangerous, forbidding new mothers to enter churches until a purifying ritual could be performed to remove the perilous *mana* of maternity that men dared not face.

One might see a connection between such male dread and our society's obsession with female slenderness. One reason men insist on the sexual attractiveness of thin women may be that such women look reassuringly unmaternal. Pregnant women look fat; fat women look pregnant. Divine principles of fecundity have always been represented by abundantly fleshy female figures, from the Paleolithic Venuses to the rippling nudes of Romanticism. Yet, despite his larger body, man seems ever in some dread of being overwhelmed by female flesh that surrounds and swallows.

Still the much-desired nonpregnant slenderness must be paradoxically combined with huge, pillowy breasts, the reassurance symbol for the infant in man—although female bodies of this description are uncommon. From the Virgin Mother on down, nearly every feminine ideal set up by patriarchy turns out to be impossible or unlikely for the average woman, because patriarchy automatically insists on the average woman's imperfection.

Whatever the feminine esthetic ideal, most human cultures show evidence of male envy of female reproductive power and of the mother's absolute, unquestionable ownership of the new life produced from her body.

Men ceaselessly endeavored to claim some comparable power for themselves. Once they discovered its function, they tried blowing up the brief moment of impregnation to a balloon of cosmic significance. That didn't work well, because the female part in reproduction is still obviously much greater. Then men tried renouncing sexuality altogether in ascetic disciplines under a motherless God, who promised them a higher existence freed from the burden of mother-given flesh. That didn't work well either, because asceticism lacked general appeal, and the guilt involved in learning renunciation of the flesh could be psychically crippling.

Finding it difficult to manage themselves, men devoted their efforts to managing women, who seem to have been too easygoing to nip these efforts in the bud. Male-dominated religions never really assented to the female idea of the sacredness of life. In their view life was more sinful than sacred. God-fearing men were told to fix their gaze on the hereafter, not the here. Perhaps only a culture trained in this attitude can contemplate the kind of madness that Western civilization is now contemplating in the interest of a maniacal strategic logic that finds it acceptable to destroy an entire planet because a few old men dislike one another and covet increases in their temporal power. Just as an individual with a death wish will eventually attempt suicide, so a death-centered society will inevitably tempt fate by following the leaders with the biggest guns.

True creation is feminine in either woman or man, as several psychologists have recently acknowledged. Patriarchal civilization denied the feminine vision of creativity, and so deprived men as well as women of their full humanity. Laurens van der Post writes, "Whole areas of history are darkened by the ignorance of men of the truth that they can create only through the feminine in their own natures just as they procreate in the world without through woman alone. [History shows] ominous evidence enough of a hidden instinctive resentment in woman over the failure of man to recognize and honor this aspect of her spirit and a backlash of vengeance and revenge over this ignorance."[17]

But the backlash may be even worse than that. On denying the feminine-creative spirit, man cuts himself off from the root of his own best social interactions and behavior patterns. He inadvertently produces many frustrations for himself, in addition to a world where love seems to have little or no practical value; a world where the generally desirable rewards are gained by cruelty or, at best, callousness. As a social system, patriarchy hurts men too. Not only does it encourage them to hurt one another; but women deprived of power can no longer do anything about it and may not even want to try.

There is a pious old saying beloved by the more woolly-minded traditionalists that goes: "God couldn't be everywhere at once, so He created mothers." The saying seems to exalt motherhood, but really doesn't. By converting mothers into the deputies of God, it still puts the idea of fatherhood first and perpetuates ignorance of the fact that the mother-child relationship is the only real, biological root of all human ideas of love, including its spiritualized aspects. It tries to deny the Bible's self-incriminating claim that God imposed motherhood as a curse and a handicap to women, to punish them forever for their foremothers' sins. Then it makes the theological mistake of depriving "omnipresent" God of his ability to be everywhere at once. Finally, it forces upon human mothers their now-familiar burden of guilt at falling short of divine perfection— that is, at not being perfectly all-giving and forgiving, ever tolerant, kind, self-effacing, and tireless in benevolent acts. Needless to say, mothers are not allowed to imitate God's other traits, such as his disastrous biblical explosions of temper, or his all-destroying curses, or his warlike exterminations of whole peoples, or his demand for his son's death. Fathers are to retain control of such traits. It seems that Mother may be powerlessly Jesuslike but not powerfully Godlike.

This is not the way our more remote ancestors viewed motherhood. Like every other mammal, the human animal based its learning on unquestioned obedience to the mother. Its first, most basic life experiences were predicated upon its absolute dependence on the mother. Its capacity for adult social and sexual connections developed through its physical, mental, and emotional interaction with the mother. Therefore mothers retained their authority throughout all human families, when children's natural gratitude for the gift of life remained focused upon life's actual giver. In many ways, far from exalting motherhood, men's ideas of God only robbed mothers of the respect that Mother Nature had made their due.

In refusing to recognize woman as the true source of an

ethic of love, man has rendered practical application of the ethic of love difficult, if not impossible, for an unacceptably large majority of people. By refusing to develop that which requires the tutelage of women, man leaves himself open to his most destructive impulses, and finds a demonic god within, apparently as perverse as the medieval demons that churchmen encouraged by their exorcisms.

Now patriarchy has run away with itself for three thousand years and has created a Frankenstein monster in fact. Men stand ready with unthinkable weapons of death-technology to assert their ultimate, irreversible victory over the forces of life. Much good may it do them, in the last instant before the final holocaust, to know that they have won: that the life-affirming power of motherhood is under their total control at last and will never rise up again.

NOTES

1. Michelle Harrison, M.D., *A Woman in Reisdence* (New York: Random House, 1982), 111, 146, 198–99.
2. Adrienne Rich, *Of Woman Born: Motherhood as Experience and Institution* (New York: W. W. Norton & Co., 1976), 176.
3. Harrison, *A Woman in Residence*, 256.
4. Wolfgang Wickler, *The Sexual Code* (New York: Anchor/Doubleday, 1973), 266.
5. Ronald Pearsall, *Night's Black Angels: The Many Faces of Victorian Cruelty* (New York: David McKay Co., 1975), 85. Andrew D. White, *A History of the Warfare of Science with Theology in Christendom* (New York: George Braziller, 1955), 1:319.
6. Harrison, *A Woman in Residence*, 243.
7. Barbara G. Walker, *The Woman's Encyclopedia of Myths and Secrets* (San Francisco and New York: Harper & Row, 1983), 146.
8. Nawal El Saadawi, *The Hidden Face of Eve: Women in the Arab World* (Boston: Beacon Press, 1982), 52.
9. E. Fuller Torrey *The Death of Psychiatry* (Radnor, Pa.: Chilton Book Co., 1974), 109.
10. Paula J. Caplan, *The Myth of Women's Masochism* (New York: E. P. Dutton, 1985), 44–45.
11. Caplan, *The Myth of Women's Masochism*, 193–98.
12. Paul Johnson, *A History of Christianity* (New York: Atheneum, 1976), 242, 305, 477.
13. Johnson, *A History of Christianity*, 487–89, 493.
14. Barbara G. Walker, *The Crone: Woman of Age, Wisdom and Power* (San Francisco: Harper & Row, 1985), 122.
15. El Saadawi, *Hidden Face of Eve*, 77.
16. Marilyn French, *Beyond Power: On Women, Men, and Morals* (New York: Simon & Schuster, 1985), 358.

17. Laurens van der Post, *Jung and the Story of Our Time* (New York: Vintage, 1975), 168, 178.

Kali Ma

When I became a mother, I was surprised to experience a gaudy vision of India's "terrible mother" Kali Ma in her classic pose: squatting over her dead consort, digging her claws into his belly, and eating his entrails. Her fangs were smeared with blood, her ornaments jingling, her eyeballs bulging at me. Against a dark background where only a few vague, unidentifiable shapes could be seen, she stood out with horrifying vividness, busily devouring her grisly meal. The skulls in her necklace clacked together with the violence of her movements. The jewels in her elongated earlobes swung and glittered. Her hair stood up and waved, Medusalike, in snaky strands with an apparent life of their own. Her shrunken breasts flapped on her bony ribs. Most shockingly, the corpse's penis stood erect and entered her vulva. With rhythmic motions of her pelvis she pleasured herself on his body, even as she also more literally ate him, like a female mantis who begins to eat her mate in the act of mating.

I wondered why the process of childbirth should stimulate my mind's eye to present me with this image, clearly drawn from pictures I had seen, yet also fleshed out with colors and details contributed by my own imagination. Was it appropriate that upon giving life I should envision this figure of death?

A long while afterward when I read more about what the Terrible Mother used to mean, I began to think the vision more appropriate than I could have known at the time. Kali Ma wasn't all horror and ugliness, though those qualities were concentrated in her outward appearance to convey an important message: namely, that one who seeks the secrets of nature cannot find them by avoiding the realities of death, rot, slime, mud, blood, excrement—all the decay on which the Earth Mother's regenerative powers feed. It was evident that every life birthed by this universal mother came to sentience with the seeds of its own demise and dissolution already contained within itself. The karmic doom of every life was to sacrifice itself, involuntarily but inevitably, to the production of new life forms that would also live their moment and pass away, producing still others in their turn. Death and life were inextricably interdependent in all time scales, from the least to the longest. This was the first philosophical lesson of archaic matriarchies. Mothers naturally understood in their guts, as it were, the principle of mature life forms given in self-sacrifice to the fostering of newer ones.

This primordial cyclic vision of the cosmos came naturally to the feminine spirit when it was still unmutilated by squeamish patriarchal ascetics, who later tried to avoid life's fact of death by renouncing the facts of life. Kali Ma was one of the oldest of deities, Virgin Mother of all the gods, according to some traditions. She was not only the life-in-death and the death-in-life but also the sexual image representing man's sole means of connecting himself with her regenerative powers as embodied in woman. She ate her consort, who was also her child, to bring him to life again in yet another incarnation out of her mysterious uterine power. Kali's yogis called this power the active principle of existence as opposed to the passive male principle. They often gave it one of her other names, Shakti, meaning "power." Every Hindu god needed a personification of Shakti, his Goddess, in order to do anything at all.

The same idea was found in all the Western nations touched by the same Indo-European traditions around the long beginning of the patriarchal era. God creators couldn't create without their Mother-spouse counterparts. Zeus could do nothing without Metis, his "wisdom," another Greek name for the Kali-like Medusa, who also represented female wisdom and was later assimilated into Hellenic patriarchy as Gorgo-Athene. Father gods of northern Europe similarly depended on the same formidable Goddess, who retained her ancient Sanskrit name in Finland as Kalma and in Britain as the Caillech. The Hebrew Yahweh depended on her as his Hokmah, "Wisdom," the same female spirit who brooded on the waters in Genesis and took the form of his spouse or Shekina (Shakti) in the Jerusalem temple. Judeo-Christian scholars chose to reinterpret her in various unfemale ways as God's "presence," "mind," or "holy spirit," concealing the original premise that she was the true creative principle, without which God could not function. Early Gnostic sects continued to worship her as Hagia Sophia, "Divine Wisdom," the cosmic mother who gave birth to the demiurge Jehovah himself.

I learned that Kali's worshipers went to cemeteries or cremation grounds to place themselves in symbolic contact with her spirit as Mother Death, that is, the principle of dissolution, as an essential prerequisite to regeneration. They claimed that no adept could ever fully know her until she or he realized her as the death bringer, tearer and devourer of her or his own flesh. Therefore her ugly, ghoulish aspect was worshiped. Similarly, medieval European pagans who were stigmatized as witches were said to have held their meetings in graveyards.

Because there could be no regeneration of life without dissolution of life, Kali's tantric yogis taught that men must willingly give themselves up to the primacy of the female principle even when it meant death. They could be rewarded by the ecstasy of connection with her, just as in the so-called little death of sexual orgasm. Sex became the paradigm of rebirth from within the female principle, for man "died" in order to beget his physical immortality, that is, offspring. Sex and death were revered together. The god always died in his sacred marriage with the Mother-spouse and so won his resurrection. He became the model for the dying-god figures of classical antiquity, all of them virgin-born from one of the Goddess's earthly incarnations, enlightened and able to work miracles, sacrificed, interred in her tomb-womb, and deified in their rising again and again as the new Son, who was identical with the old god.

Willing sacrifice of the male principle to the female was the tantric ideal supposed to be essential to true revelation and spiritual rebirth. Even the later custom of baptism, a symbolic drowning in uterine waters, was an echo of this ancient tantric notion of becoming born again. In the moment of his real death, each adept was said to be sexually devoured by his Goddess in a final ecstasy of union. The doctrine was both subtle and empirical, with many ramifications based on observable life processes in humans, animals, and plants. It was cyclic and seasonal. It made room for natural decline as well as growth, sickness as well as health—for Kali's Destroyer aspect was often called the Goddess of disease. The endless rounds of her Wheel of Time encompassed perpetual interaction and interrelationships of all living forms, from the simplest to the most complex. Nothing could be static in her universe of perpetual becomings. Life was not an existence but a process, ever undergoing subtle change—which is how modern biological science also sees it.

On the whole, it was a sensible idea of life and death as they impinge on human perceptions. Until patriarchal ascetics evolved the notion that their personal immortality might be gained by the right kind of magic, Kali and other similar Goddess figures enforced respect for natural processes. This old religion placed the male principle where it belongs in biological reality: not central, but ancillary to the many-faceted female activities of reproduction; a single instant of male "little death" as contrasted with half a lifetime of maternal care, love, and nurture, always flexibly responding to changing needs. Tantrics worshiped mother love as the universal principle of *karuna*, the foundation of all other loves and connections.

When men began to understand their role in reproduction and to glorify it into a new divinity far beyond its significance, they began to deny the death that Mother Kali, or nature, decreed for them. They could devise no better way to do this than to deny all other functions of the Mother as well: to renounce female sexuality and the pleasures of the flesh; to belittle motherhood as merely physical but not spiritual; to diabolize instead of revere women; and to make the primordial, ancestral Mother responsible for sin and for the consequent creation of death by an offended god. Naturally, it took many centuries for these ideas to gain acceptance, but eventually it happened and we all know the outcome.

I seemed to feel a special, perverse kinship with my vision of Kali. She frightened me not at all. I sensed something liberating about the very concept of ugliness and horror simultaneously expressed as feminine essence as opposed to Western civilization's unrealistic view that ugliness automatically negated femininity. The hidden message to women in that was, you must be beautiful or you can't be female. It was nonsense, of course. One might as well say to nature, you must be always springtime or you can't be natural.

Kali's worshipers had a more realistic view of both woman and nature. This may be the message that men really need to comprehend: a matter-of-fact acknowledgment that there is no escape from her Wheel, which always includes a time to die as well as a time to be born, and neither time is under conscious human control. Because dissolution is inevitable for every individual, the quality of earthly life is important and precious.

Kali as the Great Void, as she was sometimes called, represented the darkness from which we come into consciousness and to which we return. Her scriptures said that at the end of time she would devour all the gods she once brought forth. She would return the whole universe, which was her own substance, to her initial state of formlessness, uterine darkness, primal chaos. Again her spirit would brood on the infinite waters, until she was moved once more to create light, a god, a world. Her cycles were ever dissolved and renewed, even on the cosmic scale. There could be no end, because like energy itself, Kali the Destroyer could never be destroyed.

Eventually I came to realize that Kali Ma was not an inappropriate image for any woman able to feel the enormous power of childbirth, because Kali represented female power in general. The modern woman, struggling for her identity in a patriarchal world, can find much that is useful in Kali and others like her—remembering that all images of the ancient Goddess were like her, each with her Death Mother aspect (Moira, Morgan, Hecate, Cerridwen, Neith, Anat, Demeter Chthonia, Al-Uzza, Astarte, and so on). Because Kali stood for eveything men feared about the female principle, and men seem to respect only what can be feared (an observation that was abundantly exploited by male priesthoods), then Kali might command men's respect better than the prettier Goddess images: the beautiful Virgin, the all-giving Mother.

On getting past Kali's movie monster caricature, one might find a rational statement of feminine theology (the*a*logy) that the patriarchal world has found it convenient to forget. Her image states that what we call ugliness is essential to the world of living nature. Every flower must have its roots in organic rot. Every baby must be born "between urine and feces," as St. Augustine squeamishly described it, yet that baby must be accepted and loved even when it spits up or soils its diaper. Unlike St. Augustine, true human love is not disgusted by the processes of life nor even by those of death, such as aging and physical decline. Ancient matriarchs welcomed the wrinkles that men now call unbeautiful as an outward sign of wisdom. Identifying themselves with the Goddess-as-Crone, the death bringer, they felt closer to the core of things.

Kali both empowered and devoured God. In effect, her control of him was as complete as a mother's control of her dependent infant. God could not exist until she brought him into being, and everything she brought into being was fated to pass away as her Wheel turned. Hers was the mysterious uterine power that inexorably expelled every infant from its primal paradise. Hers was the equally mysterious sexual power that made a penis rise, even against the will of its owner. Hers was the deadly power that caused a body to sicken and die, also against the will of its owner. In such matters even the gods were subject to her, as one of them (Vishnu) said to her: "Thou art the birthplace of even Us; thou knowest the whole world, yet none know thee."

As even the gods had to exist within her parameters of time and essence, so men had to exist within nature. Kali made the human fantasy of transcendence irrelevant. She showed that heavens with their gods and hells with their demons were both imagined out of the rich mix of the natural world. Together with her virgin aspect (Maya the Creatress) and her mother aspect (Durga the Protectress), Kali the Destroyer represented that rich mix of reality that the enlightened person must accept because it is there.

I learned to appreciate Kali's ugliness as I learned to accept the somatic facts of my own aging and eventual death. That, of course, was the whole purpose of her image. To know life clear, one must see it all: the end as well as the beginning, the decay as well as the growth. To know life all the way, that is surely the primary purpose for living at all. What is consciousness but the precious potential for just such knowledge? To be aware is a gift. To be aware of a lifetime's totality of experience is a blessing indeed.

Like the prophylactic Medusa mask of antiquity, Kali's ugliness stands as a warning to those who trespass on her mysteries without proper preparation and mental acceptance. Like life, she is fatal. Like knowing the worst, she allays fear. Like wisdom, she appears to those who are not afraid. Like love, she brings regeneration out of crude organic reality.

After I had spent some years thinking about her, hideous Kali turned out to be one of my favorite images of the Goddess.

PART THREE

The Crone:
Meditations

The Witches

Thirteen witch women gather on the night of a full moon. They enter the house by ones or twos, embrace one another, sit down, talk. Each has brought a candle in a candlestick and a dish of food. They wear casual, comfortable clothing. One, a woman in her 60s, wears a full-length robe.

One woman is a librarian. One is a commercial artist. One is a real estate saleswoman. One is a journalist. One is a shop owner. One is a nurse. One runs a catering service. Two are teachers. Seven are married, four divorced; all of these are mothers. One is visibly pregnant.

They enter a large carpeted room. In the center of the room is a small knee-high table draped in black. On the floor beside the table are a black iron cauldron with incense burning in it, a plant in a clay pot, a feather fan, a crystal goblet of water, and a deck of Tarot cards. The women gather around the table, put their candles on it, and light them. Other lights are turned off.

One woman places a small birch twig on the table among the candles. One places a quartz crystal. One places a necklace with a silver crescent moon pendant. One places a pebble. One places a cowrie shell. One places a folded piece of paper. One places a gold ring. One places a hank of hair tied with red yarn. One places a small, naked clay image of the Goddess.

One takes the Tarot deck and spreads the 14 cards of each suit in an arc outside the circle in the corners of the room. The suit of cups is laid in the south corner, the suit of wands in the west, the suit of pentacles in the north, the suit of swords in the east. She returns to the circle. All join hands and breathe quietly in unison. Some close their eyes.

While the others remain facing center, one woman takes the goblet of water to the south corner of the room and holds it up. She speaks. "Spirits of the south, of the waters, of birth, childhood, motherhood, and love, flowing spirits of the blue sea, Aphrodite, Kore, Stella Maris, lady of the pearls of wisdom, be with us. Blessed be." The others echo, "Blessed be." She returns to her place in the circle.

Another woman takes one of the lighted candles to the west corner of the room and holds it up. She speaks. "Spirits of the west, of the fire, of beauty, heat, passion, and power, flaming spirits of sunset and lightning, Atthar, Pele, Hella, lady of the blood's urges, be with us. Blessed be." The others echo, "Blessed be." She returns to her place in the circle.

A third woman takes the potted plant to the north corner of the room and holds it up. She speaks. "Spirits of the north, of the earth, of strength and abundance and life-giving food, enduring spirit of the great mountains, Demeter, Erda, Cybele, lady of the caves, rocks, and green growth, be with us. Blessed be." The others echo, "Blessed be." She returns to her place in the circle.

Yet another woman takes the feather fan to the east corner of the room and holds it up. She speaks. "Spirits of the east, of the winds and clouds, the breath of life and the mists of death, Skulda, Cerridwen, Kali, lady of the mind, giver and destroyer, be with us. Blessed be." The others echo, "Blessed be." She returns to her place in the circle.

One says, "The circle is cast. Let nothing harmful enter this space." Another says, "We are the center. We are the still point. We are the place where all our roads cross." All answer, "Blessed be."

They sit on the floor, cross-legged, then let go of each other's hands. One woman takes the goblet of water and dips her finger into it. With her wet finger she traces a crescent shape on her neighbor's forehead. She says to her neighbor, "I, Susan, bless you, Debra. You are Goddess." The second woman smiles and answers her, "Thank you." The first woman hands the goblet of water to her neighbor on the other side, who takes it, dips her finger, and blesses the first woman in the same way. The goblet passes all the way around the circle until each woman has performed the same blessing of her neighbor.

The blessing is performed to the left, with the left hand, but the goblet passes to the right, counterclockwise.

The women meditate in silence. After a while one begins to hum quietly. Others join in with harmonizing notes. The sound grows louder. The women take each other's hands and slowly raise their arms. Together they sway from side to side. In a few minutes the humming dies away and the arms lower. One says, "Feel our blood." All concentrate on the sensation of the pulse beating in each other's palms. One says, "Woman blood is the wise blood that gives life." They spread their hands palm down on the floor, touching their own thumbs and each other's little fingers all the way around the circle.

The woman who has brought the birch twig tells the others how she found the twig and what her thoughts were as she picked it up. The woman who has brought the gold ring tells about its descent through six generations in her family. The woman who has brought the cowrie shell speaks of its ancient female genital symbolism and its use throughout the world as a childbirth or healing charm and as a medium of exchange. The woman who has brought the Goddess image explains that it is a reproduction of a Paleolithic "Venus," which she keeps on her desk as a focus for the fertility of her imagination. She describes her impression of Paleolithic mother worship. The woman who has brought the lock of hair says it is the hair of her daughter, who is traveling in a distant country. The mother expresses concern for her daughter's safety. The pebble, quartz crystal, and silver necklace are also explained. Each item is passed around for all to handle. The woman who has brought the piece of paper unfolds it and reads from it to the others. It is a poem she has written. The others listen and thank her for sharing her words.

Each woman speaks briefly of her personal concerns, recent philosophical thoughts, or her feelings at the moment. One says, "I'm glad to be here. After such a hectic week, it feels good to be quiet and centered." Another says, "I used to think I could feel that way in church. What a waste of time. Living women are much more comforting than cold stained-glass saints." Another says, "I've been thinking a lot about triangle symbolism. The triangle keeps recurring in my sketches. I've been using its Mother religion connotations." Another says, "Let's think of the three phases of the moon and their meanings." Another says, "I need energy. My husband is in the hospital with pneumonia." All murmur sympathy and hold out their hands toward her. The two on each side of her stroke her hair and her cheeks.

They decide to do a lifting charm for the pregnant one in memory of the ancient belief that this would facilitate childbirth. The pregnant one lies down on the floor. The others place their hands under her body. All breathe together three times and then raise her a few feet into the air, slowly wafting her up and down. "You're so light," one says to her. "May your child come lightly," says another. "Call on the Mother of All," says a third. They lower her to the floor.

"That reminds me," the pregnant one says. "I heard an odd thing in my natural childbirth class. That is a funny contradiction, isn't it? Natural childbirth class? If it's natural, why should you need a class? Anyway, the teacher is an obstetrical nurse who worked in maternity wards for many years. She told us, 'Women in labor often call out to Mother. They don't mean their own mothers. I don't know who they mean. The Virgin Mary, maybe.' I asked her if these are Catholic women. She said no, they could be Protestants, Jews, anybody. I didn't say anything more, but I think I know who that Mother is."

Another woman said, "Isn't that fascinating. The archetype is still in there, isn't she? Most of us just don't know how to contact her except in moments of stress. Especially that kind of stress. Why not?" The others nod. One says, "The night after I gave birth, I had a tremendous vision of a green Goddess. It wasn't a dream. I was awake. I was angry because I wanted my baby with me, and they had taken him away. She said something comforting to me, but I don't know what it was."

The oldest woman says her arthritic fingers have been bothering her. The others gather around her and take her hands. Gently they stroke her wrists, arms, and fingers. One massages her temples. One says to her, "Think of flexibility and freedom, smooth, like flowing water, like flowing love." The elder woman says, "Thank you." She smiles, flexing her hands. One says,

"Such things women did for one another thousands of years before the name of any god was spoken on earth. Sometimes it can do what doctors still can't do." Another says, "But we don't expect any miracle except the miracle of love." The others nod.

One woman says, "Do you realize that only a few centuries ago men's laws said we all could be burned alive for doing just what we are doing here?" All look serious. They are keenly aware of what holy men did to their foremothers. "Never again," one says, "must women be persecuted for wanting their own space." All repeat, "Never again." One says softly, "How they have robbed us."

One says, "My husband talks about starting a group that can include men." Another says a male friend approached her to discuss the possibility of a mixed group. The women discuss the idea. Most are opposed to admitting men. One says, "Remember, all the troubles began in the first place when men saw that the women had a good thing going, moved in on it, and then took it away from them." Another says, "Once you invite men in, it changes the whole character of the group. Some men are bound to get pushy. They want to be leaders. Some want to add drinking or drugs. It's not womanspace any more. Some want to make a sex party out of it."

"At the very least," another woman says, "they'll want to do everything skyclad." All laugh. Another says, "Maybe we can set up a men's auxiliary to serve the refreshments and run bake sales." More laughter. Another asks, "Would we like somebody to be the Horned God?" Several shake their heads. The consensus is that the group will not admit men in the foreseeable future.

The one who had joined the group most recently looks around and says, "I've been with you only a few times, but I want you all to know I think it feels right. You never seemed like strangers to me even when you were. Right away it felt like coming home, like you were family. I don't think I could have felt that way if there were men in the group." All nod their heads. They understand.

They discuss political actions they plan to take, work to be done with other groups, books they are reading, individual projects for women's causes. Some have written articles. Some are circulating petitions, arranging women's community programs, or serving on planning boards. They encourage each other's interests. They talk little about men.

One says, "I skipped dinner tonight. I'm hungry. Let's eat." They produce paper plates, napkins, cups, bottles of fruit juice and soda. Food is brought into the circle. They sit on the floor and eat, with laughter and animated conversation. They are comfortable together.

Three of the dishes are especially admired, so their recipes are collected for a group cookbook. When the remains of the food are cleared away, the women stand up and join hands in their circle around the candlelit altar. They breathe in unison. One says, "We have shared food. What each of us prepared is now becoming part of all the others. We feed each other. We are unified."

After a silence one offers to do a guided meditation. All sit cross-legged around the circle and link their little fingers together. They close their eyes. The speaker continues softly.

"Imagine that we are inside the Holy Mountain, which rises all around us in the form of an invisible pyramid with four triangular sides. Remember the triangle as a female symbol and the sigil of the Triple Goddess. A sacred river flows down each face of the Holy Mountain, the four rivers of paradise. On the south the river is blue, filled with sapphire and lapis lazuli. It is the water of love. I call on the beautiful Blue Goddess of the southern river, the mother of all flowings and mergings. Goddess, Mother, Queen, bless us and protect us in all our traveling. Blessed be."

All respond, "Blessed be."

"On the western face of the Holy Mountain, the river is fire and blood and lava and wine, red as rubies, the river of passion and abundant life spirit, the river of power. I call on the strong Red Goddess of the western river, mother of our inner fountains. Goddess, Mother, Queen, bless us and protect us in all our traveling. Blessed be."

All respond, "Blessed be."

"On the northern face of the Holy Mountain, the river is gold as the autumn harvest, a river of honey filled with amber and topaz, a golden stream of fulfillment, shining like all earth's riches. I call on the great Golden Goddess of the north, mother of the corn, the granary, and the treasure. Goddess, Mother, Queen, bless us and protect us in all our traveling. Blessed be."

All respond, "Blessed be."

"On the eastern face flows a river of milk filled with silver, diamonds, and crystals, sacred to the White Goddess of death and rebirth, who carried souls into the air as pale ghosts awaiting the next life. I call on her whose hair is white feathers, whose face is brilliant as snow, mother of the dead and unborn. Goddess, Mother, Queen, bless us and protect us in all our traveling. Blessed be."

All respond, "Blessed be."

"At the summit of the Holy Mountain is our power, raised as we come together, as the peak of any pyramid is raised by the coming together of its faces. We create this focus. We are under it. Let the image of the Holy Mountain lend us strength, clarity, and fidelity to one another."

All recite together, "Merry meet, and merry part, and merry meet again." They release each other's fingers. One says, "The circle is open but unbroken." All answer, "Blessed be."

The women stand and put their arms around each other's shoulders for a brief moment. Then they collect their dishes, coats, and candlesticks, and go out one by one into the night. Each makes a little bow toward the full moon. They get into their cars and drive away, once more transformed into ordinary modern housewives and working women, filled with ordinary concerns. Yet each retains a small, steady, sustaining core of calm, like a candle in the center of a room.

They will meet again in another 28 days.

Elemental Invocations

Women's groups and witches' covens often begin their meetings by casting a circle around themselves, invoking the four elements—earth, air, fire, and water—while facing the four directions in turn. Of course these are not the real elements but they were so identified by early civilizations from Egypt to the North Sea, from Greece to the Ganges, from Peru to the Pacific Northwest, for many thousands of years.

The elements may be represented by a potted plant or clay vessel for earth, a feather or a fan for air, a burning candle for fire, a chalice of water for water. The same elements are symbolized in Tarot decks by the four suits of pentacles, swords, wands, and cups, and in ordinary playing card decks by their modern derivatives, diamonds, spades, clubs, and hearts. Cards, pictures, or any other objects of suggesting "elemental" characteristics may be used. Some groups create a highly formal, dramatic ceremony of invocation with movement, color, and emotional impact. Invocation of the elements carries more ancient, universal associations than any mainstream religious ceremony, because the idea is so old that its origin is lost in prehistory.

The real source of the idea lies in the oldest human beliefs about the spirits of the dead, namely, that they have passed into the environment and have become part of the living biosphere surrounding their descendants. *Spirit* means "ghost" or "soul." The earliest theory about souls of the dead held that the souls were absorbed into the same medium (or element) that consumed the body and became part of that element. Our foremothers taught our forefathers to feel both divinity and sentience in earth because of the ancestors buried in it, in fire because of the cremated ones, in water because of those given to boat funerals or sea burial, and in air because the dead were sometimes exposed to carrion birds, as in Indian tree burials or in the topless funerary "towers of silence" built by the ancient Persians to receive the dead and give them to the vultures.

The theory that the dead live as environmental spirits passed into alchemy and was enshrined by Hellenic philosophers, who received ideas from the traditions of Sumer and Babylon; formed the basis of medieval alchemy and mysticism; and helped to generate the idea of the four elemental humors of the body, the foundation of all medical practice up to the beginning of the nineteenth century.

There are still many who ignorantly believe these four to be real elements, despite instruction about the periodic table in every high school science course. It is more realistic as well as more meaningful, however, to view them as our foremothers did thousands of years ago: that is, as both physical and symbolic answers to the eternal question of where the dead have gone. Those who place no credence in heaven or hell may yet find themselves responding, on some level, to these much older traditions in feeling a sense of unity with past lives, such as our foremothers felt when addressing the elemental spirits. Medieval Europe later characterized these as gnomes (earth), salamanders (fire), undines (water), and sylphs (air).

The antiquity and universality of the elemental theory stem from the primacy of the Goddess, who was always the Mother-creator of the elements. The theory also explains the confusing interchangeability of natural and supernatural entities in all religious beliefs, including modern ones. There have never been any clear-cut distinctions among ghosts, souls, spirits, ancestors, angels, demons, totems, sacrificial savior humans or savior animals, gods, genii, fetishes, fairies, revenants, avatars, incarnations, reincarnations, inspirations, possessions, druids and dryads, household sprites, or necromantic oracular communicants. Though all may seem different concepts, they have a way of sliding in and out of one another's forms like the shape shifters of old, as if people still maintained the ancient belief that divine elements permeate and animate every life of both nature and supernature.

For example, the world knows all the following common beliefs. A human body may be possessed by the devil, a god, or an oracular spirit, any of which can produce prophetic utterance, speak in tongues, or dance convulsively. One may have a guardian angel, sometimes conceived of as a dead ancestor; this descended from the Greek *daemon* or personal spirit, which later also branched out into the personal guardian demon or familiar, often appearing in animal form, such as the witch's black cat, which could also be an alternate form of the witch herself. Ghosts of dead ancestors can become angels in heaven, which in turn can become devils, as in the ubiquitous War In Heaven myth; devils, in turn, can repossess human bodies. Human ancestors may be deified to the status of gods; conversely, either gods or devils can be born in human bodies, like the

Christ and the Antichrist. With a change of earthly regime, the gods of one society become the demons of the next. An enemy's gods are one's own devils, and one's own gods are devils to the enemy. The Bible testifies to the ancient custom of carrying gods about for protection and victory in battle; early Hebrews used *teraphim,* holy relics or skulls of divinized ancestors, as their fetishes. Similar fetish worship has been carried out everywhere in Christian Europe throughout the centuries and continues to this day; it is called the cult of saints.

An ancestral soul may be reincarnated in a new human or animal body, or it may invisibly inhabit the environment. Both beliefs are common, especially in Asia. If worshiped, it may become a semidivine hero, a savior, or a god. If feared, it may become a *genius loci,* a local demon. A soul without any particular place to go may become a haunt or a vampire. Dead but not dead, it is sustained by the ghost's two elements of air (breath) and earth (body), yet lacks the animating elixir of blood, anciently supposed to combine the other two elements, fire and water.

The usual explanation for the primordial creation of blood was that a male fire spirit entered the female sea womb as a phallic lightning bolt to warm, redden, and energize the saltwater. An ancient matriarchal concept of this precious blood elixir had it that it was placed in the wombs of women by the hand of the Moon Mother so it might create new human forms as progeny. Later, male gods usurped female blood magic, claiming to make certain humans divinely immortal by means of their own blood, which conveyed the god's immortal spirit into the worshipers who ate it. Hence the common customs of sacrificing and ingesting the blood of either human or animal victims, who were understood to be deities in earthly form. Sometimes, as among the Jews and Hindus, the blood was set aside as the food of gods, because like vampires, they needed it in order to stay alive.

Even Christian baptism retains the ancient fire and water symbolism that once represented life-creating and life-sustaining uterine blood as a suggestion of spiritual rebirth. The baptismal font has always been referred to as the womb of Mary and has been consecrated in the same ancient pagan way by plunging a lit candle into the water. Thus the womb is said to be fecundated by sacred heavenly fire.

Sometimes there was supposed to be a fifth element, which the Romans called *quinta essentia* ("fifth essence," or "quintessence") and the Greeks called ether: a divine counterpart of earthly animating blood. More rarified than either air or fire, manifested mostly as light, ether was assumed to form the immaterial bodies of heavenly beings. These could be either deities or ancestral souls who had been placed in heaven to become stars, glowing with "ethereal" brilliance. Their bodies were therefore known as astral (starry). The pseudoscience of astrology arose from the belief that, like the dead everywhere, these celestial angelic ancestors made of star stuff knew all secrets and could reveal the future if properly approached. The concept of the astral body never really disappeared. Certain mystics still adduce it as a sort of semidetachable soul, which can wander away from the material body during dreams or trances or which might be envisioned as an aura.

The notion that stars and angels are made of ether also persisted long into the Christian era. Christian Gnostics claimed that Jesus was taken to heaven and given an ethereal star body by the Great Mother, Sophia, who had sent him to earth in the first place. The basic idea is still found in folklore. Angel and human remain interchangeable in such folk beliefs as a falling star is a soul coming down from heaven to be reborn in a human body. Such a star can be wished on, because any spirit in passage from one world to the other has magical and prophetic powers; it can foretell, redeem, or grant wishes. The early "Christs" and other saviors such as Tammuz, Osiris, Adonis, Orpheus, Heracles, and so on, were elevated to godhood only in their passage from life into death as sacrificial victims.

Men were so reluctant to abandon the idea of heavenly ether that even some nineteenth-century astronomers insisted that outer space must be filled with it, to account for the now outdated wave theory of light transmission. It is still called real by twentieth-century spiritualists, whose scientific knowledge tends to be minimal at best.

Aside from ether, the four basic elements provided a spirit world for preliterate people everywhere. For example, American Indians associated elemental/ancestral spirits with the four directions; these determined the orientation of camp, home place, and medicine wheel. Spirits of mothers and fathers remained in the environment surrounding their progeny, watching over everything. Sometimes the spirits entered into certain animals, plants, or artifacts in a particular way that invested them with *mana,* or magic power. This process could be facilitated or used, it was thought, by living people when the right rituals were employed.

Every move of the living person could represent an act of homage to the dead, who could also be a force of nature while they awaited reincarnation in another human or animal life. Every ceremony honored the ancestral/elemental souls of the environment, as a reminder that human beings themselves were only temporary ripples in the time stream of changing forms, whose basic components, however, were unalterable. Thus the people lived as integral parts of the ever-changing elemental biosphere with all its creatures and, of necessity, respected it. Had such a worldview been retained by our civilization, it would have had results very different from the Judeo-Christian idea that only man and woman could have an immortal soul (although at times even woman was said to lack one), and all the rest of nature was only soulless matter that God created for humanity to exploit.

Actually, even patriarchal religions inadvertently retained many details from the ancient system. No religion ever succeeded in eliminating all the elemental notions of perpetual interchange between material and spiritual worlds. Christians never really decided whether the souls of the dead could remain on earth as ghosts, revenants, demons, or possibly saints (who were supposed to hang about their relics to respond to prayers) or whether they departed directly to heaven, hell, or purgatory, and if so, when—immediately after death or after doomsday and the Last Judgment. They were never sure whether the physical body would be reconstituted in the life to come. They were never sure whether the dead could be called back to converse with the living; theologians usually denied this but necromancers and spirit mediums affirmed it. They are still unsure about demonic possession, a remarkably silly notion that ecclesiastics and their Bible took with the utmost seriousness for thousands of years. Many still think saints and gods live in holy statues or the dead live in their graves.

They are still unsure, even today, about whether their God is inherent in matter, part of the universe, or extraneous to it; able to inhabit a human body, like Jesus, having impregnated a woman without spermatozoa or not. The fundamental nature of every supernatural concept is still tied to the age-old idea of the elements and their ever-changing forms. In this area of human thought there is nothing consistent, nothing sure, nothing finally demonstrable or provable. All is opinion, and human opinions have always gravitated toward inextricable confusion between the mortal and the imaginary. The confusion betrays the fact that human beings make their deities out of collective imagining and then seek to project the result onto a reality that knows it not, in order to reinforce their vision. Millions have been killed because of a suspicion that they might disturb the collective vision. It would have been far better to leave the confusion alone, realizing that human psychology will inevitably view the world as poetic metaphor, which should never be mistaken for scientific truth. It will not add to human understanding of what is, but it may enrich humane understanding of what ought to be.

Keeping in mind, then, that elemental invocations are metaphoric rather than literal, we may tap the accreted significances of many centuries in responding to their overtones. The four classic elements are not real elements like oxygen, nitrogen, carbon, iron, zinc, phosphorus, hydrogen, gold, silver, manganese, or tin are; they are metaphors for the dissolution of the human being into its component atoms, constituting a way of recognizing continued existence in an utterly changed form or forms, as when the theory of the elements was originally conceived. This is not only the oldest theory about what becomes of the dead. In some ways it is still the best one: closer to the real world's actual events than any of the alternate theories since evolved by centuries of theological speculation. To remember our foremothers in connection with the environment that swallowed them up is by no means unrewarding.

Invoking earth we may remember all those once living, who

have passed into the soil; indeed, all those entities that made the soil out of their bodies, plant and animal as well as human. Like all other creatures we are part of Mother Earth. Our lives are supported and nurtured by her as every child's life is supported and nurtured by the mother. Eventually, Mother Earth takes us back into herself to use the dissolution of our substance to support and nurture other creatures. It is not organic or natural for us to bury our dead in impenetrable coffins, as the Egyptians tried to do to prevent the body from undergoing natural decay and becoming part of the soil's nutrients. Perhaps if we allowed our loved ones to become part of the environment, as the American Indians did, we might love our environment better. Contemplation of the earth principle was a prime source of matriarchy's cyclic concept of organic life, a concept that patriarchal religion categorically denied for two thousand years, even though modern science now confirms its basic correctness.

Invoking water we may remember all those swallowed up by rivers or seas, the ancient Celtic boat burials and Viking funerals known as the return to the womb. Others who perished by water were the many innocent women accused of witchcraft and drowned on the ducking stool. Water holds an irresistible attraction for us, whose bodies are 95 percent water and whose blood still tastes of the sea from which it came. Thales of Miletus and others named water the first of the elements, the medium of birth, the primal female deep existing before creation. The oldest Goddess bore many names of the sea, which was often called the womb of the world. Her element was used for baptismal or born-again rites many centuries before Christianity decided to copy them. It seems our prehistoric foremothers might have known something else that modern science now confirms: life first arose in the waters.

Invoking air we may remember those said to have become bodiless ghosts, the immortal self made of breath (Sanskrit *atman*), which ancient yogis desired to pass into a woman's body with a final kiss at the time of death, so they could be reconceived and born again. Similarly, carrion birds who ate the dead were called female spirits of the air, personified as Valkyries, sylphs, harpy angels, the vulture mothers of Egypt, and the bird goddesses of Neolithic Europe. Sometimes all the birds were thought to be transformed human souls. Ghosts and birds rode the winds and knew the airs of heaven, so birds were often consulted as oracles, and the cosmic Oversoul was said to consist of air.

Invoking fire we may remember a million years of cremations, whose rising flame and smoke were thought to carry souls to the heavens of light, the spheres of sun and moon. As women we should also not forget the 9 million of our foremothers burned alive at the hands of the male God's pious servants. Joan, the maid of Orleans. Manfreda, the woman who would have been pope. Margherita di Trank, said to have borne a child by the Holy Ghost. Marian Cumlaquoy, who only turned herself widdershins (counterclockwise). Rebecca Lemp, Catherine Delort, Anna Marie de Georgel: healers, housewives, mothers. And the millions unnamed. Even in our own century: women who went into the ovens at Auschwitz, Dachau, Buchenwald, Treblinka. Women dying in the fires of Hiroshima and Nagasaki, London and Essen and Cologne, not to mention the pitiful villages of Korea and Vietnam; innocent women and children killed by all the fires of men's wars. Women may be roused to passionate action by the knowledge of fire as warmth and light, the blessing of civilization, turned into a curse by civilization's misuse of it.

Finally, we should remember the metaphor of the center: the maternal hearth fire, for which the Latin word was *focus:* the meeting place of the four elemental directions and of past and future, where spirits of tribal mothers gathered to watch over their clans. We should remember that the idea of the elements arose in the beginning from a feminine sense of the oneness of all things, human and inanimate, from the feeling that we all partake of the same nature, the same components, united through the ages by the birth-giving blood bond. As in the past and always, the center is where the women are.

The center is holy; it is the Self. The Self is where divinity lives, because divinity has no other home.

People, places, or things become holy only when human words declare them to be so. We are always ready to consecrate what we find individually or collectively meaningful. We project

reverence or respect toward objects that have no inherent usefulness on the basis of emotional cues that tell us what to feel.
Simple examples of this process are shown by ceremonial clothing: royal robes, ecclesiastical vestments, military uniforms. Respect is given to the costume rather than to the person inside
it, who is really an actor in theatrical garb that defines the character.

In the same way, a plaster statue of Jesus may be revered
by the faithful, even though it may be inferior in esthetic merit.
Though churches have always tried to bind the best available
artistic talents to their service, still a good deal of ecclesiastical
art is crude or tasteless. No matter; the pious will respond as
if it were a Michelangelo as long as they are given to understand that it is holy.

Men's words create holiness. Holy water is usually just tap
water with certain words having been spoken over it. Holy medals are ordinary metal thought to have been mysteriouisly en-
hanced by words that convert them into fetishes. Holy altars
are ordinary constructions consecrated by words that purport
to attract the attention of God. So it goes with every sacred
thing, even when the object itself is a deliberate fraud, such as
thousands of fake saints' relics that burden Europe's cathedrals
with the bones of pigs and goats, old shreds of unidentifiable
cloth, and decayed human teeth, hair, and mummified fingers
of unknown origin and unbelievable legends.

Speeches that consecrate the four directions, the four corners of the earth, and the corresponding four pseudoelements
are no less valid than speeches that make bread, wine, water,
bone, or stone into holy objects. Indeed, our world would be
better served by consecration of the natural environment, after
the manner of American Indian and other primitive religions.
To consider nature a holy repository of ancestral spirits, inter-
changing and interacting with living humanity at all points, is
to develop new respect for what we should have respected all
along: the priceless legacy of the terrestrial Mother, on whom
the lives of our own and all other species depend.

Alas, we have polluted earth, water, and air alike. We have
even polluted the fire that used to be seen as purification by
burning dangerous chemicals and setting off hideous explo-

sions. We have befouled the elements that ancient Stoic philosophers worshiped as the divine *stoicheia,* the building blocks of the universe. This is the sin of men against Nature. Perhaps one day Nature will exact a fearful retribution, which men will be forced to carry out against themselves.

Yes, let the elements be honored, before it is too late.

Out Of Body

It has become increasingly clear that what is popularly called an out-of-body experience is by no means uncommon. This inner adventure used to be considered bizarre, mysterious, or restricted to a few special people said to be either psychically gifted or crazy, depending on one's point of view. Yet it seems accessible to many, if not most, people under certain conditions.

Perfectly ordinary folks have reported the experience in circumstances of severe illness or injury, a passing brush with death. Children have been describing the experience for years, though they usually discover that their elders are either bored or disturbed by such fantasies and so encourage them to repress them. More and more people, however, now study Asian techniques of meditation or trance that conduce to the out-of-body experience.

Ancient mystics who invented these techniques believed that their souls traveled to distant places, leaving their uninhabited bodies behind. Perhaps what really happens in such an experience is both simpler and more complicated than that. It may represent yet another fascinating glimpse into the fathomless depths of the human mind.

A psychological phenomenon that has been so often described surely deserves recognition by those who call themselves psychological scientists, even though they tend to avoid what they can't handily explain. Dreams can't be handily explained either, yet dreams have to be recognized, because everyone can dream. Lesser but still significant numbers of people are spontaneous visionaries and visual fantasists, well able when awake to see "things that aren't there," clearly and in great detail, without impairment of their sanity. Most graphic artists have this knack, but psychology still doesn't quite know what to make of art.

For millennia shamans, prophets, and other mystics have viewed the soul journey as an essential prerequisite to personal enlightenment. Founders of religions almost always have such an episode featured in their legends. Buddha left his body under the bo tree and traveled beyond space and time to discover his life work. Mohammed claimed to be guided by the angel Gabriel on his famous Night Journey, riding the flying horse of the moon—which innumerable mythic seers had ridden before him. A sojourn in the otherworld, the underworld, the heavens, the western paradise, or the land of the dead is central to the story of nearly every known savior god, hero, visionary, or saint: Orpheus, Osiris, Dionysus, Adonis, Tammuz, Vishnu, Aeneas, Odin, Heracles, Jesus, Taliesin, Thomas Rhymer, the Areopagite, St. Theresa, and Dante, to name only a few.

I can't place myself in such legendary company, but I too am used to the out-of-body experience, having slid into it easily more times than I can count. I offer a subjective description, which is our only handle so far on this particularly interesting aspect of psychological introspection, which may be as universally realized as the great archetypes.

My memory (faulty creature) insists positively that I have traveled unthinkably far through interstellar and even intergalactic space and have seen things never before viewed by human eyes. Such memories are as clear as any others—clearer than most, in fact—and seem to be as broadening as any real travels.

During these experiences my physical body has been comfortable; not sick, not injured, not comatose or near death. For me the trigger is usually music coupled with a certain floating, serene, contemplative mood. The music should be melodic but unobtrusive. I've had results with Debussy, Sibelius, Mahler, Richard Strauss, Ralph Vaughan Williams, Kitaro, and some of the more evocative cinema sound tracks.

Of course the experience is always unpredictable. A certain passage of music may stimulate it once but then never again. Or a different, familiar passage, which never stimulated it before, may suddenly do so. The mood must be just right, but what the components of its just-rightness may be, I can't say. Nothing seems accessible to conscious control. The experience always takes me by surprise and each time seems to be the first time. The sense of wonder is never diminished.

I move away from myself, not gradually, but with the speed of thought: that which the ancients called the fastest pace in the universe, far outstripping the speed of light. Sometimes I see my home planet receding behind me into the depths of space; sometimes not. My home planet seems to have virtually no significance in the cosmic scheme. It is a mere dust mote, a particle, an atom lost in emptiness. Even its native sun is a small fifth-rate star soon vanishing in vast, cold gulfs of ultimate darkness.

I am singularly alone.

The universe around me is splendid with sights I would never normally conceive. There are giant explosive suns, luminous gas clouds light years in diameter, flights of great dark planets, swarms of drifting objects so far apart that their distances couldn't be encompassed in all the billions of years elapsed since the birth of my home planet. I am at a different place in time also. Everything I know has disappeared either into the future or into the past. All I perceive is completely alien on a scale far beyond any possible human comprehension.

I, the perceiver, comprehend it only because I am no longer human. Alone now for eternity, I have no body, no mind. I exist as nothing more than a pattern of energy able to travel through these dark immensities where nothing material could survive. I see, but I have no eyes. I respond to what I see, but I have no nerves with which to respond. I don't feel cold, but I am aware that the space around me is colder than any earthly thought of coldness.

Certain things threaten my entity. A close approach to a star is terrifying. From several million miles away in space, almost any star is a holocaust of violence beyond violence, a vast oven of devouring explosiveness where matter and energy are indistinguishable. I wonder how it can possibly hang together. I think it would destroy me if I were sucked into it. I have no control over this. I drift in space like a jellyfish in water. I can never choose a destination.

Sometimes I visit planets in other, distant solar systems. The landscapes there are indescribable. There are colors like no other colors I have ever seen. Even the geometry is strange. Though I see traces of artificial structures, I never see any other living thing. I am always alone. I know I will always be alone. This doesn't particularly distress me; it's just the way it is. I am neither blissful nor unhappy. My emotions simply don't fit human terms.

Neither does my intellectual comprehension fit human terms. For example, I neither see, nor need to look for, any limits to it all. My universe holds no end, nor even a concept of an end, but it is equally devoid of the concept of endlessness. It defies all categories and descriptions. It just *is*. Human language could never find words to correspond with this existence. All human ideas lose meaning.

With all this alienation and detachment, still I am very much rooted in my own physical being on earth. I don't lose contact with reality. In real time I remain alert, awake, normally conscious. I know where I am. I am not dreaming or entranced. If someone speaks to me, I immediately shake off the vision and return to an ordinary state of mind. And yet, so rich is the vision that I am often reminded of things I have seen "out there," just as one receives flashes of real memories through passing colors, shapes, or sounds. With the reminder comes a dim, momentary spark of the same odd, alien, detached but receptive state of mind.

From a subjective point of view, I could convince myself that some indefinable part of me went wandering in space and time, forever alone and dehumanized to a condition of weird, alien glory. From a more objective point of view, I am sure that the most creative part of my mind has put it all together for me without my conscious participation in any way except one: that is, my education in my own culture's current understanding of the universe, a peculiar mixture of science and science fiction. Therefore, unlike a majority of mystics, I can't find the out-of-body experience true for myself or anyone else, despite its amazing vividness. Its building blocks are obviously not facts but thoughts. Descriptions handed down from ancient societies show that each individual out-of-body traveler sees what his or her contemporary culture expects to see. Followers of the Osirian Mysteries rose into a heaven with trees and rivers in the sky and golden halls and meadows of the gods, without leaving the sight of earth far below. Early Christian mystics such as St. Paul were caught up into one or another of the concentric planetary spheres that represented the prevailing erroneous picture of the heavens in their time, and they conversed with angels. Dante visited the kinds of hell, purgatory, and paradise that his contemporaries would have expected. Hindu yogis achieve the same kind of oneness with the infinite Atman that they have been led to expect. In the out-of-body state Christian believers can see Jesus; pagans can see the Great Goddess; Jews may attain comprehension of the Shekina; and Moslems may feel themselves united with Allah. It makes little difference. We become our own kind of god and find him or her or it within the most unpredictable part of the mind.

The point is, no one sees reality. No soul traveler ever perceived the true nature or distance of sun, moon, or stars before they were discovered in the real world. What I see in the depths of space-time is not what truly exists there, but what I suppose to exist. There is no humanness about it, because none of the facts I learned have ever led me to expect any.

Still, I'm glad to have a mind capable of putting together such wonders for me. Sometimes I feel a sense of privilege, just as both ancient and modern mystics believe themselves set apart by their visionary ability from the common run of humanity and even manage to awe the rest of humanity into believing the same. But I suspect the soul journey is less rare and impressive than most people think. Humanity has recorded endless variations on the waking dream, the courting of vision through meditation, trance, fasting, drugs, or physical exercises. Given appropriate conditions, almost anyone can do it. It's only a matter of finding the right combination of circumstances.

The phenomenon has never been adequately studied, because its essence is subjectivity. We don't know how to study the subjective. Most investigators tend to wave it away into those areas of psychological limbo embraced by faith or occultism. Yet as a human phenomenon, it deserves as much attention as any other human phenomenon. There must be some meaning in it, because anyone who approaches it tends to perceive it as profoundly meaningful. It is primitive in the sense that it is created by a primitive part of the mind from materials donated by the more advanced parts.

Is it useful as prophecy, insight, inspiration, genius, or as a guide to behavior? Maybe. I don't know. Certainly some people have believed it radically altered their lives. It never altered mine, because it seems too far away and unrelated to anything mundane. But because it is so difficult to describe and impossible to picture, I can well understand the Asian sages who said, "Those who know the Way don't speak of it; those who speak of the Way don't know it."

Past Lives

The ubiquitous Eastern doctrine of reincarnation has become a staple of certain Western occult traditions, some of which even make a practice of describing people's past lives. Among those who do this are psychics who claim to have acquired their powers while serving as priests or priestesses in ancient Egypt, Babylon, or even that never-never land Atlantis, all of which they can "remember" with the utmost clarity. Lovers are sometimes encouraged to think their mutual attraction first arose centuries ago in previous lives. Strangers who take an immediate liking to one another may believe their rapport began with a close relationship in past incarnations. Conversely, instant dislike is sometimes said to stem from hostile interactions in a former life.

In addition, many Westerners have adopted the Tantric

concept of karma as a way of accounting for the apparent injustices of this world. If the innocent suffer, it is because they committed unknown crimes in a previous life. Animals may be viewed as reincarnations of humans or vice versa. Almost all the various implications of the world's oldest notions of earthly rebirth after death are still alive and well today, somewhere.

I don't number myself among the believers, though I have had several of the same kinds of experiences that believers adduce as incontrovertible evidence of past lives. One of the most vivid of my apparent preexistences offers to my mind's eye and memory a girlhood during the late nineteenth century in Vienna—a city I have never yet visited. On what basis do I identify the city as Vienna? Nothing definite. I only know it as one knows things in dreams and as children know what they are told.

Nevertheless, I remember Vienna as clearly and perfectly as I remember the girlhood of my own life in the present. It seems I was the petted child of a cultured, well-to-do family. I lived in a four-story stone house on a quiet street, with six front steps and a tiny dooryard with flowerbeds behind a knee- high wrought-iron railing. The front door had a carved fanlight and large glass panels veiled by a starchy white curtain. The interior of the house was full of heavy, dark mahogany furniture and paneling, potted plants, patterned rugs, and tatted, crocheted, embroidered, or lacework mats and runners on everything.

My mother and father I saw mostly at meals, seated at opposite ends of a big dining table covered with a thick cream-colored linen cloth. I remember a time in my life when I was too inexperienced to control my eating utensils, and so my place was covered by a double layer of coarse woven stuff with a ruffle around the edges to protect the tablecloth from my spills. The table's legs were fat, polished, and carved in fanciful shapes, including odd gnomelike faces within wreaths of wooden leaves. Like all children, I had particularly clear impressions of the lower parts of the furniture.

My daily attendant was not my mother but a live-in nurse, who always wore a long-sleeved blue-and-white striped cotton gown, which resembled bed ticking. Over this she wore a white pinafore apron. She had pockmarks on her cheeks. I don't recall her name (nor, for that matter, my own or my parents' name).

When I saw my nurse putting on her black wool coat and hat, I used to get excited, because it usually meant that we would go for an outing. We would walk in the streets or drive in a carriage behind two fat bay horses whose round rumps gleamed like mirrors as they bobbed along. We would pass the great river with its ornate bridges, broad fountained plazas, great stone palaces, and buildings such as the opera house, covered with fascinating sculpture.

An outing would finish up at a café, where we would sit at a tiny white table on the sidewalk and eat amazing confections piled high with whipped cream. I loved whipped cream. So did my nurse. She would plop great spoonfuls of it into her coffee. Many of these memories involve sweet foods, cakes and candies of all descriptions, which overflowed on every holiday and birthday, as well as figuring largely in the daily diet. No one ever hinted that such things might be fattening.

My parents sometimes gave parties, and food and wine and rich desserts poured forth from the kitchen, which was a dark little dungeon of a place on the floor below ground level (though I don't remember finding out until much later that old European houses often had kitchens below ground level). For several days before each party, my mother closely supervised the servants' work in the kitchen amid a general air of excitement. I enjoyed the bustle and constantly got underfoot, until I was ordered to leave.

When my parents gave musical evenings, I would sneak out of bed in my long white flannel nightgown and stand behind the balustrade at the top of the stairs, where I could hear the harmonies of piano, harp, violins, and, I think, flutes. There would be two or three dozen people seated on small gilt chairs facing the performers in the library. I distinctly recall that one evening there was a large group, and several people had to be seated near the hall doorway within my view. I saw a graceful lady in a long black satin dress adorned with black feathers and bugle beads. Several jet necklaces poured down her bosom. Jet earrings dangled from her ears. She wore white feathers in her hair and long white kid gloves on her arms. She carried a black feather fan with a jeweled handle. I thought she was the most elegant creature I had ever seen.

My memories of the house and my life within it are about what one would expect a child to remember: intensely detailed flashes with little continuity and no clear comprehension of adult existence. Apparently the life was a childhood only. I never grew up. I seem to have sickened and died at an early age.

I remember long tedious stretches of living continuously in bed under a huge eiderdown quilt that felt oppressively heavy. In one corner of my room there was a rocking horse with the head of a swan instead of a horse. I looked at it constantly, but seldom got out of bed to ride on it. I was visited by a solemn, ugly, side-whiskered doctor with a gold pocket watch in his waistcoat. I hated and feared him because he did unpleasant things to me, though he tried to distract me meanwhile by dangling his gold watch before my eyes.

I had toys to play with in bed. One of my favorites was a jointed wooden doll with red circles painted on her cheeks. But often I felt poorly, and my toys failed to give pleasure. Either my parents or my nurse would tell me stories about the heroes of old, the Nibelungen, the Rhinemaidens, trolls, fairies, swan knights and talking animals. I remember thinking that when I grew up, I would go to the famous rock in the Rhine river to see the water nymph who still lived there. But as I grew older I only wasted away by degrees, so the outings were fewer and the days in bed were longer. I don't remember dying, but the Viennese child never did become a woman.

When I visited Europe as an adult, I found myself frequently haunted by an odd, indefinable air of familiarity about things that should have seemed unfamiliar: the design of parks and streets, the glass doors and little dooryards of German and Swiss urban houses (I did not visit Austria). The food, the manners, the culture and tradition, the whole ambience seemed unwarrantedly familiar. The German language struck soothingly to my ear, even when I understood not a word of it. Somehow it seemed that I *ought* to understand it, and if I just listened a little harder its meaning would come clear.

In addition to this Viennese childhood, I have numerous

other pseudomemories of the sort that reincarnation buffs would pounce upon as evidence of past lives. Most are only fragments. A very old one features a section of yellow stone wall bathed in hot sunlight. Wearing a one-piece garment of white linen, I sit on powdery-dusty ground leaning against the wall, my hand resting on the cool, dewy shoulder of a clay jar full of water. I feel pervaded with calm happiness and well-being. In fact, anything that reminds me of that scene gives me a strange sense of inner peace.

Or again, I remember a spring or pool that I seem to have visited many times. It lies in a natural hollow of the ground at the foot of a white marble staircase. The water is cold and very still. It looks black, because no sunlight can touch it. The hollow is overhung by thick bushes, vines, and trees. A white marble rim runs all the way around the basin, its inner surface green-ish-black with a soft, wet mantle of algae. Opposite the stairs a marble statue of a faun with a vase pours a shimmering trickle of water into the pool. The atmosphere is one of summer's deep shade, all cool black, green, silver, with the music of falling water and the slightly shabby grace of a classical antiquity some-what neglected: the bushes untrimmed, the statue a bit chipped. Though I never saw it for real, it is a scene that I love to revisit.

Most pseudomemories match these descriptions: that is, they tend to be intensely detailed and vivid, but random, ar-bitrary, isolated from context. None of us know what such impressions mean. They are just *there*, part of the old furniture in the attic of the mind, which may store its detritus much less purposefully than modern psychologists believe. How can one describe pseudomemories? Bits of the inner drama, stage sets created for a play never enacted, shards of dreams whose or-igins were forgotten, passing thoughts hooked out of the stream of consciousness and incongruously varnished like stuffed fish on a plaque before being consigned to that mental attic.

I don't for a moment doubt the human brain's ability to create any number of "past lives" in rich detail and immense credibility without even bothering to inform its owner of the working of the creative process. After all, we can even solve problems and create artworks in our sleep. The unconscious never ceases to reshuffle and redeal our mental card decks to present us with fresh arrangements. We take for granted the lavish visionary powers that enable some of us to create stories, novels, drama, sagas, and all other kinds of fiction out of next to nothing. Why should we doubt our own creative potential? False memory or *deja vu* is common enough, and mythmaking in every possible permutation and combination is what the human mind does best.

And then, what it does next best is to believe.

Mortality

"If you don't believe in God," my friend asked, "What do you suppose will happen to you after you die?"

"Nothing," I said. "Happening implies existence. What can happen to a person who doesn't exist?"

I saw her struggling with the concept, trying to put her mind around it and failing. To some people, personal nonexistence is simply incomprehensible. "But *something* of you will go on," she said solemnly.

"What makes you think so?"

"It just doesn't make sense that life should be meaningless."

"I didn't say life is meaningless. I think life is full of meaning, good and bad. It's death that's meaningless, at least for the dead person, simply because there is no more mind to invent or perceive meanings."

"Then you don't think some part of you can survive after death?"

"What part? My mind, my personality, my soul, my self, whatever you want to call it, is my brain's functioning, just as music is the functioning of the musical instrument. Where is the music after the instrument is destroyed? Where am I after my brain is dissolved? Where was I before I was born—nowhere."

"I wouldn't want to think that way," she said. "It seems terrifying."

"To me it seems much less terrifying than the eternal torture that Christian authorities say God has prepared for the vast majority of human beings. Pain terrifies me, not death. I think it would be really unbearable to have to believe in that traditional hell."

"Yes, but what about heaven?" she asked. "Wouldn't you like to think of spending eternity in a completely happy place?"

"Sure, I'd like it," I said, "But improbable things don't become probable just because it's something I'd like. Furthermore, in all the descriptions of heaven that I've read—and there have been many—not one ever made it sound like a place where I could be happy."

She looked shocked. "Why do you say that?"

"Well, think about it. How do *you* picture heaven?"

"I see it as a lot of beautiful light and music and peace and singing praises and people feeling joyous because they're able to look at God directly. It must be a place more beautiful than anything we can imagine." She gave me a small smile. "I guess that's pretty traditional, isn't it?"

"Exactly. If something is more beautiful than anything I can imagine, then obviously I'm not going to imagine it. Therefore it can have no meaning for me. In regard to the traditional ideas, I'd be intolerably bored by spending all eternity in a blaze of light, singing praises to a God of whom I've never even approved. I'd be climbing the walls in a week, let alone eternity."

She laughed a bit nervously. "Then what would be your idea of a happy heaven?"

"One that included all the things that have made me happy in my experience. Sunshine, colors, tastes, music, trees, warm furry animals, blowing wind, mountain landscapes. Love. Laughter. Friendship. Things like that. Sensual things. Feelings of good health and strength of body. Satisfaction of my curiosity."

"Well, maybe heaven is for each person the very things he or she likes best."

"That's a nice thought, but equally improbable. The things I like best are quite earthly and perceptible through the senses, which a dead person no longer has. Anyway, traditional views of heaven insist that sensual enjoyments are inimical to it—except for certain Eastern heavens made up by and for men, who can spend all their time there copulating with gorgeous female angels."

She gave an ironic snicker. "The male fantasy to the letter, huh? But how can you stand the idea of dying if you think that's just the end of you and there's nothing more?"

"It's not a pleasant idea, but it's bearable. I believe the real ingratitude, or hubris, or conceit lies with those people who think life worthless if it can't last forever. To become conscious at all is a precious, wonderful piece of luck. It shouldn't be belittled or regretted just because it has a finite beginning and end. In fact, I think we would respect life more if we understood its brevity and uniqueness."

"Then you don't think there's any ultimate meaning to life?"

"Why should life need a meaning outside of itself? Nature doesn't deal in meanings; it just *is*. To the entity living it, life is either worth living or it's not. If your life holds enough of the satisfactions you crave, either for yourself or for others whom you affect, then it has good meanings. If not, not."

"How about the good people who never manage to get any satisfaction from their lives because of bad circumstances, even though they do the best they can?"

"That's sad, of course. Also sad are the people who have every advantage and still can't be contented. It's sad that our lives are seldom long enough to suit us. Lots of things are sad. Deep down, most people know this. When death comes, they say it's too late, because they know that's the end of possibilities. But officially, our culture denies this."

"Don't you think those denials might be based on some perception of truth?"

"I think they're based on fear. According to William Gibson, from the time we first recognize death, some fear of it is in every brain 'like a fretful grain of sand, and around it man has created many pearls of wisdom, mostly false.' Look at the enormous power of self-delusion in those early Christians who didn't believe any of their elect would die at all, because the Gospels promised that Judgment Day would come first. So when Christians died, survivors insisted that they were only asleep, even when their bodies rotted."

"I grant you, there's been a lot of silliness perpetrated on this subject. Yet maybe there's a basic truth somewhere in the traditions. Deathbed conversions are notorious. How do you know even you might not change your mind when death is staring you in the face, and maybe you'll see something you don't see now?"

"I'm 99 percent sure I won't change my mind as long as I'm still sane. I'm afraid of dying because I think it will probably hurt, but I'm not afraid of being dead. Oblivion doesn't scare me. After all, I've gone through periods of living oblivion every night of my life. Who remembers what a dreamless sleep feels like? It's just nothing. That's not scary."

"But it's so final. Never again to feel or know anything at all. Doesn't that bother you?"

"Of course it bothers me. That's why I want to appreciate every day of my life as much as I can, to enjoy my consciousness while I have it. It bothers me that the world will go on showing sunsets that I'll never see, and people will write good books that I'll never read, and whatever descendants I have will live lives of which I'll never be aware. But there's nothing I can do about it. I live as I can and wait."

"Religious folks would say there is something you can do about it. You can be saved."

"*Saved* is another one of those words, like *meaning*, that are never defined. Meaning what? Saved from what? If there is no heaven, then being saved won't put me there. Obviously, no one is literally saved from dying. It would be sort of fun to wander around the world as an invisible ghost and watch what goes on in the future, but that's only a primitive fantasy. So what sort of actual saving does religion offer?"

"I guess the usual belief is that saved souls can live on, in another place, in a better life than this one, because they believed what the church taught."

"Which church? They all teach different things. Anyway, that always struck me as a peculiar bargain. What it really means is that you support the church financially, and in return the church gives you a more or less indefinable promise, which no one has ever been able to verify nor ever will. Some contract. The church gets much the better part of the bargain, trading mere words for hard cash. If an individual acts like that, it's a crime, and the person's a con artist."

"Maybe the point is that what you believe can affect what happens to you after death."

"That's just another way of saying whatever you can imagine must come true, just because you imagine it. This is the universal delusion of the admittedly imaginative human animal, who, after all, has always created gods in the human image, and demons too. Still, one's thoughts alone can hardly affect any real postmortem events. Believers, disbelievers, semibelievers, all are subject to the same laws of life, death, and decomposition."

"That's so, from a materialistic viewpoint. But maybe there's another viewpoint based on different facts."

"If so, I've never seen such facts demonstrated, nor even clearly stated. The nonmaterialistic believers tend to get tangled up in ideas they can't express without circular reasoning and assertions that they can't demonstrate. Death is eminently demonstrable, but any similarly objective indication of life after death has always had to be faked."

"Are you saying all religious authorities lie?"

"No, I'm sure many of them are sincere. But many others, probably the smartest ones, realize that it's just another business, running on hype and public credulity. They may rationalize their insincerity by telling themselves it's good for people to believe, that people need it or want it and can't be happy without it; therefore even ecclesiastical lies can serve good purposes. I'm not convinced, however, that a majority of people need to build their happiness on such a shifty foundation. I know I'd rather be told what's really happening than live in a fool's paradise, which is what most paradises seem to be. I mistrust clerics who claim all dying people want the hope of an afterlife to comfort them. It's been shown that many clerics, like many doctors, fail to pay attention to what dying people want. Trying to block out their own fear of death makes them inexcusably insensitive."

She looked thoughtful. "That's true," she said. "When my

mother was dying of cancer, she told everybody around her—including the doctor and the minister—that her only wish was to die immediately. In fact, she talked of nothing else. We all contradicted her. No one listened, no one took her seriously, no one tried to help her do what she wanted. Instead, we let her suffer horribly. I've always felt guilty about that."

"Our whole society should feel guilty about that. Again, it began with a rule made by the medieval Christian church for its own self-aggrandizement. Suicide was declared a mortal sin to prevent those accused of heresy from killing themselves before the inquisitors got to them, and if they did it anyway, to give the Inquisition an excuse to take their property away from their heirs. There are still legal remnants of this inhuman system. It's especially inexcusable nowadays, when a painless death could be easily provided for anyone who requested it. We'll do it for our pets but not for our relatives."

"Yes, there's a lot of hypocrisy surrounding the whole subject," she said slowly. "I've often felt that, but I've never been able to articulate it. Maybe most of us are afraid to even talk about death, because the very words might somehow magically bring it on."

"Quite so," I said. "People have always given their own words more credit for affecting external reality than words deserve. Not only magic charms were based on this notion, but all the invocations, evocations, prayers, blessings, curses, exorcisms, and the alleged power of the Logos. Even extreme unction—supposedly the only essential attention to the dying—was only a matter of words. The priesthoods were always pretending to talk their gods into or out of everything by torrents of verbal arguments and appeals, even commands—for man has always secretly thought himself capable of issuing orders to God."

"Well, that may work, if your idea is correct, because it means that man is just issuing orders to himself after all."

"Granted. But why not address the words to the only ears that really hear them instead of filtering them through an abstract object of belief that few people can perceive well, even when it's been described to them all their lives?"

"I don't know. Maybe we try to put things at one remove from ourselves, so we don't have to deal with them directly."

"That's typical of patriarchal religions. Haven't you noticed how men often avoid dealing directly with our crude biological realities?"

"You're right," she said. "It's always the women who change the diapers, tend the sick, wash off the puke, and clean up the messes. I guess women weren't as frightened by the idea of natural biological decline as men were. Women do make room in their experience for life's down side."

"So did matriarchal religion, as you might expect. Like the Indian Goddess, Kali Ma, the Destroying Crone. This aspect of the Goddess was ugly and scary because she represented approaching death. Yet the process of enlightenment in her devotee wasn't complete until she or he mastered this ultimate revelation of her. As Death, she must be adequately grasped, understood, and accepted. So the rituals celebrating the Crone were held in places of death, such as cemeteries and cremation grounds."

"Wasn't that supposed to be a custom of witches too?"

"Yes. There's reason to think that some, at least, of the medieval witches were only carrying on pagan rites in honor of the same Crone under some of her Western names such as Cerridwen, Skadi, Morgan, Hecate, or Kalma—'Kali Ma,' you see. The nonlinear view of the universe seems natural to women. Where time and space are always cyclic, life and death could be accepted equally as parts of the whole or temporary eddies in the stream of time. So there couldn't be any we or they, saints or sinners, souled humans as distinguished from nonsouled animals. All were part of the same power that our foremothers called Goddess. The patriarchs hated the Goddess, and, by extension, women, because the lives they gave birth to were doomed to death. Men wanted to live forever. They couldn't accept biological reality. Hence the myth of female sinfulness, supposed to have brought death into the world as a result of Eve's original offense."

"But that really made God responsible for death, didn't it? According to the book of Genesis, it was God who threw Adam and Eve out of Eden before they could discover the fruit of immortality. He didn't want them to be like him and live forever."

"That's right. Another expression of the typically patriarchal blame-the-victim attitude, like the husband who beats his wife and says it's her fault for annoying him. The patriarchs and church fathers unanimously blamed Eve for the existence of death and held God innocent of the whole thing. They even made God reverse his ruling later and admit some humans to the immortality he originally denied them, provided the people on earth killed his son with remarkable cruelty. Don't smile, I know it doesn't make sense. But men have managed to convince themselves that it does."

She laughed. "It is silly when you think about it, isn't it? How do you suppose the whole religious idea could be revised to do away with the silliness and make clearer pictures of reality so we can deal more directly with the world's problems?"

"All my life," I said, "I have hungered for a church I could attend in good conscience without leaving my intelligence on the doorstep; a divine image I could relate to without betraying my femaleness; a morality of which I could approve, without compromising my standards; and a symbol that could point the way to a peaceful world, a world where people could trust one another, a world without fear. I think such a world lies beyond the comprehension of our present patriarchal, militaristic, violent society, which has been bred to such notions as sex equals sin and death and only men can make the rules. I think a new version of Goddess religion is sorely needed, not only to help people face death with dignity, but also to teach people what it means to be responsible for one another."

Her eyes took on a faraway look. "Yes, I think there are many women who yearn for that," she said, "even some who can barely envision it and hardly understand what's wrong. Most of them have never heard of the Goddess. Do you suppose they can learn about her and the ideas connected with her soon enough to make a difference?"

"It's worth hoping for," I said. "But I also hope it would mean an even more profound change in the way we think about spiritual matters: a change from the childish literalism that needs to envision a Parent Out There telling us what to do. I think intelligent humanity has outgrown that and is probably ready to recognize that all deities are symbols of the inner human mind, collectively perceived. I'm tired of hearing religious concepts addressed to only the lowest common denominator. I'm tired of *dumb* religion. I might be more accepting of religion in general if there were any intellectual stimulation in it. But the religion I grew up with, Christianity, the religion of my society, demands so much belief in the absurd that it insults my intelligence—not to mention my common sense."

"Some parts of the Bible are pretty unbelievable," she reflected.

"Surely. Fundamentalist types want everyone to attribute 'divine truth' to such rubbish as sticks turning into snakes, a river turning into blood, dry passages appearing through a sea, the sun moving backward, demons living in human bodies, animals and bushes speaking human language, food raining from heaven, cities falling flat at the sound of a horn, dry bones standing up and putting on living flesh, water turning into wine instantaneously, blind men cured with spit, virgins impregnated by spirits, words causing a tree to die instantly, and corpses rising from their grave. When anthropologists report such beliefs among primitive people, you can smile and dismiss them as quaint, benighted myths. But in our own so-called civilization, millions of people are expected to take such things literally as sacred history. This notion boggles my mind."

"It does seem foolish," she admitted. "How do you suppose they manage to preserve this literalism?"

"In one sense we're still living with remnants of the witch-hunting era, when unbelief was declared a crime punishable by the worst death anyone could imagine. The fear generated in those centuries is still with us, internalized, as unspoken and perhaps even unrealized taboos. Many of us are still children fearful of offending Big Daddy, who has the big stick. Then, churches have succeeded in brainwashing many into believing that every decent person must have a religion. Atheism is supposed to be deviant. Even liberal Christians expect atheists to keep quiet, not to offend the cherished delusions of the faithful. The faithful, however, don't return the favor. They offend the sincere convictions of intelligent unbelievers at every opportunity. There is an inexcusably arrogant assumption that these convictions just don't exist."

"Yet you constantly hear people admitting that they don't

really buy all that stuff in the Bible or they don't go to church of if they go, they take it all with a grain of salt. Still, they won't use the word *atheist* because the religious types have managed to load it with bad connotations."

"Yes. I have a feeling that atheism is not nearly as deviant as the churchgoers would have you believe. I have a feeling that atheism is so widespread as to be almost a norm among educated people, and theism is more like the deviant. Nor is atheism associated with immorality and crime, as churches want you to think. Most people who describe themselves as atheists are honest, law-abiding, taxpaying citizens, faithful spouses, good parents. It has been shown that the proportion of believers to nonbelievers is greater among criminals than in the general population. Maybe it's understandable. To follow a faith that demands constant denial of demonstrable facts would hardly tend to develop the habit of truthfulness."

"Do you think it will improve matters to return to the Goddess religion, whose followers were equally credulous back there in its prehistoric heyday?"

"I think so, because a restored Goddess religion would not demand the same kind of primitive credulity. That religion never tried to preserve itself by squelching scientific curiosity or by persecuting truth seekers in general. Like the rest of matriarchy, it was tolerant. Remember that it was the Christian church, in the early centuries of our era, that first began to close schools, burn libraries, destroy the records of the ancient world's scientific technologies, forbid reading—even of the Bible—and generally foster the onset of an illiterate, superstitious Dark Age. If Goddess religion had not been suppressed but had undergone the same development over the past two thousand years that God religion has, we would be much further along in our understanding of the real world and perhaps also of ourselves. Women, and men too, would know about the Goddess within, the archetype we all carry around and keep trying to conceptualize, simply because we are all born of woman and not of any god."

"Then you see the Goddess as a reality?"

"Only in a metaphorical sense, but it's a powerful metaphor.

We don't know what to call the Mother archetype within ourselves. Our male-dominated culture gives us no verbal handle
on it. As you know, we verbalizing animals can believe in almost
anything for which we invent a word. The Goddess words were
silenced. Yet something is still there, in the collective unconscious of women especially, something that we need, for which
many of us feel an inarticulate hunger. That's the foundation
of the women's spirituality movement. I hope the movement
will continue to develop and will avoid the pitfalls of excessive
credulity so as to retain that commonsense acceptance of reality
that men's religions insisted on denying."

"Including the reality of death?"

"Precisely. Marilyn French put it very well." I took my
much-thumbed copy of her *Beyond Power* from the shelf and
found the quote: " 'To create symbols that suggest that some
people live forever, is to implant in human experience a false-
hood so profound as to distort it utterly.' Such ideological dis-
tortion led to terrible destructiveness. Paradoxically, the denial
of death seems to foster a cruel society that holds life cheap.
Patriarchal gods tend to be death-centered without being death-
tolerant. Their myths are full of pain, sin, sacrifice, aggression,
and Oedipal rivalries, not to mention war, torture, and sadistic
hells. Nowadays there are even some men who come right out
and say a rebirth of feminine spirituality is the only force that
might be capable of reversing the world's appalling slide toward
man-created apocalypse."

"Yes, we all fear that, for ourselves and our children," she
said seriously. "I have trouble trying to imagine how men can
bring themselves to contribute to it. The whole concept seems
insane. The men involved seem like a sort of collective Hitler,
driven mad by too much power."

"The power to kill," I observed. "That was what man first
claimed in his envy of woman's power to give birth. Too many
men still think it's their only real significance. But there are
other forces at work in the collective psyche, even the male half
of it. The signs are all around us, mostly unrecognized."

"What signs?"

"For instance, take a minute to think about the insatiable

and apparently senseless male obsession with women's breasts. Everywhere you look you see breasts and more breasts—magazine covers, billboards, posters, ads, television, movies, art. No other part of human anatomy gets so much attention, not even genitals of either sex, which you might expect to attract more interest as obvious pleasure centers. This is a single-gender obsession. Emotional response to the sight of male nipples is virtually nil, yet female nipples evoke fascination you could almost call worship. Now remember, one of the holiest figures in the ancient world was Many-Breasted Artemis of Ephesus, nursing mother of everything, who had a torso full of breasts. Even the Bible says she was worshiped by all Asia and the world. Reverence for the female breast was overt then, and early fathers of the church went to ridiculous lengths to grab some of it for their own deity. The *Odes of Solomon* talked about the Father's milk-filled breasts. St. Ambrose of Milan mentioned 'the nourishing breasts of Christ.' Underneath all the macho strutting, the patriarchal male secretly yearns to come home to the nurturing Mother whose breast is still his primary symbol of love. In such a context it surely made more sense to say Goddess is Love than God is Love."

"I've often suspected that this breast fixation reveals the infant in man. There's always this craving to suck, even if the breast is dry. But that's a sensual pleasure for women too."

"Of course. That's true for all mammals. The erectile tissue is there to make suckling enjoyable for the mother, so she'll be sure to do it and the young will get the nourishment they need. But nature doesn't intend this for the benefit of the adult male. In humans, something else is going on: a hidden craving for spiritual nourishment by way of body sensations. We know sex and religion are linked in the unconscious, just as we link the physical and the spiritual under the blanket term 'love.' Ancient religious practices show us that the dream of immortality takes form for men through intimate connections with woman's body. Paganism was shamelessly overt about it until Christianity began to claim that woman's body is the gate of hell instead of the Pearly Gate of paradise. In either case, though, it had to do with the afterlife."

My friend's eyes suddenly shone with new insight. "Their

symbols of immortality are still female-maternal!" she cried. "The baptismal font is called a womb. The waters of regeneration are waters of rebirth. Nobody's born without a mother! And what's the symbol of immortality in the Eucharist but a cup of blood—wasn't that a womb symbol practically forever, long before Christianity adopted it?"

I nodded. "The Holy Grail," I said. "Object of every hero's quest. Medieval Christians' transformation of the Cauldron of Regeneration, which was a Goddess womb filled with moon blood, the blood of life. In visions it was always carried by women. Psychologists have often said the whole quest-for-immortality idea is bound up with a wish to get back into the mother's womb for rebirth. Jung suggested that as the real basis of so-called Oedipal desires."

"Then in all these centuries they really haven't come up with anything to replace the maternal imagery. The Goddess is still there in a lot of disguises."

"In a way. Most of her symbols were usurped by the church because of their proven evocative power. Unfortunately we're taught not to analyze patriarchy's takeover of female attributes, even when it's as silly as the 'nursing father' in the eleventh chapter of Numbers. That was probably another of those Hebraic reversals of Egyptian scriptures, such as the ones that promised Pharaoh that in the afterworld he would suckle the Goddess's breast forever and never be weaned. Baby's paradise! But it's seldom pointed out that the baptismal font is called Immaculate Womb, or that the milk of human kindness comes only from that endlessly fascinating female breast. Of course, mother love doesn't cure mortality. It only represents most of the things that make life worth living."

"Well, wasn't that a basic idea of Goddess religion? To make life worth living here and now, to enjoy the real world while we have it?"

"Yes. And we want our children to be able to enjoy it too. We don't want to hand them a world ruined by men's greed and carelessness, or worse yet, a world made totally unlivable by men's insane aggression. I think men need to recognize all those Mother symbols for what they are, to bring back the female principle to religious consciousness, to stop dithering about sexuality and start getting all that violence under control. Otherwise, God's green earth may not be green very much longer."

"Maybe your Goddess church really is what we need. Maybe it really is urgent for women to begin making their own theology."

"Thealogy," I said. "Goddess knowledge. Here's to it."

We raised our teacups and drank.

Intuition

"I think," said my friend, "you have backed into this feminist movement. You're a feminist more by nature than by ideology. Freud's theory of the passive-masochistic 'typical woman' would have to choke on you and spit you out."

I laughed and poured her another cup of tea. "The worst of it is," I said, "I couldn't be palmed off as the exception that proves the rule. I'm not an exception. Surely the passive-masochistic woman must be the rare exception, just as much as such a person would be among men. It isn't human—or animal—to want to be hurt. This masochism thing is only what men project upon women so they don't have to feel as guilty as they deserve to feel for putting women down."

"But how about your classic earth mother type? You know, the all-giving, all-forgiving, eternal nurturer, accepting the good and the bad, loving even those who exploit and rape her? Aren't there women like that? Wasn't that even a typical image of the Goddess herself?"

"Hardly. It's another male projection from the kind of men who think the earth exists just for them to exploit and rape. Ancient ideas of the Earth Mother included fear about her possible vengeance if she was insulted, as a child fears to insult Mother. She was seen as the primordial lawgiver. The tablets of the law, handed down on the mountain, were originally hers, you know. She was implacable about punishing lawbreakers, those who hurt others. Why, she punished even the gods if they got out of line. In Greek myths, gods swore their binding oaths by her name, because only she had the power to hold them to their word."

"But feminists today downplay all that avenging Fury stuff. Most women want to join men, not scare them off. Doesn't equality mean that no one should be made afraid, that we should all be fair to one another? Isn't that what women are aiming for?"

"Sure, but they probably ought to aim higher than that. There are some areas where women are not equal to men, but clearly superior. Morality, for instance. Women commit less than 10 percent of violent crimes. They accept responsibility for the welfare of others better than men do. They're more humane, patient, aware, and sympathetic. They regard world peace as an overriding priority. Anthropologists have shown that societies where women set the standards of behavior are not warlike, cruel, rigidly ascetic, or riddled with neurotic anxieties. When women run the show, everybody is made to feel comfortable. Besides, it's natural that women should establish the society's standards of behavior, because it evolves inevitably from the mother's authority in teaching her children."

"You think that's why the Goddess became the first lawgiver?"

"Of course. Men have always wanted a superparent to tell them what to do, and Mother was the only parent they knew of until late in the development of civilizations. It wasn't until the gods came on the scene that murder, rape, and warfare became regular aspects of human culture."

"Then you're assuming that these activities are natural to men?"

"Not necessarily. Sexual competition is, because we see that among male animals too. But human social conditioning can be planned to contain male competitiveness in the area where it belongs, so it doesn't overflow and spread to become the bloated, obscene thing it is now, gobbling up every part of life for both sexes."

"Don't you think Christianity has tried to establish the kind of morality you advocate?"

"Certainly not. Historically, Christianity has always betrayed women—even with well-nigh unbelievable brutality, as in the witchcraft centuries. Today's Christianity still tries to block women from being the primary leaders. It still proposes literal belief in a male savior and a male God. Any ideology that encourages women to take their orders from a male authority is going to trample on them, sooner or later."

"But there are many feminists who call themselves Christian, who believe in reforming their religion from the inside without upsetting the basic structures of faith."

"Good luck to them. To my mind there isn't any baby in that bathwater. A woman who needs to worship a male God is just projecting her own animus somewhere into outer space, letting him tell her what to do. I use the term in the Jungian sense, not because it describes anything real, but because it's reasonably familiar. Actually, we're dealing here with concepts for which the accurate terms have yet to be invented."

"Well, to keep to the same terminology, would an anima projection be any better? I mean, would men be more likely to obey a female image of supreme authority?"

"It would depend on how they were trained. Most people are trained to be credulous, to think they need some kind of authority figure 'out there.' For this, female is just as good as male and probably better. But perhaps we could go a step further and teach people to live with the concept that the authority figure is not outside but inside, even though it can be collective as well as individual. That puts responsibility where it belongs, on us. We should know that human beings make their own fate in this universe, so we can responsibly decide what we want our fate to be and work toward it."

She gazed into the middle distance, tapping a finger on her cheek and considering her own thought. Presently she said, "You're very tough-minded. Many people might find that responsibility too much to bear. It may be more comfortable for them to envision somebody out there who cares and is willing to help."

"Perhaps so, but even a slight acquaintance with scientific truths can make that impossible. Beliefs of that sort are too vulnerable to evidential disproof. That may be why you find the more credulous types now tending to retreat into true silliness, such as wise, benevolent beings from other galaxies showing up on earth in time to save us from our own stupidity. Yet the canonical God fantasies are really not much above that level and maybe even more injurious because of the neurotic guilt feelings they impose."

"Then why do you think so many people have this urge to believe? If it's an inborn trait of the human organism, then what purpose could it serve in terms of survival?"

"Ah, that's easy. It's our substitute for instinct."

"Come again?"

"Genetically, human beings have lost most of the instinctive behavior patterns that guide other animals through their life cycles. With our more complex brains, we are supposed to be able to figure out for ourselves what we need to do to survive and maintain our species. To some extent this is true of all the higher mammals, so their behavior patterns are never quite uniform; there's always room for individual variations."

"That's so, but how does it fit in with human beliefs?"

"Consider the so-called spiritual experience, or vision. Psychology hasn't even begun to deal with that phenomenon, although it's actually fairly common. Whatever form it may assume in the mind's eye, there is one emotional characteristic that it always has: a sense of absolute, transcendent certainty or rightness. This feeling can be so strong that it may permanently alter the course of a person's life, for it is not forgotten. There isn't anything else in ordinary experience that can carry such conviction."

"Well, I can't say I've ever experienced that."

"You probably have, only you never identified it as such. The 'flash of intuition' is one manifestation of it, somewhat milder, but the same idea. Sometimes it happens during actual unconsciousness. Haven't you ever had a dream that seemed like some transcendent revelation of a great power, from which you could solve all your problems, write the perfect poem or the perfect symphony, paint the perfect picture, or understand the secrets of the universe? Then when you wake up, the revelation you thought so miraculous turns out to be a perfectly absurd idea as your sensible waking mind sees it?"

"Yes, I've had that happen."

"A religious revelation puts the mind through the same process while it's awake, with the critical faculty operative but not interfering. I think this is the same way a lower animal subjectively experiences the working of its instincts. That animal's brain is genetically programmed to tell the animal exactly what it must do, without any possibility of doubt, and that this is right and certain and unchangeable. In short, this is God. The animal obeys because it has no other choice. It can't modify its behavior as an individual to suit changing circumstances. Modifications can only be made through the evolution of the species."

"Okay, I follow you so far."

"Even if it gets the animal in trouble because of adverse changes in its environment, that kind of certainty must make an animal feel comfortable. When brains got more complex we human animals lost some of that comfort, because we came to know anxiety and worry about making the right choices. Our reasoning faculty is not yet so highly developed that it is a perfect substitute for instinct. We can still find irrationality more comfortable, exciting, or appealing, on occasion, than what we perceive to be reasonable."

"Are you saying our brains still retain some of that capability for instinct and crave it even though we can override it if we want?"

"That's it. Whenever you make contact with that leftover, primitive brain, instinctive way of knowing, you can have what is called a religious experience—an intense form of intuition. As with your dream, the actual content of the experience may seem absurd, which is why such an experience can never be accurately described. Any attempt at description necessarily omits the individual's emotional response, because that's purely subjective and belongs to the individual alone; yet that's the real essence of the experience. The whole phenomenon bears out what the more intelligent mystics throughout the world have always said, that deity is wholly within, not without, to be found only by digging into deeper levels of the mind than those of which we are usually aware."

"That's quite a theory. With that you could revolutionize the philosophy of religion, to say nothing of its practice. But it doesn't explain why many people are willing to believe things they haven't experienced directly, things that are taught them by others."

"I think they like even the *sound* of certainty, in a world where nearly everything else seems unsure and unpredictable and there are so many decisions to be made all the time. None of us can know when any one of our seemingly sensible decisions might turn out to be terribly wrong. A million drivers of cars each year can testify to that—to give only one example. We can't trust our commonsense thinking the way an animal can trust its instincts. We are too aware of the possibility of mistakes. So we're uneasy, always slightly off balance, neurotic animals in search of a sureness that our evolutionary ancestors left behind long ago."

"Therefore as children grow up they think their elders have that kind of sureness—until they find out otherwise—just because the elders are the teachers?"

"Precisely. Then when the disillusionment with human elders sets in, many of us project the original trust onto something else and so create the big parent figure that can rule everybody. Trouble is, that parent figure is wrong just as often as we are."

"Well, so much for God. I think you were led into feminism first of all by your propensity to judge God as wrong. Once you've rejected the male authority figure, everything else follows, right?"

"Right. That image-of-God notion means a lot to the male priesthoods. It's the basis of their claim to lord it over women, in both senses of the word."

"Then you think women need their Goddess image as a basis for establishing their authority, as men did?"

"Probably. It can't hurt. But I hope and trust women will have enough sense to avoid the pitfalls into which men's religions have stumbled."

"Such as?"

"For one thing, the tendency to spread the faith by violence, to oppress or kill the unbelievers—an almost universal characteristic of patriarchal enthusiasts. For another thing, the tendency to take it too seriously, until one is believing even one's own nonsense. Religion isn't right for everybody. We need to remember that the human capacity to diversify is the essence of our potential. Patriarchs always try to enforce conformity— in the home, the school, the workplace, the church. Even as revolutionaries they do it: you know, liquidate all those who don't cleave to the party line. Especially dissident women. The only important thing is that we as a species must learn to live together without hurting each other. We flatter ourselves that we are brighter than dolphins and whales, so if they can do it, why can't we?"

My friend looked down at her teacup and sighed. "I wish I knew," she said.

"Me too," said I. "Now we both wish we knew."

We both sighed, remembering a distant age when women did not feel helpless to influence the moral teachings of their society.

"One thing I do know," I said. "Our intelligence still has a long way to go. In some ways it's a product of deficiency rather than augmentation."

"How do you mean?"

"The paradoxical reason for our species' achievement of intelligence is preservation of the immature state. It's been said that a human being is essentially a fetalized ape, with permanent characteristics of immaturity such as an overly large cranium, lack of body hair, and lifelong retention of the infantile learning capacity. We go on storing new information in our heads for a lifetime, but an ape or other animal slows down its learning to almost a standstill when it is full grown."

"Yes, I've heard of recent studies that show how brilliant babies are."

"With our lifelong preservation of childishness for the sake of our awareness, responsiveness, and learning capacity, we also show other symptoms of lifelong childishness that aren't so beneficial, for instance, those typically patriarchal tendencies that we deplore: greed, selfishness, lust for power, inflated egotism—all serving to disguise a childlike dependence. Men especially depend on women to nurture them, because each man sees something of the mother figure in each woman. Just as Mother is the foundation of a child's life, so most of us never quite lose the need for a parent concept at the roots of our consciousness. Hence, religion. We make a deity for ourselves to obey and then fool ourselves into thinking the deity has ordered or approved whatever it is we want to do. We don't want to take the responsibility for initiating the action. All the time we wonder if we dare make our own decisions, and if some unforeseen punishment might come as a result."

"Then you think the divine Father is a less satisfactory substitute for the divine Mother, who used to exist as a mental projection of the primary caregiver?"

"Yes. A child's mentality is responsive, reactive, relational. The child must have the Other as a guiding authority. Normally, the religious imagery of the Other would be based on the real primary caregiver, the mother. Humanity's evolution of a Mother Goddess was inevitable, given the perception of childbirth as life's creation and given the deep sense of dependence on female life support. The paternal God came much later, as a male effort to copy everything previously decided about the nature and function of the Mother. Eventually, men did with deities just what they try to do in the patriarchal family structure: cut off the natural authority of the Mother figure and try to eliminate even the memory of it. Only it never quite works, because the inner child never forgets that first lesson learned with the skin and the eyes and the guts, namely, that Mother means life."

She looked into my eyes and smiled. "You certainly do have some interesting intuitions of your own," she said.

I laughed. "Yes, the sense of absolute, transcendent certainty. Nothing else quite like it. My inner child knows what it knows."

"If learning is childlike," she said, "may you never grow up."

Meaning

Patriarchal religion has been far more successful as a profit-making endeavor than as a salutary influence on human behavior or as a deterrent to warfare and crime. In fact, it has been the ideal scam. It provides no product and no service essential to the economy. Yet through centuries of assiduous propagandizing, it has convinced most of the world that its non-product is necessary even to the most basic of life's events, such as birth, sex, and death. It holds the minds of billions in thrall to the premise that they can't live without it, that life holds no meaning without religion. What it actually gives are only words, and mightily ambiguous words at that.

Christianity gets around its ambiguity by announcing that true faith must never question or try to clarify these mysterious meanings. This order does not apply to ecclesiastical official-dom, which spends a great deal of time redefining its concepts according to prevailing conventional wisdom, so as to take maximum advantage of current trends. Those whose business it is to keep Christianity palatable by constant rearrangement of its doctrines are not usually accused of bad faith. The accusation applies only to laypeople who learn enough to become confused. Those laypeople who wonder what the church's words really mean are already out of line.

It is important for the faithful to be kept ignorant, not only of the theological precepts of their own sect (especially as contrasted with those of other sects), but also of the very nature of the universe in which they live. Knowledge of earth's geology, the history of its life forms, its infinitesimal significance in the cosmos as it is now known—all these dispense with the biblical sort of God, who threw the whole thing together in six days and was invented by men almost entirely ignorant of the

world around them. To preserve those ancient errors, patriarchal religion has unwisely chosen to be the enemy of science.

Some people turn away from science because it's not easily
comprehended, and they can't or won't make the mental effort
required to master its disciplines. Simple notions of salvation
and sin, divine and devilish are much easier to understand.
Besides, religious convictions may seem more stable. They don't
have to be subjected to constant revision in the light of new
evidence, as scientific theories must be. One may cling to any
absurdity one likes, defending it as an unassailable article of
faith, without feeling that it must be logically justifiable. Most
people don't care much for logic, anyway.

Some insist that only religion can give meaning or purpose
to their lives. Apparently they find life meaningless or pur-
poseless unless they can think it is validated from without. Life
by itself is not enough. This is generally opposed to the feminist
view, which finds life valuable for its own sake, just as a mother
loves her child not because it matters to the world at large, but
only because it is there and it is hers.

Yet when advocates of religious meaning are asked, "What
does life mean, then?" they never seem to know. The usual
response is that God knows and that makes everything all right.
If God doesn't tell them the meaning they call essential to their
peace of mind, however, then they are perhaps even less secure
than one who regards life as a happy accident, treasuring it
simply because it is.

As a rule, religionists confine their considerations to human
life. They don't care about any possible meaning in the lives of
porpoises, elephants, ants, trees, jellyfish, bacteria, grasses,
earthworms, mosquitoes, or radiolaria. With oddly medieval
tunnel vision, they ignore the rest of the living planet as if it
existed for only one out of its swarm of species. It seldom occurs to them that we humans are but one life form among
millions, or that the only discernible purpose of any of these
life forms is to go on reproducing itself as long as conditions
permit.

Such people lack, and may even reject, basic information
about geologic time spans and the evolution of earth's species.
Because this is considered dangerous information (anything

that raises doubts is dangerous), its dissemination is usually opposed by fundamentalists.

Noting that if the earth's lifetime is compared with the height of the Eiffel Tower, then all human existence equals the thickness of the skin of paint on the knob at the tip of the tower's spire, Mark Twain once dryly remarked that, of course, any fool could see that the tower existed just to support that skin of paint. This is the kind of foolishness professed by those who would like to subordinate all other species to the human one and to view all those millions of years as a mere prelude to the coming of the skin of paint—that is, us. Innumerable species have come and gone, many lasting much longer than our species has lived so far, and what was their "purpose"? They only existed and then ceased to exist.

The dinosaurs lived a hundred million years, more than fifty times as long as humans have lived; therefore, they were fifty times more successful at surviving. Now they are gone. Even more successful are those archaic creatures that still exist today, after species lifetimes that make humans seem ephemeral indeed: sharks, dragonflies, horseshoe crabs. Even the fish are Methuselahs compared with us. Yet we are so conceited as to imagine that all those billions of creatures were only God's preliminary models and assorted failures on his way to devising a species that would finally notice him.

But why should this allegedly all-powerful, all-knowing God have so bumbled about, creating so many life forms that he subsequently found unsatisfactory and destroyed? Even more to the point, why should he find it necessary to be noticed by any life form whatsoever?

The notion that God basks in the continual flattery of praising, praying human beings is one of our most childlike delusions. Should the creator of our unthinkably vast cosmos need tiny human voices to feed his ego? It might have been all right for a biblical *ba'al,* who lived in a box or a stone cairn and "walked in the garden in the cool of the evening," chatting with his creature; but surely we are less naïve today than the ancient scribes who envisioned that.

The answer of course is that man wants constant flattery to feed his ego, and man makes God in his own image. This explains how psychologists keep discovering profound revelations about human nature in studying the deeds and characteristics assigned to gods. There is meaning in religion, but it is not quite the sort of meaning envisioned by those who want to take their religion literally.

Most feminists seek a more practical sense of meaning in religion. They hold that religious imagery and ritual should shape social behavior in more intimate, effective, and encouraging ways than just providing myths about commandments on stone tablets, copies of old seasonal savior sacrifices, or primitive parables. Because social behavior is inextricably bound up with sexuality, motherhood, and family relationships, they say, religion should recognize the centrality of the female in all these areas, should restore the female image to its proper place, and should provide more workable guides to handling social interaction in the here and now. A remote, punitive father god and a passive, victimized son god just don't have much to do with it.

Thus it is important for women to restore the Goddess to the central position in their the*a*logy, cleansed of all the mortalizations, diabolizations, and trivializings that patriarchal theologians have imposed on her. At the same time it is important to recognize that she is a symbol, an archetype, a product of collective consciousness, made "real" by human invocation, not by the Nature she personifies. Nature is essentially neutral. It may be understood in any way we prefer, according to our interpretations.

There are, however, genuine discoveries to be made about Nature. Many have been made, but many more still remain. Our planet is no human psychological archetype. It exists for real and we depend on it utterly. We need to find out as much as we can about how it works. The best way of doing this that has ever been devised is the scientific method.

Some feminist groups evince a tendency to denigrate all scientific discovery as a product of patriarchal, exploitative thinking. Some would like to do away with scientific inquiry in favor of shamanistic magic or mystical techniques such as meditation and trance. Some go beyond the perception of symbol and ritual as foci for the setting of goals into the realm of primitive sympathetic magic itself, where symbolic enactment is believed to bring about real events quite apart from their psychological component. There is a kind of credulity here that may be as destructive to the ultimate aims of feminism as Christianity's flat denial of what Galileo saw or what Darwin realized turned out to be destructive to orthodoxy.

Like prayer, magic works through the mind when it works at all. Unlike scientific methods, however, neither prayer nor magic can work without the intervention of the mind. A scientific procedure is empirically reproduceable and verifiable. It will always work. If it doesn't, then it isn't scientifically accurate. Magic presents no such certainty. Sticking pins in a clay poppet won't really injure anyone. Singing a certain song over a cornfield won't really help the crop. Amethysts won't prevent a drinker from getting drunk. Menstrual blood is neither a poison nor a panacea. Charms written on paper and swallowed are not really medicine. And so on, down the endless lists of magical misapprehensions that our culture has gathered in its centuries of ignorance.

Still, the human mind loves to make connections, even where no literal connections exist. As is often said, our ability to use language depends on this very faculty. This is an area of psychology that has hardly begun to be investigated, because we are so close to it that we find it almost impossible to back off far enough to see it. It is a deep part of ourselves, all the connections we make in thinking, feeling, verbalizing, conceptualizing. It is our poetry of being. Once the connections are made we resist unmaking them. That would be like unlearning our language, taking ourselves apart.

This sensitive psychological realm is precisely what enlightened feminism must explore to find out how human society can be changed, how humanity can learn to control its self-destructive behavior patterns, and how ritual and visualization can be related to our daily conduct. We have no guideposts to that realm except the imagery that we have naturally evolved but have not yet understood. As a species we have not yet even crossed the threshold. A whole interior world remains to be investigated in the decades to come—if we survive long enough.

Many people find the concept of humanmade deity difficult to grasp, even when it is tacitly understood, for instance, when a scholar discourses on the nature of God and in the process changes it. Many take the simplistic viewpoint: God is either *out there* or he is not. If you believe he is, you're religious. If you believe he isn't, you're atheistic. Similarly, the Goddess must either be or not be in objective reality.

But this is kindergarten thinking. We understand objective reality according to our own concepts, just as we understand the earth's surface by parallels of latitude and longitude, which don't exist anywhere but in human minds. Deities, and other anthropomorphisms of natural forces, are also mental short-hand, convenient hooks on which to hang our sense of wonder.

We find it pleasant to see the sun not only as a nuclear inferno but also as a bright-faced, golden-haired Apollo riding across the heavens; or the moon not only as a dry sphere of rock, but also as a silver Diana with three aspects echoing the life stages of every woman: Maiden, Mother, Crone. Having created the poetry, we like to use it as if it were an illuminating truth.

To maintain our collective sanity, however, we must recognize the difference between the nuclear inferno and the face of Apollo, between dusty space rocks and the Dianic bow, between the real world and the deities we impose on it. God and Goddess are equally our inventions and equally subject to collective alterations. The fact that construction work on the Goddess image has been forbidden for the past two thousand years, while work on the God image went on undisturbed, does not alter their essential similarity as creations: the one from the female half of humanity, the other from the male half. Now it is time for work on the female deity to be resumed. The world needs her, perhaps even more than it ever needed him.

It is time, too, for the real meanings of these images to be understood, even though to seek such understanding is to plumb a hidden psychological realm that we often don't care to think about. New truths are to be sought not in the light of what is already known, obviously, but in the dark beneath the disguises of pseudomeaning, where things yet remain to be discovered.

Theologians generate rivers of words to disguise the fact that they have no idea what their God means, nor what he is, nor what he knows, nor what he does, nor what he communicates, nor what he wants. Opinions differ so radically on every one of these points that any impartial observer can see that God has never succeeded in making himself clear to humanity about any religious issue whatsoever, no matter how trivial—let alone the larger issues of salvation and sin, good and evil, the meaning of life and death.

In reality, life and death would carry on in their usual way even if no meaning were attached to them, just as they carried on for a previous two billion years before man came along to give himself airs about occupying the tower's ultimate skin of paint under God's eye. It seems perverse in the extreme to postulate any deity who lays such significance on the matter of following the right religion but then fosters infinite confusion about which one is right. The most junior copywriter on Madison Avenue could give this God lessons in getting across a clear, unambiguous message that all can understand.

God's adherents seldom even credit him with enough sense of fair play not to puzzle the majority of people with deliberate obfuscation and then viciously punish them for being puzzled. God's adherents have been known to make him as absurdly tyrannical as a father who beats his infant son for not knowing the multiplication table, yet they call him the epitome of justice. Voltaire remarked that reading the works of theologians seemed to him like spending time in an insane asylum. The arguments may be closely reasoned, but their fundamental precepts make no sense.

If the muddle of man's theology means anything, it is that man makes God in his own image or in the image of the idealized father-controller within, which Freud called the superego. Then man seeks ways to project that image outward onto a reality that does not deal in meanings. God differs from himself and can never be consistent because men's minds differ from each other, both individually and in the context of changing times and social trends. The Old Testament war God can become a twentieth-century peacenik. The vengeful witch-burning God of the Middle Ages can become a loving father to all.

The pitiless judge is credited with infinite mercy; the inventor of hell is supposed to be kind; the slayer of his son is seen as the best possible parent.

Though theologians pretend that God is immutable, in practice the God concept is endlessly fluid, showing beyond a doubt that it is artificially created out of changeable human minds. God is like a dragon that each of us can envision differently: green-scaled, red-scaled, leathery-skinned, winged, nonwinged, fire-breathing or not, clawed or hoofed, two-eyed or four-eyed, horned or not horned, and so on. We can play with the dragon concept in such ways because none of us has ever seen the real thing nor ever will. Despite the fact that dragons do not exist and never have existed, each of us has a mental picture that we can label dragon, just as if it were as real as an elephant or a codfish. Deities partake of this same immunity to consistency, being equally unreal and yet even more talked about. Like the meaning of life, the matter of picturing dragons or gods is a wide-open field.

It's possible that restoration of the Goddess image to the same central place it used to occupy in collective conceptualizing may bring more meaning to life than any other symbol now regarded as sacred. Certainly the Goddess image would do more for the self-respect of women than the God image has done, because any patriarchal deity has always been either implicitly or overtly inimical to the female principle. Under the Goddess, however, life was seen as a blessing and an end in itself, requiring no transcendent meaning. Under the Goddess, life was not supposed to require validation from without. Life could be seen as a purposeful production of more life; a celebration of sensual enjoyment, sexuality, feeling, and the poetry and mystery of being; the cherishing and nurturance of future generations; and the responsible custodianship of the planet they must live on. All these are implied by the symbol of the Goddess more directly than they were ever implied by the God, who indeed was generally more hostile toward such concerns than otherwise. The Goddess stood for spontaneity, playfulness, love, joy, and absence of guilt over harmless pleasures. This does not mean mere thoughtless hedonism, for useful work is one of the greatest of pleasures as well as a basic human need. Goddesses, like mothers, fostered work that would help others and not merely exploit their baser impulses for money.

So it seems likely that an established Goddess religion would be less greedily exploitative, less defensively opposed to general learning, and less prone to lying and dissimulation than patriarchal religion has been. Under the Goddess, religion might become like motherhood itself, a trust maintained for love instead of a business run for profit. What is now called religion has only one real meaning: its bottom lines are money and secular power, always under the control of men. Perhaps it is time for the sex that understands altruistic morality to resume the reins of moral leadership in a world that doesn't know where its next meaning is coming from and lives in fear of its own present leaders.

Of course there are monumental difficulties involved in the effort to unseat the money-based hierarchy. The Father culture of today may be even worse in some ways than the Big Brother culture of Orwell's famous fantasy, *1984*. That year came and went without any overt symptoms of the repressive socialism Orwell envisioned, but no one noticed that there was (and is) a similar brainwashing system in effect, far more insidious than Orwell's.

It might be called repressive capitalism. It is keyed to mindless enjoyment instead of mindless obedience. Instead of incessant control, its technique is incessant offering of pleasure, rendering the masses intellectually inert and emotionally malleable through marketing. This culture's messages are transmitted day and night through every possible medium. No individual can escape them. Verbally, graphically, constantly, they suppress analytical thought and stimulate insatiable greed.

The signs are everywhere. A lackadaisical educational system graduates functional illiterates, who find reading too bothersome. Their attention span is not much larger than it was when they were 3 years old. Huge numbers of them emerge from the educational system with a significant portion of brain cells permanently destroyed by the drugs that are now energetically marketed even in grade schools. Through drug use as well as through permitted intellectual inertia, many have become psychologically and physiologically stupid and will never discover how much they don't know.

Government never really opposes this astronomically profitable drug traffic, which maims millions of young minds every year. Its distribution system would never have become so completely effective if law enforcement agencies didn't receive their piece of the profits. Governments don't really want a thinking population. They want a controllable population. Bureaucracy needs its constant supply of robots. Our country doesn't need Orwellian brainwashing exercises to turn its citizens into automata. It has better methods, which masquerade as freedom from discipline, even in the very process of eradicating the possibility of free thought.

Ignorance, illiteracy, a pop culture that fosters mental laxity, drugs and alcohol aggressively pushed, especially upon the young, and a constant bombardment of the senses with so-called entertainment that replaces, for the average seven hours a day, the time children used to spend in reading, learning, or relating to people instead of to a television tube: these are obvious downhill pathways of our society.

Television is a prime carrier of the new no-think culture. Collectively, television programming presents patriarchal interests first and foremost: vicious violence, hostility, crime, war, abuse of women, adoration of money and crass hedonism, contempt for intellectual sophistication unless it is strictly technological. Over all presides Father God in various showy guises, stage managed by his most unctuous priests, the big-bucks evangelists. The one word never seriously spoken where any television audience can hear it is *Goddess*.

The bottom line of all this is money. Women, as the society's primary consumers, must never be allowed to analyze the system they uphold, just as most patriarchal thinkers said women must never be allowed to judge the men their ceaseless marital labor supported. Women must not even communicate their own ideas to one another, lest some of the powerful ones at the top of the pyramid feel some shakiness in their seats of power when some of the bottom blocks defect.

We're told that women have come a long way since they began agitating for the right to be real people, two centuries ago and more. In truth, it's been no more than a first half-step. Women's perceptions of what's wrong with the world and of what their children need to grow into mature individuals still go almost as unnoticed and unrecorded as in the early years of the Industrial Revolution. Feminine comments are sought by marketing researchers not to find out how women think but only to find out how women can be more effectively manipulated.

Perhaps the most depressing part of feminist thought today is the inevitable discovery that it has all been thought before and said before and continually rendered invisible and inaudible by the male control of religion, education, and communications. Feminist scholars such as Matilda Joslyn Gage and Elizabeth Cady Stanton put their fingers directly on the spiritual lesions of patriarchy more than a century ago. History has heaped veritable mounds of suppression over the work of many women, their names virtually unknown today: Charlotte Perkins Gilman, Vera Brittain, Barbara Bodichon, Mary Ritter Beard, and dozens more whose discoveries were deliberately lost. Dale Spender has given profound meaning to her own life by retrieving some of these foremothers from the obscurity men decreed for them and pointing out how cogently and passionately they argued for reforms that never came, in her recent book, *Women of Ideas (And What Men Have Done to Them)*.

Much more feminine effort is needed to combat the male experts who seek to bury women's experience and insight. Men having found their primary meaning largely in money, it is left to women to redirect society into less destructive patterns. There are indications that women see past the dollar signs to the real impact of pernicious commodities and entertainments; that women detest the rapism, pornography, gore, and violence of popular drama; that women hate the waste and agony of war. It remains only for women to find their highest meaning in eliminating these evils from their world and preventing such threats to their children.

If there is an ultimate meaning to life, the established spiritual authority has never yet presented it in any consistent form. Woman's perceptions and woman's morality must take charge of the future if there is to be any future.

Opiate of the Masses

On the few occasions when I have mentioned spiritual ideas in a casual or social context, I have been surprised by the apparently fathomless naïveté with which such subjects are approached even by intelligent, educated people, who are quite capable of rational analysis of almost any other subject. One reason for such naïveté is that spiritual ideas are seldom discussed in a social context, the clergy having convinced most of us that it is ill-mannered and presumptuous for laypeople to talk about them.

Like many modern bad luck taboos, this taboo dates back to the age of persecution, when it was bad luck indeed to be overheard discussing, doubting, or questioning any detail of the theological party line. Still, the average degree of reticence today seems excessive, inexplicably so, because we're told that spiritual or religious notions should underlie an individual's whole approach to life and therefore should be important enough to be considered with care and chosen on an informed basis, rather than out of the ignorance, credulity, or superstition that seems to characterize so much of the average person's religious thinking. The degree of naïveté shows that the average person's religious education is really no education at all, but a propagandistic brainwashing aimed at quenching curiosity and inhibiting analysis of the implanted ideas. In effect, it is like a military system: God's orders can't be questioned even when they sound crazy.

A high school teacher of medieval European history once told me that he never mentioned religious ideas in the classroom because he might get in trouble. I asked how one could teach medieval European history without mentioning religious ideas, because these ideas figured so largely in shaping events. He replied, "I can say the church did this or that, approved of one thing or another, but I stay away from theological and sectarian issues. If I went into those, before you know it there'd be some Bible banger demanding that I either shut up or get fired before I corrupt the tender minds of our young people. Tender minds which, I might add, can be muddled almost to the point of idiocy by drugs before some parents even take notice."

Despite desperately defensive religious attitudes along such lines as these, most people seem uninformed about the theological assertions of their own sect or unable to say how its opinions differ from those of other sects. Thus it becomes obvious that few people bother to check out what a church actually stands for before they join it. Once I asked a Presbyterian, whose church was founded on the doctrine of predestination, what the current teaching is about that doctrine. He said, "What's predestination?" Church members claiming that all their beliefs are founded on the Bible often seem unaware of what the Bible says. Others are vague about what deity means at all. A churchgoing Methodist woman once said to me, "Well, I definitely believe in Something, but I don't know what it is."

Both history and science contain multiple threats to the church-sponsored programs of noninformation, and therefore both are regarded with suspicion by those who profess the Truth, which invariably turns out to be an antihistorical and unscientific Truth. Somehow it is seldom noticed that thousands of others are simultaneously professing a different Truth, and some even have hard evidence. Many believers learn to turn off their brains whenever an uncomfortable either-or choice drifts past. For instance, if a Garden of Eden buff notices a *National Geographic* article on human evolution, he or she simply gazes at the ceiling instead of at the magazine or else reads it as a kind of fairy tale version of the biblical reality, even though the two versions do not resemble each other in an allegorical or any other way.

However earnestly a religious organization advertises itself as an educational institution, it should not be forgotten that religious organizations mold rather than educate. Religious training suppresses, instead of encourages, creative thought.

We should remember that nearly every book of any scientific importance during the past three centuries was promptly placed on the Catholic Index of Prohibited Books. In 1922, one year after Anatole France won the Nobel Prize for Literature, the church placed the whole corpus of his works together on the index.

As a result of the brainwashing process implicit in religious training, confusion, misapprehensions, and misinterpretations of theology abound among lay believers. A surprising number of people who think themselves devout Christians profess a belief in reincarnation, apparently unaware that the notion has been most bitterly opposed by orthodox Christianity from its very beginnings. One woman told me, "I know I'll come back in another life. Jesus says so." I asked, "Where does Jesus say that?" She answered, "Oh, I don't know. Somewhere in the Bible. I'm sure it's there, because the Bible always says what's true." This was a woman with a college education.

There is an amazing quantity of plain benighted superstition among the avowedly religious. I heard one of those televangelist preachers declare to the whole television audience, in no uncertain terms, that the air all around us is inhabited by millions of invisible devils.

Lesser fundamentalist fry pour similar absurdities into credulous ears via radio stations that broadcast Christian messages 24 hours a day, seven days a week. I have heard some of them tell the sick that serious or even terminal illnesses can be healed if the patient has enough faith and (not incidentally) sends enough money to the radio station for the right kind of prayers. Of course Christianity has been working this particularly cruel kind of con game for two thousand years now, but that's no excuse for letting it continue.

Televangelism is especially pernicious. It reaches many. It distorts much. It brings cultist irrationalities, forcefully presented, into the living rooms of the ignorant and impressionable. It promulgates the same old simplistic all-male God through the elegant, expensive, professionally staged posturings of his all-male prophets, who blatantly put down women, science, higher education, and social reform, as well as intellectual freedom.

Fundamentalism is the religion of millions in boob tube land. There is no alternative. The other side not only never gets equal time, it never gets any time at all. As far as television is concerned, religion means mainstream patriarchy and nothing else. As in so many other fields, television has failed once again as a medium of real education. It ignores the richness and complexity of "alien" spiritual, philosophical, and religious ideas created throughout the ages and throughout the world. It never touches upon the heretical controversies that have given humanity real food for thought. It never allows debate upon the eminently debatable premises of mainstream belief. The purpose of such fundamentalism is not to educate but to manipulate, so its God is as forcefully pushed as all its other commercial products.

As a commercial product (or nonproduct), God is the greatest moneymaker of all time. Through God, more men have grown rich off the labor and pain of their fellow creatures than through any other means in history, even war. Nowadays, while most toilers in the vineyards groan under their burden of taxes, the God men rake in billions and pay no taxes at all. Not only do they not support their fair share of the bureaucracy, they do not even produce anything useful in return for their enormous profits. Their only actual product is hot air.

A habit of these hot air merchants that gives much food for thought is their blandly implied assumption of personal Godness, betraying what man has always secretly believed: God is really himself. Again and again the preachers tell us what God says and what God means by it, what God's intentions and plans are, what God thinks about everything and everyone, and what God's political views require. (Somehow God's political views always correspond exactly with those of the speaker.) Never for a moment does any one of these men pause to contemplate the absurdity of this assumption. In precise imitation of the most primitive shaman, they are sure their own inner voice is literally the voice of God, and, of course, in a real sense it is. Never do they imagine that other people might have equally valid inner voices saying altogether different things.

It might be said that like man, God has now entered the

technological age and has become one of its most aggressively marketed commodities—if anything entirely without substance could be called a commodity. Selling God has become a big-bucks game, utilizing all the most sophisticated persuaders a busy persuasion industry has developed.

The pernicious persuaders insist on the same thing men have always wanted: mental, physical, and emotional subjection of women; opportunities for man to act the bully within the family; enforced ignorance about human (and particularly female) sexuality; suppression of real knowledge and of individual creative thinking; and personal power to sway masses of people at will.

The world expressed horror at the suicidal massacre initiated by the mad prophet Jim Jones, but that he could persuade so many people by his word alone to lay down their lives was a demonstration of the kind of power many God men secretly crave—and military men already possess. Man tends to love especially the Godlike power to order the ultimate sacrifice from his "sons." To many men this is the only proof of love that their nagging inner insecurity can find credible. Of the power to nurture and encourage mature independence they know nothing. Such spiritual generosity is left to women, who are usually taught never to interfere with the independent development of man or to attempt to influence him toward a less patriarchal attitude.

There is a darkness over the civilized world today: the kind of darkness that, always before in history, has heralded a plunge from a pinnacle of culture and enlightenment into a fresh wave of barbarism, with its corresponding loss of skills, arts, and information. We see the signs in a newly aggressive ignorance, a creeping tide of superstition and credulity. People cling to extravagant fantasies hardly different from the nonsense that was current at the beginning of Europe's Dark Ages.

People are reluctant or unable to read, to learn, to test their notions against nature's realities, to know their own history. Many want immediate answers to the impossible questions, not caring whether the answers are even credible. Rational assessment of ideas seems beyond their reach. Many who might have been thinkers turn to drugs that so insidiously cripple their capacity for thought that they can't feel it happening until it's too late.

It seems that collectively we don't want to understand ourselves. We may laugh at primitive people for their faith in fetishes, idols, and amulets, yet many of us have exactly the same sort of faith in saints' relics, plaster Virgins, gold crosses, healing charms, and horoscopes. Even those who renounce traditional beliefs often turn to equally silly substitutes drawn from the same primitive roots. A majority turn away from the hard, demanding discipline of real research, because they are unwilling or unable to concentrate as consistently as this requires. It's easier to listen to the miracle tale than it is to check it out. It's easier to let other believers validate one's belief than it is to discover where it came from in the first place.

It seems that most of us would rather be amazed than informed. Because our minds can be organs of entertainment, our spiritual beliefs are often based on whatever happens to entertain us; we learn how to be entertained. That's why so much religious symbolism and ritual boils down to sexuality in one way or another. Sexuality has been humanity's primary means of entertainment from the beginning, and its specific manifestations (or lack of them) are learned. Sexuality is also an intimate aspect of the Self, which so many male traditions either overtly or covertly declare identical with God.

The corresponding female traditions, however, have been lost or distorted because of patriarchy's war against them. Thus women have been robbed of their sexual, maternal, nurturant, and personally powerful Goddess, who actually symbolized the most entertaining, creative, loving, and esthetically rewarding aspects of life.

It's time we gave up literal belief in our various superstitions and false sacred histories and began to use these things as keys to understanding ourselves, which is the only way they can truly serve. Patriarchy is a disease that can't be cured by more of the same. We must achieve a new outlook on spiritual matters. Then, and only then, humans as a species might learn to live in peace with each other and with the planet that supports them.

Utopia

W oman's Utopia is not like man's. The emphasis lies on different events and qualities of life. Yet I suspect that men's and women's Utopias have the same end product: a world without war, violence, cruelty, or greed. But by what means might such an ideal be achieved or even approached?

Here is where men's and women's visions diverge. Many men see Utopia as a perfection of material technology, producing such abundance that no one need lack the comforts or even the luxuries of civilization. Men tend to believe in universal acquisition as a universal panacea. Moreover, work should be minimally demanding, so every person may enjoy ample leisure to play.

Most women, on the other hand, realize that cultural problems originate in collective emotions, and proper structuring of emotions is the only hope of solving such problems. Women's Utopia therefore addresses such structuring more directly. Accumulation of better things is beside the point. Women generally crave an accumulation of better feelings and gut level experiences.

Accordingly, my Utopia is a world God never made and never could make. Only real women could make it and only if men helped instead of hindered them. Men's hindering of women's cultural instincts arose from male fears that women in positions of real social power would oppress the other sex, as men have shown themselves all too willing to do throughout the centuries. Yet it is highly unlikely that a civilization focused on women's primary concerns, love and motherhood, could be as oppressive as one based on men's primary concerns: aggressive conflict in play or in earnest, winning or losing accompanied by concomitant rewards and punishments.

Even if such aggression comes naturally from the male

mammal's instinct to compete for the privilege of mating, among civilized humans it obviously no longer serves its natural purpose, which is to ensure that only the healthiest, strongest males are permitted to reproduce. Patriarchal laws have seen to it that even the least promising specimens of manhood may "own" women and children, even abuse them, thereby perpetuating a culture of fear, anger, and mindless aggression. Male competitiveness is clearly counterproductive in a civilization that stands ready to destroy its entire planet in a few seconds of fatal decision on the part of a few dominant (but not necessarily superintelligent) males.

This incredibly dangerous potential must be brought under trustworthy control before it's too late. Who is there to control it when the accepting-or-rejecting function of the male's natural judge, the female, has been eliminated by centuries of patriarchal suppression?

Life in a female-oriented Utopia begins with each woman's decision to conceive, in her own time and at her own pleasure, subject to certain basic laws: a potential mother should be physically mature, economically secure, and emotionally prepared. If these conditions are not met, at the woman's choice any accidental pregnancy may be terminated without trouble, because the quality of life is considered more important than the quantity, and it is a tenet of the culture that no child should ever come unwelcome into the world.

A potential mother may choose to conceive her child naturally, with a beloved husband or lover, or she may choose to be artificially inseminated from a sperm bank, whose donors must meet high standards of physical and mental health. During a first pregnancy she attends routine childbirth classes at her local Birth Temple, watches a number of actual deliveries, and talks to new mothers and their helpers, the Birth Priestesses.

Birth Temples are an essential feature of this Utopia: a combination of church, medical school, family planning center, and fully equipped lying-in hospital, staffed by trained female doctors and nurses who are also mothers and whose calling is regarded as sacred. As priestesses, they engage in practical observance of the principle of motherhood—reverence for life—on which the society is founded.

Those who elucidate the doctrines of religion or morality are usually elder women associated with the Temple. Their writings and speeches are the scriptures and teachings of a society in which the giving of life engenders as much interest as the taking of life engenders in our own.

Direct personal experience of Utopian morality begins at each child's birth, which usually takes place in the Temple's innermost shrines, the birthing chambers. There are delivery rooms prepared for every eventuality up to and including full-scale operations. There are the latest facilities for diagnosis and treatment of special problems. There are labor rooms carefully decorated with soft fabrics, soothing music, scented oils for perineal massage, and other niceties in the hands of helpful, reassuring, experienced nurses. Also a choice of furniture is available so the laboring woman may stand, sit, squat, or lie down when and as she wishes.

This is woman's space. Prospective fathers may enter, but only in proper reverence and gratitude for being allowed to witness the miracle of birth. No man is permitted to control his wife's labor, as some husbands today are taught to do. His function is purely supportive. If he cannot fulfill this function, he must withdraw and leave it to others. Indeed, men are not admitted to this branch of medicine unless they can show themselves willing to work under close female supervision and can pass personality tests demonstrating innate gentleness and kindness. It is a coveted privilege for a male doctor to become a priest or helper in the Birth Temple.

Childbirth is accomplished as naturally and gently as possible, never hurried for the convenience of the attending physician or subjected to assembly line techniques. The Temple recognizes the uniqueness of each woman and of each birth. An adequate staff size ensures that each mother will have the encouraging presence of her own doctor-priestess for as long as necessary. The Temple never forgets that the mother is there because she wants to be; that she has the right to take full charge of her body's holiest function; and that all others are present only to help her as unobtrusively as they can.

If the mother is conscious immediately after the birth, her infant is laid in her arms and left there. If she is asleep, the baby is cuddled against the body of someone else, where it can hear the heartbeat and feel body warmth. No healthy full-term infant is left to cry in a lonely crib. Whenever it is awake it is tenderly held and rocked. Elderly attendants of the Temple, male and female, perform this function in their rocking chairs.

Boy babies are not circumcised, because of general recognition that this custom originated in the Oedipal jealousy of adult men and in their resentment of possibly pleasurable stimulation of small unmutilated penises during mothers' cleansing. No unnecessary pain is to be inflicted on babies or children. That is one of Utopia's firmest taboos.

Being wanted and cherished, young children are freely doted on and given much freedom, but never allowed to annoy or injure others. As in some primitive societies whose child-rearing techniques are more successful than our own, it is simply assumed that all children want to take responsibility for themselves as early in life as they can, and the adult role is to provide good examples of mature behavior. Various types of family groups (and there are many) treat children as their collective joy and still consistently support the ultimate authority of each child's true mother.

Because affection is not withheld from them, either as a punishment or for any other reason, children don't grow up greedy, selfish, or robbed of their confidence. They are disciplined with gentle but effective techniques that encourage good behavior as a sign of maturity, preventing the resentment and inner rebellion that overly harsh punishment causes.

Children are not given violent entertainments or toy weapons. They do not play killing games. Utopian society is strongly opposed to showing children how to hit, hurt, or kill, in the same way that our own society is opposed to showing children explicit sexual acts. Conversely, Utopian children may view sexual acts (for example, on television) that emphasize affection, tenderness, and shared pleasure. Sex is not evil. Masturbation is not an abuse. Sadomasochistic practices and rape would be generally incomprehensible, because the severe repressions and harsh punishments required to entangle eroticism with such violent perversions are not part of the culture.

With the onset of sexual maturity, the young are trained by older lovers, who may be teachers affiliated with a Love Temple, like the ancient *alma mater* (soul mother) or priestess of Aphrodite. Teenage boys are initiated by older, experienced women. Teenage girls are guided toward their full sexual potential by older men carefully trained for the purpose. Sexual initiations are cautious and gentle, geared to the budding capacities of the novice.

Such official sex education occurs in a religious or semireligious setting, because sex is viewed as a solemn sacrament, even though it may be approached in a spirit of play. The special pleasures that can be generated between individuals by sensual and sexual means are taken as symbolic of the unity of all things in joy of being—an expressed understanding of the capacity for enjoyment as a true essence of life and a way to appreciate all of nature's gifts.

Utopian society recognizes the appalling error of confusing sexual pleasure with sin, guilt, fear, and hatred. Instead Utopians are trained to relate sexuality to their most altruistic feelings of love, tenderness, affection, caring, and sharing. A sexual encounter therefore may reveal the divine in, and to, the particular partners who properly adore one another's specialness as well as the expansive feelings toward all creation that typically accompany passionate love.

Love Temples are founded on much the same rationale as were ancient shrines of the Great Mother. Behind their sensual rites—which make full use of music, color, light, procession, artistic decoration, pleasing scents and textures, and other aids and comforts—lies the basic maternal theology of spiritual wholeness and growth arising first in every life from the vital interaction of mother and offspring, later from the equally vital interaction between loving adults. It is part of the conventional wisdom that adult sexuality arises directly from the all-important relational satisfaction of sensual needs in infancy. Thus sex acts must be founded on gentleness, nurture, and trust. Interpersonal violence is as grotesquely incongruous in a sexual relationship as in the relationship between mother and child, for violence is seen as an expression of hatred, arising from emotional sickness, not health.

The life force manifested in women, as mothers and lovers, is viewed as sacred in its particular closeness with the underlying unity of nature. Males best experience communion with this sacred power through physical, emotional, and intellectual contact with females. Still, Utopians do not rule out the possibility of genuine nurturing love between males in a homosexual relationship. Recognizing the fact that approximately 10 percent of human beings (and other mammals) are fundamentally homosexual from birth, Utopians make no attempt to change this orientation when it spontaneously appears. Each individual is given the opportunity to try heterosexuality first in a positive, supportive setting, but if it doesn't take, no one cares. Homosexuals male or female are fully accepted members of the society. Their sexual preferences are no more noticed in ordinary social relations than the similarly private activities of any heterosexual persons.

With such training, along with child-rearing practices that allow psychic space for each child to develop self-esteem and self-confidence, Utopian society hardly ever produces sociopaths or seriously violent people. Thanks to strong taboos and constantly reinforced respect for the life principle, murder is about as rare in Utopia as cannibalism in our own society. War is simply regarded as mass murder (hence inexcusable), and hunting is irresponsible murder of wildlife. Utopians don't *enjoy* killing in fantasy or sport. Their Mother theology is as free from violence as our own Father theology is permeated by it.

Because nothing is ever perfect, however, there are always a few who deviate even from the wide range of acceptable behavior. A violent person may appear even in the gentlest milieu, perhaps because of some brain malfunction or unfortunate accident. Utopians found guilty of violent behavior receive psychiatric treatment. If judged too incompetent to understand and correct their inner conflicts, they must be incarcerated for life and put to useful work in a place where they can do no harm.

Men found guilty of the exceedingly rare crime of rape are subject to castration—performed painlessly, in a hospital, not in a spirit of vengeance but simply to prevent repetition of the crime. The same operation may be performed on men guilty of any especially noxious violence, because such men are regarded as unfit to reproduce themselves or to assume responsibility for the welfare of children. No man who is abusive toward a child is ever allowed to be a father.

Our own macho society would naturally regard these precepts and practices as unacceptably emasculating, in both the literal and the figurative sense. Our own massive cultural error, however, of equating masculinity with cruel aggression is precisely what cries out for correction in today's world. The myth that maleness equals meanness must be done away with completely and forever if the human world is ever to be made safe for human beings.

Utopians define masculinity and femininity only in relation to each other; that is, a man is masculine when relating in a certain way to a woman, just as she is feminine in her relationship with him. The sexes define each other. People outside the context of their sexual relationships are just people, with few practical distinctions between male and female. Jobs, interests, hobbies, tastes in art or dress are not gender-specific. Anyone may like, do, or be whatever he or she pleases without regard to gender. Utopians understand that there are no human activities inevitably restricted to only one sex except the activities of begetting and bearing offspring.

Utopians also believe that although sexuality is a true expression of universal love and appreciation for nature's beauty, as well as for the collective spirit of all that is good in humanity, no individual should be forced into a sexual relationship if chastity is more to his or her taste. People make such decisions naturally and independently, without either undue obsessiveness or unwarranted anxiety. Those with powerful sex drives have no difficulty satisfying them; conversely, those whose interests are largely nonsexual are not not pressured to be sexier than they care to be. It is considered unkind to push people in any direction against their natural inclinations, as long as their inclinations are harmless to others. All mature people are considered wise enough to understand their own tastes. Utopians value diversity, not uniformity. In their view, a great miracle of terrestrial life is the fact that every creature can be different from every other.

Given this honoring of diversity, it might be expected that Utopian marriages and family groupings take many forms.

Young people may get together experimentally in couples or groups to test their relational skills. Those in special professions, such as those who are temple personnel, may make familial groups of people not necessarily genetically related. Mothers may form alliances with the men who fathered their children or with other women or with their own parents or siblings for whatever they judge the best emotional environment for their youngsters. There can be all-female or all-male marriages, sexual or nonsexual marriages, childrearing or childless marriages. There can be marriages for companionship, professional collaboration, economic advantage, or learning experience. Extended, tribal families are usually considered best for the well-being of all family members. Nothing, however, prevents Utopians from living alone or as an isolated couple or as a nuclear family, according to preference. All people are envisioned as belonging to a single megafamily born of Mother Nature.

A family group is viewed as an economic and productive unit of the society no matter how the work load is divided among members. Income is fairly shared. For example, a wife raising children and keeping house for a husband who goes out to work, as in the familiar conventional family, is considered just as productive a worker as he is, if not more so. Therefore at least half the income, pension, and other benefits are payable directly to her. There is an additional increment for each child, because the raising of responsible future citizens is considered a more important social contribution than the actual end products of the husband's daily labors. Conversely, a woman who goes out to work while her husband keeps the house and tends the children is expected to share the income equally with her spouse.

Free choice of work is important for all people. Human interests vary enormously. Not all women are interested in being mothers. Not all men are interested in being breadwinners. There are men whose parenting skills and inclinations are more highly developed than that of their wives; such men should take over the childcare. There are women who are intellectually creative or skillful in the political and organizational sense; such women should be free to devote their time to public rather than private life.

Personal interests can be assessed even in early childhood, when each child is given various types of toys. If a little boy wants to "mother" baby dolls or help care for a new infant, why should anyone deny him?

The legal family exists without necessarily coinciding with the biological family. Open family groups function to prevent anyone's having to live in loneliness. It is easy for a lonely person to be adopted by a congenial family group, to contribute his or her earnings to its general good, to provide services and have services provided. Families can be tried out for several years at a time, just as jobs are now.

It is generally recognized, however, that the best environment for growing children is a stable constellation of familiar, trusted relatives or close friends in a physical setting that is not often changed. Businesses should move their employees as little as possible in order that feelings of continuity and constancy can be developed by employees and their youngsters.

Old people are better provided for in Utopia than in our own society, which too often isolates, ignores, and even physically threatens them. Like children, the elderly need protection, respect, and something useful to do. Utopians believe every family needs its grandparental figures, who can spend time with the very young, mediate the disputes of older children, and teach everyone how to cope with old age, which awaits all who live long enough.

In a society that emphasizes the quality of life rather than its quantity (or duration), it is only natural to find Death Temples corresponding to Birth Temples, where life can be ended as tenderly and humanely as it was begun. Those who have painful, wasting illnesses or who have lost their capacities to the point where they no longer wish to live have the right to go to a Death Temple to be attended by trained personnel, which correspond to ancient priestesses such as the dakinis, vilas, or death angels.

Death Temple decor is beautiful and soothing. Visits and classes are encouraged. Death is seen as a return from the temporary life of consciousness back into the universal womb of nature from which one emerged. Each client understands that release from pain into eternal nothingness is available any time it is wanted.

After an individual proven to be of sound mind has made the decision to die, has set his or her affairs in order, and has said farewell to loved ones, Temple attendants provide a painless death in a comfortable, pleasant environment. Corpses are either cremated at once or buried naked in the earth to decompose as quickly as possible, according to nature's law for all organic life. There are no funerals, because Utopians think it pointless to provide ceremonial honors for those no longer able to enjoy them. Ritual celebration of a death takes place before it, not after, with the fated one as guest of honor.

Basically, my Utopia is a world of more rational taboos than the ones we have now; a world where greed, jealousy, aggression, and excessive acquisitiveness are curbed; a world where warfare does not seem a feasible way of settling any problem; where people are more effectively taught to respect the physical and emotional integrity of others; and where women are accorded as much social significance as men, if not more.

There were such societies once, of a primitive type, a long time ago, before the patriarchal spirit invaded our world and gradually turned it into the battleground of hostile gods. Dominance of male over female is perhaps the worst thing that has ever happened to the human race. Male values engender guilt, fear, anger, and, ultimately, a psychotic disregard for the goodness of life for its own sake. Female values foster respect for sentience, sensibility, sensuality, and the qualities that enhance life and make it worth living.

So, a feminist Utopia. All very well, but how to get from here to there? Answer: we don't. Every Utopia is only a dream. It might be endlessly elaborated on to provide endless hypothetical solutions to every social, economic, or legal problem, but dream worlds, however minutely detailed, remain dream worlds.

All one can hope is that some of the values women prefer may gain more significance in our real world; that some of the practices women like may become more common; and that some of the morality women feel to be right may come to prevail. Together with many other thinking persons of the perilously poised modern world, I find the absolute rule of male values a Frankenstein monster that may well devour us all unless it is soon declared a devil rather than a god. There must be another way to go, or else the human race will find itself at a dead end—in every sense of the word. And we may take all the rest of our living world with us into oblivion. What hubris can ever justify men's assumption of the right to do that?

In a sense it might be said that, just as a male creature is made by a "flawed" or incomplete female (X) chromosome, so the collective creature of male-dominated culture contains inherent flaws capable of destroying the whole organism. Our world certainly shows collective tendencies toward immature behavior, avoidance of social responsibility, runaway greed, little-boy braggadocio, limitless power seeking, and a mad compulsion toward conflict, cruelty, and destructiveness that can only have fatal results. The feminine tendency to give posterity's welfare the first priority is conspicuous by its absence in our society; so is the feminine willingness to communicate, comprehend, and work out a nonaggressive *modus vivendi* with others.

Our world doesn't recognize the basic relatedness of all human beings. Instead, it seeks always to divide the We from the They, like little boys excitedly choosing up competitive teams—a seemingly innocent playfulness that can acquire dreadful overtones when carried into adult life. Our world fills us with suspicion and mistrust of our fellow humans, unfortunately often justified, because their own suspicion and mistrust can cause attack. Too many of us are fear-biters, like mistreated dogs. Women and children in our cities feel constantly threatened and are told as a matter of course that they must be always on guard against other adult male members of their own species, who are quite capable of killing them for no special reason. Not even sharks are quite so consistently vicious as this.

There is little rational pity for victims, but attackers have plenty of irrational excuses, ranging from "She was asking for it" to "God told me to." Throughout history the God men made in their own image has been telling them to destroy large numbers of their fellow human beings almost incessantly. Most of the pages in our history books are filled with wars for the glory of God.

It is believed that the dinosaurs became extinct because they couldn't adapt to changing conditions. Their fatal flaw was their large size, evolved in a more fertile age, when there was plenty of food. When the climate changed and food supplies declined, smaller animals survived on less nourishment while the giant reptiles starved.

Our species may be facing a similar extinction because of its own fatal flaw: not bigness, but male destructiveness. Whatever advantage that quality may have been for primitive hunters is now wiped out in a civilized world where such destructiveness can only turn against the wrong objects, tending to damage rather than preserve the species. Men have not adapted well enough to the changed world they made for themselves. They don't really understand the high degree of cooperative behavior—as exhibited by dolphins, for example—that collective living requires. From nature's point of view, the human male is an insane animal. He is the only animal that attacks females of his own species more or less routinely. He is the only animal that rapes. He is the only animal that engages in vast, mutually destructive group wars against his own kind. It is time for man to realize that most of his collective insanity can be regulated only by the comparatively less sociopathic female of his species.

Compared with the dinosaurs, who existed fifty times as long as humanity so far, we haven't had much of a run through geologic time. Yet perhaps we've had all we need to prove— maybe in this very century—that despite their intelligence, men are too crazily aggressive to survive on this earth. The toys these boys play with now are much too big for them. This is implied in the statements of our so-called leaders when they say the arms race is out of control, as if it were some natural disaster threatening humanity from without, instead of a danger entirely subject to the decisions of male humans. Little man's eternal craving to be a big god may well end with an all too literal doomsday.

Though neither Utopia nor Paradise can be realizable in

this, the only world we have ever known or are ever likely to know, still as pretenders to the title of earth's most intelligent creatures, we really ought to have enough sense to stop building our own hell.

Sea Vision

I was walking on a beach at midnight, accompanied only by my dog. A full moon threw its lemon-silver path across the water to the horizon. Blowing sand hissed faintly along the shore. The beach was empty. There were no lights, no signs of human habitation. It could have been a primitive, Paleozoic earth or a time before history. The scene had no identity in time.

I sat down in a clump of dune grass and watched the moon path. Viewed from different angles, it could change. Sometimes it looked like a heap of jewels miraculously floating on the sea. Sometimes it looked almost solid, a Yellow Brick Road of light leading to a never-never land beyond the sky. In minute detail it resembled cold fire. Wavelets stirred the reflected moonlight with the same curling, twisting motion made by the red glow worms of hot coals on a hearth.

As I watched, this illusion of fire grew stronger, until I seemed to be looking at a multitude of real fires.

Then came one of those soundless clicks that lock one into a new angle of vision. The scene changed. The water surface disappeared, as if the sea bed were exposed.

I seemed to be looking down, as if from a mountaintop or an airplane, into a great valley filled with fires. Each fire arose from a low stone altar that was surrounded by people. Among the many altars stood archaic-looking temples, ornamented with circles and aisles of sphinxes, pillars, arches, towers, stepped platforms, fountains, and elaborately landscaped gardens. It was night, and the people looked as small as ants from

my vantage point; yet I could see them, down to the details of
their clothing and jewelry.

Some sort of ceremony was in progress. There was a flat,
faint, clanging sort of music played on instruments like none
I had ever heard before. There was a sweet perfume of incense
rising from the altars, which were tended by women. The people looked busy but serene, each one knowing what to do and
when to do it.

Then the scene changed suddenly.

There was the same valley in daylight: a hard, glaring, pitiless noonday that whitened the very rocks. The fountains had
gone dry. The gardens were dead. Dessicated brown stalks rus-
tled slightly in a weak breeze, where only a moment ago I had
seen lush trees and shrubs covered with fruit. Some of the altars
still sent up thin, pale gray columns of smoke, but their fires
were out. Some of the temples were partially ruined. Their
sides were caved in, their pillars fallen. What had been an aisle
of fine sphinxes and palm trees was now leveled to the ground.

In this desolate scene the people were leaving the valley in
long, straggling lines. Some were leading cattle, sheep, or don-
keys. Their backs were bent under heavy burdens: sacks, bun-
dles, furniture. They walked slowly, with their heads down.
Even the children seemed dispirited. They looked like war ref-
ugees, people plodding numbly along to nowhere in particular.

I raised my eyes from this depressing scene to the empty
sky and saw a flat white disc of—was it the sun? No, it was the
moon after all. In the disc was a pale shadow of a face, apparently formed of pearly smoke. A strangely familiar face.
Where had I seen it before?

As I realized that the object in the sky was the moon and
not the sun, that it was really the middle of the night and not
a glaring noon, the vision faded and the valley dissolved beneath the returning waves of the sea. I became aware of a chilly
sea breeze. My dog, tired of running about on the sand, had
seated herself beside me and pressed against my shoulder. I
could feel her shivering a little. When I got up I felt stiff, as
if I had been sitting in the chill for a long time. Yet it seemed
no more than a brief moment.

I looked again at the face on the disc of the moon. It wasn't the usual man-in-the-moon face. Its shadows and hollows were not in the familiar places. It was symmetrical, a female face seen head on. Where had I seen it before?

Then I remembered. I saw it many years ago, in my vision of the tree woman in the pine grove. It was the face of the Mother merging with the face of the Crone, as if I saw the same woman at different times of her life two or three decades apart.

Moon and sea together seemed to have given me a vision like that of *La Terre Gast*—the Waste Land. Could it be the past, the future, or a timeless dreamland? I had no idea. It was there, vivid but equivocal. I still don't know what to make of it, except that it seems to have been both a revelation and a warning.

Above it all, the face in the moon communicated to me a certain thought without any words. With that odd certainty of visions I understood that I would see her at least once again. Her Crone image would be the last thing I would ever see, and it would be like an image in a mirror. I would see her on the day of my death.